GRAVE TALES
Tasmania

By
Helen Goltz & Chris Adams

GRAVE TALES – TASMANIA

First published 2022
Publisher: Atlas Productions
Greenslopes QLD 4102
Web: www.atlasproductions.com.au

A catalogue record for this book is available from the National Library of Australia

Cover images (please see individual chapters for full source details):

Top row: Lily Poulett-Harris, Wikipedia; Errol Flynn, National Library of Australia; Mark Jeffrey, Libraries Tasmania; Thomas Midwood, Libraries Tasmania; Sylvia McArthur, kindly provided by the McArthur family descendants.

Bottom: Henry Stock, State Library of NSW; Correll Allison, Allison family tree, Ancestry; Roy Cazaly, Wikimedia; Mary Grant Roberts, Libraries Tasmania; Martin Cash, State Library of New South Wales.

*"If history were taught in the form of stories,
it would never be forgotten."*

Rudyard Kipling

Contents by cemetery or location:

Contents by story:

Authors' note:

We have taken great care to be respectful to the people featured in *Grave Tales* – in the telling of their life stories, and to any living descendants. Our intent is to save our history and share the tales of the many lives that have gone before us. **Please note:** where naming errors have appeared in quotes and newsclippings, we have left them as they were originally written or intended.

Also, we were unable in this volume to give specific details to all the **Cornelian Bay Cemetery** gravesites as the cemetery grounds do not feature row or site numbers, only sections e.g. EE, NK, etc. It is a beautiful cemetery and some of the graves featured in this book will be identifiable by photo in that section. Enjoy the challenge if you wish to visit after reading the story.

Donation:

We are proud to donate $1 from the sale of every *Grave Tales: Tasmania* paperback to providing gravestones or restoring damaged gravestones for the people we feature in our *Grave Tales* series. Please connect with us on our website or Facebook pages to read about beneficiaries.

Introduction

This is the ninth book in the '*Grave Tales*' series in which we tell the stories of ordinary people who were caught up, either willingly or otherwise, in extraordinary events. In this volume we look at Tasmania and some of the people who are featured in its history. Most now lie in resting places around the state, hence the title '*Grave Tales*'. Others are only remembered by memorials in cemeteries and public places.

Fittingly, the oldest cemetery in Tasmania stands in the heart of Hobart, in St. David's Park. It was used from settlement, in 1804, and is the burial ground for many of Tasmania's earliest settlers. Its location was indicative of early church-run denominational cemeteries which, as they grew, lapsed into poor condition. By 1843 they had become public health hazards: they were too close to the city centre, and the soil was so rocky that graves could not be dug deep enough.[1]

With all good intentions, the search was on for a new cemetery to serve Hobart, and while a site had been suggested—the Old Government Farm at Cornelian Bay on the Derwent River—nothing actually happened for 20 years. Finally, in 1872, Cornelian Bay Cemetery was opened. The first person buried there was 12-year-old Bridget Ryan, who died of typhoid fever. A replica of her headstone still stands in the cemetery. It is estimated that there have been 100,000 burials and 60,000 cremations at the cemetery since it was established.

Bridget Ryan, 12, was the first person buried in Cornelian Bay Cemetery.

Over the years it has been discovered that there are many convict-era graveyards scattered across the city of Hobart which have been covered over and used for other purposes. As an example, Campbell Street Primary School is believed to stand on a graveyard that contains as many as 5000 convict remains. In Launceston in the state's north, old cemeteries have been located and their current usage made public. For example, the upper Charles St. Launceston General Cemetery, which operated between 1841 and 1925, is now a park and the Prisoners' Burial Ground, Peel St., Glen Dhu which operated between 1846 and the 1870s is also now a park. And there are plenty more across the state.[2]

As Cornelian Bay and Carr Villa are the only operating cemeteries in Hobart and Launceston respectively, many of the people featured in this book are buried there. Cornelian Bay is the resting place of some famous, some not so famous and even not so Tasmanian… like the man whose name will always be associated with Aussie Rules footy, Roy Cazaly – you know… up there Cazaly – who finished his days in Tasmania.

And a lady called Mary Grant Roberts who almost saved the thylacine—the Tasmanian tiger—by mistake. There is a bushranger by the name of Martin Cash who avoided the hangman's noose and escaped three times from the inescapable hell-hole, Port Arthur convict settlement.

And there are memories of the swashbuckling film star, Errol Flynn, who made more than 60 films and TV series, and was always recognised as a Tasmanian whereever he went. We hope you enjoy this volume.

Chris Adams

References:

1 Jones, Callum. Tas that was – Cornelian Bay Cemetery, *Tasmanian Times*. March 2021.
2 Cemeteries & Churches & Things. *Launceston Cemeteries*. https://monissa.com/ccphotos/launceston-cemeteries/

A memorial for those buried in the paupers' graveyard which lies behind. The undulating grass and the indents are where bodies lie.

The gravedigger of Dead Island

Mark Jeffrey

Interred: **Mark Jeffrey**, 31 August 1825 – 18 July 1894[1] (aged 68 years).

Location: Pauper A, Number 516.

Cemetery: Cornelian Bay Cemetery and Crematorium, Queens Walk, New Town, TAS 7008.

The Isle of the Dead, Port Arthur. Above: Note the two people amongst the graves in 1890. One appears to be a priest. Below: Taken in 1910. Source: Libraries Tasmania.

By an unofficial count, there are around eleven hundred people buried on what is known as Dead Island or the Isle of the Dead, which is located just a little over a kilometre offshore from the once savage penal settlement of Port Arthur, Tasmania.[2]

Here location indicates the social status of the occupants of graves. The free lie in the north-west corner where there are still some headstones to be seen. These resting places range from prison officials to those of invalids, paupers and lunatics. There are seamen, soldiers and their families. Convicts, on the other hand, were almost exclusively buried at the island's lower southern end where headstones were largely banned.

This is the story of one man who should by rights have been buried at that southern end of the Isle of the Dead but instead the grave he prepared for himself lay open, tended to, but empty for years after his death.

Runaway boys

In 19th-century Britain, security in life was little better than tenuous and to give any real thought to what a future may hold was folly indeed. So it was with a youngster named Mark Jeffrey who was born at Wood Ditton, near Newmarket, Suffolk, in 1825. He was the son of John Jeffrey, a gardener, and quite a successful one, who rented land and a house from a local medico, Doctor Norton.

The life of Mark Jeffrey and his younger brother, Luke, should have been comfortable, but while being a successful market gardener, their father had the insufferable habit of

Convict and colourful character, Mark Jeffrey, 1870.
Photo by Thomas J. Nevin. Source: Libraries Tasmania.

beating his sons while he was drunk. No doubt the boys had considered leaving the family home, and when in 1840 Doctor Norton, from whom John Jeffrey rented, suddenly died and the family was left with nowhere to live, the boys ran away, not able to stand the violence any longer. Mark was 15 and Luke just 12.

But what would they do to survive? There are several versions of how the boys kept body and soul together. One was that Mark was no stranger to defending himself with his fists. He worked the carnivals and fairs around the Fens district in the amateur boxing tents, eventually finding his way to London where he became involved with the 'wrong crowd', drank excessively and joined up with a gang of burglars who preyed on London society.[3]

The second version of how the boys ended up in the burglary game also has Mark, who at 15 was said to be almost 6 feet tall (1.8m) and weighed in at 15 stone (95kg), working the amateur boxing tents. However, at St Ives in Cornwall, they met up with a nefarious type by the name of Tom Hart who convinced Mark and Luke that burglary had the best of both worlds – good pickings and little chance of being caught.

What happened next must have given the boys some cause for doubt. It was no later than the very day after Hart had convinced them that there was little chance of being 'nicked', that he introduced them to his brother, who had just been released from jail on a burglary conviction.

Regardless, Tom and John Hart and the Jeffrey boys teamed up, purchased the tools necessary for their newly adopted trade, and set to work. It didn't take long before they had a sizable result from a robbery at a place where the boys and their father had once worked. Mark and Luke knew there was gold and silver, jewellery and cash on the premises which belonged to Mr Jones. From the proceeds of this venture, they retired temporarily to Barnwell, near Cambridge, where they discovered a world of drinking, fighting and prostitution.[4]

In his autobiography, modestly titled, *A Burglar's Life: Or, The Stirring Adventures of the Great English Burglar Mark Jeffrey; a Thrilling History of the Dark Days of Convictism in Australia*, Jeffrey describes the brothers' view of the suburb of Barnwell, compared with Cambridge, whose civic fathers were apparently uncompromising on streetwalkers: "I may here mention that women of lewd character were not allowed to parade the streets of Cambridge, for which offence they were at once apprehended by the police. The suburb (Barnwell) possessed a potent charm for us, and we were never weary of sporting our figures in its vicinity. Indolence and dissipation at length made considerable inroad upon our ill-gotten gains, and it behoved us to adopt some means to replenish our coffers." [5] Therefore, it was back to the life of crime.

Nicked

No matter which version of Mark Jeffrey's decline into a career of dishonesty you give credence, the outcome was bound to be the same and predictably, on their fifteenth burglary job they were 'nicked'. In rapid succession, they were charged, convicted, sentenced to 15 years transportation and found themselves in the now long-defunct Millbank Prison awaiting their conveyance to a far-off place.

And it was here that the first incident occurred that gave some idea of what the future would hold for the guards and officials who would be charged with overseeing the decade and a half-sentence of Mark Jeffrey… and why he would become known as 'a terror to those in authority'.

For their upcoming trial, Mark Jeffrey had secured the services of an eminent legal counsel in his attempt to have him and his brother acquitted. But the tactic came to nothing when the prosecution gave the court details of all 15 of the robberies that had involved the brothers, courtesy of their fellow thief, John Hart. This treachery was too much for Mark, and he attempted to attack Hart on the courtroom floor. He was physically restrained, but all that achieved was some delay in Mark Jeffrey's confrontation with John Hart. That took place when Mark was sent to work in the tailoring shop at Millbank Prison and he found himself face to face with Hart. Jeffrey's blistering verbal attack was reportedly so menacing that Hart collapsed as though he'd had a seizure. Within three days he was dead with no physical involvement from Mark Jeffrey who was charged with manslaughter on the grounds he had frightened Hart to death. This was later dropped after Mark argued Hart had brought about his own death through his actions.[6]

It was during his time in Millbank Prison that Mark Jeffrey's world began to revolve around food… the quantity of rations allocated to him was meagre and the authorities must have wondered what would happen in days to come.

In his book, he wrote: "One day, when more than usually hungry and exasperated, I seized an additional piece of bread from the turn-key, as he was serving out the allowance. 'You have one piece,' he said. This was provocation enough for

Above: Millbank Prison in London by Thomas Hosmer Shepherd, published 1829. Source: Wikimedia Commons.
Below: An illustration of the Warrior convict hulk, moored at Woolwich, in the Illustrated London News in 1846. Source: National Archives UK.

me in the condition I then was, and I immediately retaliated by knocking him down. For this act I was sentenced to three day's solitary confinement."[7]

Toward the end of his time at Millbank, Mark contracted cholera and was close to death. The illness left him weak and angry because it also meant he was permanently separated from his brother, Luke, his only real friend, who was transported to Swan River, Western Australia, during the time Mark was struggling to survive. And even when he regained his health, matters did not improve. Mark Jeffrey was transferred to the prison hulk, *Warrior*, which was lying on the Thames River at Woolwich.

The starving wild beast

The British Government was highly aware of the cost of keeping prisoners aboard hulks on the river and so convicts were sent to work to help cover costs. It also meant they were fed as little as possible of the cheapest fare available. It mainly comprised ox-cheek, either boiled or made into watery soup, biscuits which were often green with mould and a form of porridge made of legumes called pease. But whatever it was, there wasn't much of it. The warders knew that Mark Jeffrey was a lamb when his belly was full, but a wild beast when he was hungry.[8]

From the *Warrior*, he was sent out to back-breaking manual work, probably at the Woolwich Docks. This led to him becoming involved in fight after fight over food when his lack of rations resulted in violent attacks on his fellow prisoners. As a result, his rations were cut even further as punishment, driving him into terrifying rages. During this time he became so depressed that he wrote a letter to the government asking that it should execute him. It refused.

Finally, Mark Jeffrey's time on the *Warrior* ended when the authorities loaded him, and 59 other prisoners, on board the merchant ship *Eliza,* for the torturous trip to the other side of the world. A trip made harrowing by not only the weather but the conditions in which the men were expected to exist.

This extract from the writings of the surgeon, John Andrews, onboard the *Eliza*, gives some idea of what life was to be like: "All being men of desperate and very bad character were immediately on their arrival on board confined below in the prison cells – four cells being fitted up for the safekeeping of fifteen in each cell. These cells were very dark, close and hardly ventilated so that the men were in a short time within them when they felt the want of air, of faintness and giddiness. Fits of an hysterical, epileptic character quickly attacked most of them. I was subsequently obliged to get them on deck as soon as possible."[9]

After 115 days, the *Eliza* finally reached Hobart on 6 April 1850, with the loss of four lives on the way. They took those who needed hospitalisation from the vessel until it set sail for Norfolk Island, its final destination off the coast of New South Wales, some 12 days later. Mark Jeffrey was among those on board, bound for what Marcus Clarke in *For the Term of His Natural Life* described as "Hell in paradise".[10]

Hell in paradise

Every man who was sent to Norfolk Island to labour until he was close to death soon understood the instructions of the New South Wales governor, Ralph Darling, that: "every man should be worked in irons that the example may deter others from the commission of crime to hold out (Norfolk Island) as a place of the extremest punishment short of death."[11]

And clearly, Darling's view that reformation of the convicts was not on the agenda of the Norfolk Island penal settlement was achieved, along with its aim of 'breaking' any convicts who may dare to challenge the system. After the convict mutiny in 1834, the Vicar General of Sydney, Father William Ullathorne, went to Norfolk Island to comfort the mutineers due for execution. He was given the duty of telling each of the mutineers who would hang and who would be reprieved.

He said it was: "the most heartrending scene that I ever witnessed… each man who heard his reprieve wept bitterly, and each man who heard of his condemnation to death went down on his knees with dry eyes, and thanked God."[12]

Thirteen mutineers were hanged, over two days, 22 and 23 September 1834, in the presence of other convicts.[13]

Mark Jeffrey seemed to do reasonably well at Norfolk Island… well, perhaps that should be restated as… didn't seem to

Above: A portrait of Father William Ullathorne, no later than 1889. Source: Wikimedia Commons

be as brutally treated as others there. In fact, some of his treatment is hard to understand. When he first arrived on Norfolk he was employed as a gardener and did well until one day the issue of food arose again. In reality, it had probably never gone away. But in this particular event, the cook where Mark was staying refused him extra food, at which point Mark attacked the cook and eventually left him unconscious.

Above: Norfolk Island convict settlement at Kingston in 1848.
Source: National Library of Australia.

Remarkably, Mark's next role was that of a policeman, appointed by the commandant of the island, John Giles Price. While Price warned Jeffrey that his temper would get him into serious trouble, Mark Jeffrey wrote of him: "He thought for a moment, and then said the best thing he could do for me was to make me a sub-constable: 'You will get wheaten rations instead of corn cracker,' he added, 'and plenty of tea and sugar instead of hominy.' (Dried corn) I consented to this arrangement, and the commandant permitted the appointment to be made. A suit of clothes was procured for me, and I was placed on duty in the lumberyard with another constable."

Mark's role as a policeman didn't last long. He was sacked after being accused of sleeping on the job. His demotion saw him put into the stables to look after the horses and again he would have the daily struggle to get enough to eat.

Life at Port Arthur

As transportation from Britain to Van Diemen's Land ceased in 1853 and was replaced by penal servitude in Great Britain, there was little need for the penal settlement on Norfolk Island. The last prisoners were returned to Port Arthur or Hobart in 1855.

Back in Tasmania, Mark Jeffrey fell on some good luck once again when he was given the job of improving the Port Arthur Chaplain's agricultural efforts by applying his horticultural skills working in his garden. Mark's efforts raised the production levels of the potato patch, the harvest from which was sold to miners on the Victorian goldfields.

The grateful Chaplain gave Mark ten per cent of the profits, and there are no prizes for guessing what Mark spent it on. Let's just say he didn't go hungry while at that job.

Above: The guards at Port Arthur, c.1866. Source: Libraries Tasmania.

Sometime in this period, Mark was granted his ticket-of-leave, a document issued to any convicts who had served part of their sentence with good behaviour. It gave prisoners limited travel rights throughout the colony and allowed them to work for themselves, providing they stayed in a specified area.[14] It well may have given Mark the right to move around more freely, but he didn't hang on to it for long.

The trouble began when he and some friends were travelling home from a night of drinking in Richmond in what he described as "a state of merriment and full of life". He later wrote about what happened next. "When we had got about a mile out of Richmond, I commenced to sing a song, and meeting a gentleman – whom I subsequently found to be a police magistrate – on the road, accompanied by two ladies, I accosted him, and requested his opinion of my song. He called me a blackguard, and with that I gave him a playful spank on the face, asking him jocularly how he dared insult me."[15]

Mark and friends may have been in a state of merriment… what transpired after the "playful spank on the face" indicated the magistrate wasn't. Mark's ticket-of-leave was revoked, and he was sent to Port Arthur for life.

When he arrived back at Port Arthur, the Governor sent him to work with constables who were snaring kangaroos and selling them to locals. This, the amount of food available, and the company of the constables suited Mark well and kept him away from the fights and punishments he had incurred at Port Arthur previously. In around 1870, Mark was conditionally released once again but struggled, being found guilty of attacks around Tasmania and sent to various jails many times.

In 1871 he was involved in a pub brawl, fighting a man who had insulted him. He maintained it was simply self-defence, but when the man's death led to Mark's conviction for manslaughter, he was again sent to Port Arthur for the third time… and again for life.[16]

And again, because of his violent rages brought about by his extremely short temper, Mark spent long periods in solitary confinement. This further aggravated the damage to his legs that heavy irons had caused during earlier imprisonments and on Norfolk Island. He felt it was an injustice and lashed out, causing substantial damage in his efforts to wreck the cell in which he was confined and attempted to murder a doctor who was treating him. By now the officials who ran the prison wanted him out of sight, and so despatched him to the Isle of the Dead as the resident gravedigger.

Living with the dead

There are only two men known to be resident gravediggers on the Isle of the Dead. The first was an Irish convict, John Barron, who was convicted twice for receiving stolen goods and sent from Limerick to Port Arthur.[17] He managed the lonely task for over 10 years until he was pardoned in 1874. And then there was Mark Jeffrey. We know little about Mark's time on the island, but of Barron's occupancy, there has been some recording of what life was like on the Isle of the Dead.

Anthony Trollope was an English novelist who wrote a series of books about an imaginary English county called Barsetshire. In the early 1870s, he toured Australia and New Zealand on a writing mission that was directly aimed at the traveller of the day. While he was in Tasmania, he went to Port Arthur and gained some insights from John Barron as to what Mark Jeffrey would have gone through.

Surprisingly, what Trollope wrote wasn't a story of terror or fear, but that Barron had enjoyed many freedoms not readily available in Port Arthur proper. He was very much the monarch of all he surveyed. "He was no prisoner at all but might wander where he liked… go to bed when he pleased and get up when he pleased, might bathe or catch fish, or cultivate his flower garden. He had been there for 10 years digging graves in absolute solitude without being ill a day."[18]

Whether Mark Jeffrey had the soundness of mind to see life on the *Isle of the Dead* through the same looking glass as John Barron, we will never really know, except to say that while he was on the island, he claimed to have had a strange visitation. According to Mark, one night he was in his dwelling hut when the devil (or his 'satanic majesty' as he was referred to by Mark Jeffrey) appeared and had a conversation with him. There is no record of what the conversation was about, but Mark said he was so disturbed by it he requested immediate removal from the island.[19]

It is clear from his book that Mark Jeffrey was in no state to be left alone for days on end with digging graves and tending to his own, which he had dug at the southern end of the island, the only tasks to keep him occupied. What he believed would eventually be his own resting place must have become something of an obsession, as he is reported to have even repeatedly patted down the edges to keep the worms out.

But he laboured under the weight of his overwhelming view that his life had been one of cruelty, as he wrote: "One sentence sums up my life: I have lived long; I have suffered long."[20]

Above: Mark's biography which tells his version of his colourful life, 1893. Source: Examiner (Launceston, Tas.) & National Library of Australia.

Dead and buried

Mark Jeffrey died in 1894 aged 68, but ironically after all the years of grave preparation, there was some confusion about where he was buried. As he died in Launceston, it was believed he was buried in that area, however, the Southern Cemeteries records show he was interred in Hobart's Cornelian Bay Cemetery in the Pauper A section, grave number 516.[21]

We know little about the fate of Mark's brother, Luke, who had been transported to Western Australia, except that he shot himself when he was about 55 years old. He and Mark had never met again after their days in Millbank Prison.[22]

Such is the life of a burglar who got caught.

How to find Mark's grave in the paupers' section of Cornelian Bay Cemetery:

Mark Jeffrey is buried with many paupers in a section of this beautiful cemetery but there are no distinct markers to determine where Mark rests. The area is a large, undulating green lawn *(pictured)* housing many bodies. There is, however, a memorial stone in remembrance of those buried in this section without their own headstone and remembrance.

Above: Mark aged 68. His legs were troubled from years in irons. This photo is from his biography.
Source: Examiner (Launceston, Tas.) & National Library of Australia.

References:

1 Death of Mark Jeffrey. (19 Jul 1894). *Launceston Examiner (Tas: 1842 - 1899)*, p.6. Retrieved 25 June 2021, from http://nla.gov.au/nla.news-article39586455

2 Ross, Lynette. *Companion to Tasmanian History*. Isle of the Dead. Centre for Tasmanian Historical Studies. https://www.utas.edu.au/library/companion_to_tasmanian_history/I/Isle%20of%20the%20Dead.htm

3 Godfrey, Barry, and the Digital Panopticon project team, *Jeffrey, Mark, 1825-1903*, The Digital Panopticon. Retrieved 9 July 2021 from: https://www.digitalpanopticon.org/Jeffrey,_Mark,_1825-1903

4 Wayback Machine. *Mark Jeffrey Wood Ditton's notorious burglar.* Retrieved 9 July 2021 from URL: https://web.archive.org/web/20050824212243/http://www.wood-ditton.org.uk/markjeffrey.htm

5 Jeffrey, Mark, *A Burglar's Life; or, The Stirring Adventures of the Great English Burglar Mark Jeffrey; a Thrilling History of the Dark Days of Convictism in Australia.* J. Walch & Sons, Pty Ltd. Retrieved 9 July 2021 from URL: http://handle.slv.vic.gov.au/10381/183230

6 Wayback Machine. Op.cit.

7 Jeffrey, Mark, *A Burglar's Life, etc. Op.cit.*

8 Port Arthur Historic sites, *Meet Mark Jeffrey.* Retrieved 9 July 2021 from URL: https://portarthur.org.au/wp-content/uploads/2017/12/Mark-Jeffrey.pdf

9 Willetts, Jen, Convict Ship Eliza 1850. *Free Settler or Felon.* Retrieved 9 July 2021 from: https://www.freesettlerorfelon.com/convict_ship_eliza_1850.htm

10 *For the Term of his Natural Life.* Marcus Clarke. Australian Journal between 1870 and 1872.

11 Norfolk Island — the "Hell in Paradise" of an 18th-century penal colony, *Five Minute History*, 2016. Retrieved 9 July 2021 from: https://fiveminutehistory.com/norfolk-island-18th-century-hell-in-paradise/

12 Wikipedia contributors. (2021, June 5). History of Norfolk Island. In *Wikipedia*. Retrieved 14 June 2021 from: from https://en.wikipedia.org/w/index.php?title=History_of_Norfolk_Island&oldid=1026946129

13 Wikipedia contributors. (2021, Jan 25). Norfolk Island convict mutinies. In *Wikipedia*. Retrieved 15 June 2021 from: https://en.wikipedia.org/w/index.php?title=Norfolk_Island_convict_mutinies&oldid=1002724979

14 Tickets of Leave/Certificates of Freedom/Pardons, *National Library of Australia.* Retrieved 9 July 2021 from URL: https://www.nla.gov.au/research-guides/convicts/tickets-of-leave

15 Jeffrey, Mark, *A Burglar's Life; etc.* Op.cit.

16 Godfrey, Barry, and the Digital Panopticon project team. Op.cit.

17 Axton-Thompson, Carol, John Barron, *Convict Records.* Retrieved July 13, 2021 from URL: https://convictrecords.com.au/convicts/barron/john/129747

18 Trollope, Anthony. *Australia and New Zealand.* 1873 Cambridge University Press. Retrieved 9 July 2021 from: https://babel.hathitrust.org/cgi/pt?id=mdp.39015010728460&view=2up&seq=2&size=150

19 Wikipedia contributors. (2021, January 23). Mark Jeffrey. In *Wikipedia, The Free Encyclopedia.* Retrieved June 22, 2021, from: https://en.wikipedia.org/w/index.php?title=Mark_Jeffrey&oldid=1002220131

20 Jeffrey, Mark, *A Burglar's Life; etc.* Op.cit.

21 Death Of Mark Jeffrey. (1894, July 19). *Launceston Examiner (Tas: 1842 - 1899)*, p. 6. Retrieved 25 June 2021, from URL: http://nla.gov.au/nla.news-article39586455

22 Wayback Machine. Op.cit.

Images:

- (1890). Photograph - Port Arthur - Isle of the Dead - Headstones. *Libraries Tasmania.* Retrieved 9 July 2021 from URL: https://stors.tas.gov.au/PH30-1-4553

- (1910). Photograph - Port Arthur - Isle of the Dead. *Libraries Tasmania.* Retrieved 9 July 2021 from URL: https://stors.tas.gov.au/NS1029-1-258

- Nevin, Thomas J., 1842-1923, (photographer.) (1870). Mark Jeffrey. *Libraries Tasmania.* Retrieved 9 July 2021 from URL: https://stors.tas.gov.au/144584489

- Millbank Prison: Millbank T. H .Shepherd, 1829. *Wikimedia Commons.* Retrieved 9 July 2021: https://commons.wikimedia.org/w/index.php?title=File:Millbank_Thomas_Hosmer_Shepherd_pub_1829.jpg&oldid=243959980.

- National Archives UK, an illustration of *Warrior, Illustrated London News*, 1846. Retrieved 9 July 2021 from: https://www.nationalarchives.gov.uk/education/resources/19th-century-prison-ships/convict-hulk/

- Portrait William Ullathorne, before 1889. *Wikimedia Commons.* Retrieved 13 July 2021: https://commons.wikimedia.org/w/index.php?title=File:Portrait_of_William_Bernard_Ullathorne.jpg&oldid=569087951.

- Searle, E. W & Beatties Studio. (1848). Norfolk Island convict settlement at Kingston in 1848. *National Library of Australia.* Retrieved 9 July 2021, from URL: http://nla.gov.au/nla.obj-142181355

- Port Arthur, Guards c.1866 [picture]. *Libraries Tasmania.* Retrieved 9 July 2021 from URL: https://stors.tas.gov.au/AUTAS001131821464J2K$init=AUTAS001131821464

- Jeffrey, Mark & Examiner (Launceston, Tas.). (1893). *A Burglar's Life... Dark Days of Convictism in Australia.* Retrieved July 13, 2021, from http://nla.gov.au/nla.obj-2625635185

25

Above: Sylvia's grave in Balfour Cemetery, West Coast, Tasmania.
Source: kindly provided by the McArthur family descendants.

The young letter writer
Sylvia McArthur

Interred: Sylvia McArthur 16 October 1897 –
5 November 1912 (aged 15).

Location: This is a small cemetery with only a few
remaining graves.

Cemetery: Balfour Cemetery, Alexander Street, Balfour,
West Coast, TAS 7321.

This story was suggested by Ash Laan, who first heard of Sylvia from her father, Martin Laan, of Balfour. Our sincere thanks to Edie McArthur, the McArthur family, and Balfour historian, Patrick Bakes, for all their kind assistance.

Above: Sylvia McArthur.
Source: kindly provided by the McArthur family descendants.

"Dear Dame, I have not written to you before, although I have been going to do so for a long time...."

Sylvia wrote and signed off:
"Hoping you will think my letter fit for publishing."[1]

...and so began Sylvia McArthur's correspondence to Dame Durden's *Young Folks* page in the Launceston *Weekly Courier* on 11 January 1912. Dame Durden's page featured letters and poems from children to the age of 16. She would actively encourage new letter writers and offer prizes such as five shillings for the best story on 'How I Spent Christmas Day'. Violet Munro wrote of the fruit ripening, the weather being windy and her family's trip to Devonport for New Year; Agnes O'Keefe from North Scottsdale wrote of the school's Christmas tree; and Englebert Lewis told of the wet weather and having to bring the cows in.[2] Each letter received two or three gracious lines from Dame, welcoming their contribution and responding with interest as the letter dictated.

Life changes for a young girl

When Sylvia was seven, her mother, Catherine, 27, died from an illness, leaving four daughters – Florence, Sylvia, Gladys and Laurel 'Mavis' – and her husband, William. Her grandmother brought young Mavis up for her first four years until 1908 when William married[3] 20-year-old Marion Delaney. Sylvia, now 11, had the love of a new stepmother and soon found herself sister to two younger half-brothers,[4] Willie and Alan.[5]

Above: Sylvia (sitting on cushion) with her mother, Catherine, father William, sister Florence (on Catherine's lap), and sister Gladys (standing). Source: kindly provided by the McArthur family descendants.

But three years later in 1911, more upheaval was to come when Sylvia, now 14, left the only home she had ever known in Zeehan and with her family moved to the mining town of Balfour. Her father, William, accepted work as an engine driver[6] at the Murray Brothers Copper Reward Mine.[7] Copper was the currency, and Sylvia and her family were arriving two years into the 'boom' time. Their new township was right next to the mine where her father would work.[8]

Typhoid and timing

Typhoid was no stranger to the people of Tasmania – an epidemic had affected the island in the late 1880s and early 1890s. In 1910-1911, the 'new' town of Balfour experienced the deadly virus again and Dr Ingram was called from Stanley to be the local doctor in Balfour, arriving in February 1910 as the epidemic was getting underway.[9] Two deaths and 16 cases were recorded in 1910 and the two victims were buried in the Balfour Cemetery.[10]

There is much written about Sylvia having had typhoid but no evidence to support it. On her death certificate, it is not typhoid that is listed as taking her life. Sylvia's family was very fortunate to have arrived after the terrible typhoid outbreak which had all but finished around Easter 1911.[11] The Balfour family left Zeehan on 17 October 1911[12] and arrived to enjoy the spring months of 1911 in their new home town.

The journey and arrival

Sylvia's first letter to Dame Durden told of the McArthur brood's arduous journey moving from Zeehan to Balfour

– a trip by sea, coach and train, with a stay at a station. Today, the trip would take three hours by car and a ferry trip, 143km (89 miles) or six hours if you were driving from Hobart to Balfour. But in 1912, with no defined road, deep water entry point, or rail to the area, the journey with weather delays took two weeks.

Sylvia tells Dame Durden:
"The weather prevented us for nearly a week."

Dame Durden replies:
"I hope to hear from you often, Sylvia.
Tell me what Balfour is like."

Those six words would inspire Sylvia to capture the essence of her small town – then a thriving mining town in the heart of northwestern Tasmania, now a ghost town.

Tell me what Balfour is like

"I shall be very pleased to comply."

Sylvia wrote to Dame Durden in her next letter published 1 February 1912.
"The scenery close to the town is very nice, on one side, as the Franklin River wends within one mile of the eastern side, with numerous little fern gullies and glades running down towards the rugged bank of the stream. On the western side, right on to the sea, is open button-grass plains... there are many wild flowers blooming amongst the heath."[13]

Sylvia describes the industry in her town:

"One hotel – the other was burnt down two days before Christmas – a store, a butcher's shop, one baker, besides boarding houses and private buildings, a police station and a state school."[14]

Dame Durden replies:

"I read your description of Balfour with a great amount of interest, Sylvia. I hope the railway will soon connect your township with Circular Head, then I assure the district will advance rapidly. Thank your father on my behalf for the photographs. The editor was very pleased at receiving them and they are to be reproduced in the 'Courier'.

–Dame Durden."[15]

And they published them with a credit to Sylvia's dad in the corner. In her next correspondence, Sylvia agrees:

"We live in hope of the Stanley-Balfour railway being completed someday, so that we may have better means of transit with the larger centres of civilization.

Sincerely yours, Sylvia McArthur, Balfour".[16]

The loneliness of a teenage girl

Sylvia adapted to her new town and blended family – she referred to her father's young bride, Marion – nine years Sylvia's senior – as 'Mum' in correspondence.[17] But her letters reveal her loneliness and a homesick feeling for Zeehan. Sylvia had left a large school in Zeehan to attend the school in Balfour comprising one teacher and 23 students, none of whom were girls Sylvia's age.[18]

In Western Tasmania.

Above: Sylvia and her father sent his photos of Mount Balfour life to Dame Durden and they were published with a credit in The Weekly Courier, 1 February 1912, p18.[11] Source: Libraries Tasmania.

Sylvia wrote to Dame Durden about her schooling experience:
"I do not go to school, and the day does seem long. I would very much like to go to school again, only there are no big girls here, and I would be just as lonely as I am at home."[19]

A photo taken by her father, William, captures Sylvia with children from the Balfour school. William was a keen photographer and a wordsmith. Sylvia shared the love of creativity and expression with him and he forwarded his photographs for the paper's use to accompany Sylvia's letters. They create a wonderful record of Balfour at the time of its heyday. She tells Dame Durden:

"You will find my photograph in the school group. I am in the back row, the fourth from the left hand side; the laddie in front of me is my little brother Willie. I remain, sincerely yours,

Sylvia McArthur, Mount Balfour."[20]

Above: Sylvia - back row, fourth from the left. Little brother, Willie, is in front of her. Source: kindly provided by the McArthur family descendants.

Her loneliness surfaces again in her correspondence of 18 July 1912, when she recalls the celebrations for Empire Day in Balfour, and the year prior when they lived in Zeehan. Sylvia tells Dame Durden:

"Empire Day went off very slowly here; even the poor school children did not have a half-holiday – not like the grand time we had at Zeehan last year. There we had sports all the afternoon, and a fire in the evening. The elder girls handed round tea, buns, lollies, and fruit; really, I don't think I will ever forget that day. Have you been to Zeehan, Dame? It is a bonnie place, I think."[21]

Celebrations in Balfour for a young woman of nearly 15 were few and far between. Sylvia writes:

"I think we are going to have a dance here one night this week; that would indeed be a treat, for we only have one on an average about every five months. Of course we would have more, only there is nobody who will volunteer to play the accordion; if it were a piano, for instance, it probably would be different. But the piano which was used for dances was destroyed when the hotel was burnt down at Christmas."[22]

A family affair

As Sylvia's first year in Balfour progresses from January to June 1912, she writes Dame Durden of her family members including her sister, Gladys, now studying in Hobart, and of her own love of reading.

"I read with great pleasure the letters from your correspondents, especially from Janie King, in Hobart. My sister Gladys is at the same college as Janie, and mentioned in her last letter to me having made her acquaintance."[23]

And of her brother, Willie:

"He will be three in July, but he thinks himself quite a man. He can sing almost anything."[24] Adding in her next correspondence: *"He told me to tell you he can sing 'Don't go down in the Mine, Dad', 'All things bright and beautiful', 'Meet me at the corner, Darling', 'God Save the King' and dozens of other songs."*[25]

Dame Durden replies:

"Tell Willie that he must write or dictate a letter to me. I would love to hear him sing."[26]

Sylvia's letters reflects a girl of maturity, aided no doubt by her life lessons and a love of reading.

"Do you read many books, Dame? I do. I very much like Ethel Turner's books, and think I have read most of them."

Dame Durden replies:

"Ethel Turner's books are most interesting and popular."[27]

Ever the inquiring mind, in the latter weeks of May 1912, Sylvia takes a trip down the mine with her father, informing Dame Durden of her adventure:

"*It was the first time I had been down a mine that I can remember. I think it a funny feeling one has whilst going down in a cage. Whilst I was down below a gentleman took a flashlight photograph of us. We all looked like ghosts, for our faces were so white.*

However, I would not like to leave Balfour without being able to say I was down a mine. Believe me to be sincerely yours,

Sylvia McArthur. Balfour."[28]

Dame Durden replies:

"*I have been down several mines in the course of my travels.*"[29]

We soon learn of the demands of the job on her father, and his separation from family.

Above: *William and Sylvia in the mine. Source: kindly provided by the McArthur family descendants.*

Sylvia wrote of her father's work in the mines:

"My Dad is working 12 hours a day now, and he gets very tired, but it is a long shift, isn't it? Will close with love to your many correspondents, and also to yourself."[30]

Dame did not comment on this aspect of Sylvia's letter as, no doubt, many a worker would have been producing similar hours in 1912.

The last letter

Sylvia's last letter to Dame Durden was published on 3 October 1912. There was a concert in Balfour and despite the poor weather, the hall was crowded, and everyone in attendance *"voted it the best held at Balfour up to the present."[31]* Sylvia closed by advising the fishing season had started and sent her love. On 21 November 1912, on page 3, Dame Durden wrote the following:

["Readers of the 'Page' will join me in tendering deep sympathy to the sorrowing parents of dear little Sylvia M'Arthur. Sylvia was one of the most beloved of our correspondents, and all will be sadly shocked to hear of her death. Not only was the dear child a writer of interesting letters, but she frequently sent me photographs of the Balfour settlement, and these have from time to time been published in the Courier, Farewell dear little Sylvia: the Father has taken you unto His loving care, but we will miss you. Following are some touching verses written by the father of our dear departed friend.]

Dame Durden."[32]

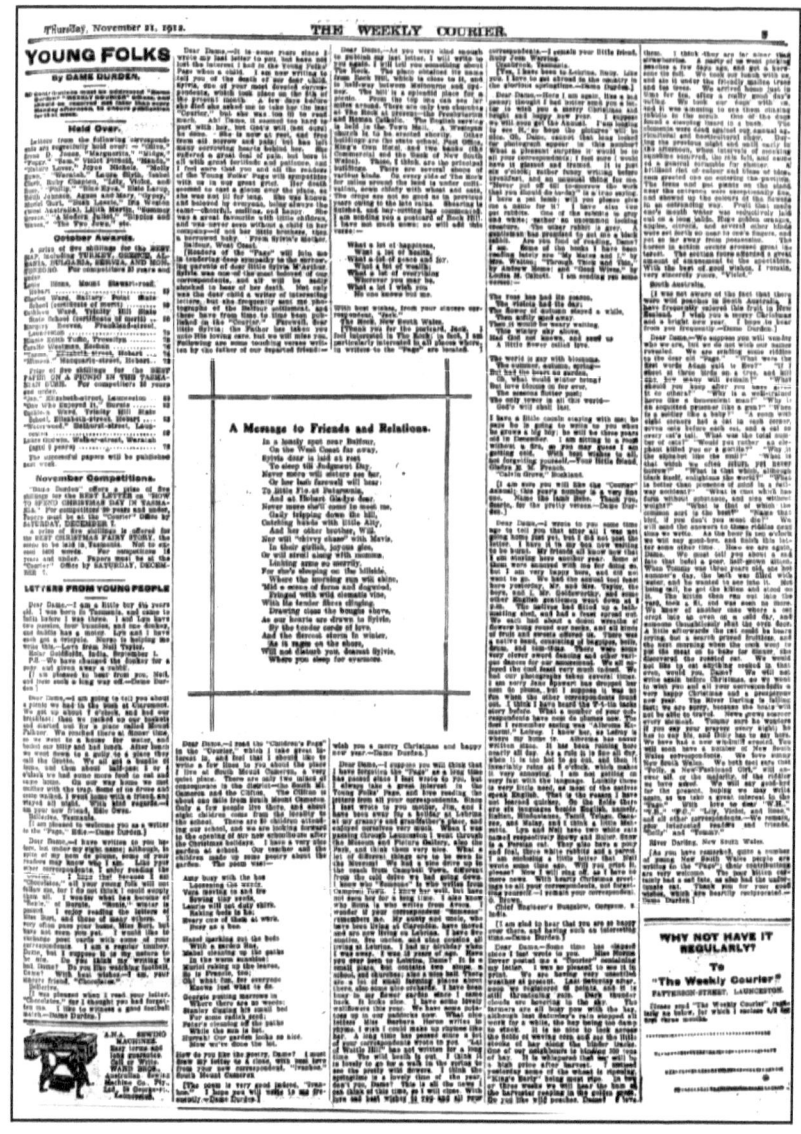

Above: Sylvia's stepmother's letter and her father's poem (centre) are given pride of place in Dame Durden's page on 21 November 1912.[35] Source: The Weekly Courier, Libraries Tasmania.

Dame Durden published a letter from Sylvia's stepmother in full: It read:

"It is some years since I wrote my last letter to you, but have not lost the interest I had in the Young Folks' page when a child. I am now writing to tell you of the death of our dear child, Sylvia, one of your most devoted correspondents.... Ah! Dame, it seemed too hard to part with her but God's will (not ours) be done. She is now at rest, and free from all sorrows and pain; but has left many sorrowing hearts behind her. She suffered a great deal of pain, but bore it all with fortitude and patience.... She was known and beloved by everyone, being always the same – cheerful, smiling and happy. She was a great favourite with little children and was never seen without a child in her company.
From Sylvia's mother, Balfour, West Coast."[33]

Her father penned a poem which was also printed on Dame Durden's page, paying tribute to his beloved daughter:

In a lonely spot near Balfour,
On the West Coast far away,
Sylvia dear is laid at rest
To sleep till Judgment Day.

Never more will sisters see her,
Or her last farewell will hear:
To little Flo at Patersonia,
And at Hobart Gladys dear.
Never more she'll come to meet me,

Gaily tripping down the hill,
Catching hands with little Alty,
And her other brother, Will.

Nor will 'chivvy chase' with Mavis,
In their girlish, joyous glee,
Or will stroll along with mumma
Linking arms so merrily.

For she's sleeping on the hillside,
Where the morning sun will shine,
Mid a scene of ferns and dogwood,
Fringed with wild clematis vine,
With its tender fibres clinging,
Drawing close the boughs above,
As our hearts are drawn to Sylvie,
By the tender cords of love.

And the fiercest storm in winter,
As it rages on the shore,
Will not disturb you, dearest Sylvie,
Where you sleep for evermore.[34]

The *Zeehan and Dundas Herald* wrote that Sylvia: "was under the care of Dr. Clark, but no serious symptoms manifested themselves until a few days ago. Despite medical skill she gradually sank and passed peacefully away."[35]

The *Circular Head Chronicle* ran a tribute to Sylvia on 6 November 1912 noting two deaths in Balfour had saddened the town:

"Another death occurred here today in the person of Miss Sylvia McArthur, second eldest daughter of Mr W. McArthur, aged 15 years. She had been ailing for three weeks, from a complication of complaints. The two deaths so close on one another has cast a gloom over the field. Both the deceased were well known and highly respected."[36]

And on Saturday 9 November 1912, in the *Zeehan and Dundas Herald*, the following appeared from Sylvia's parents:

"Mr and Mrs W. McArthur, of Balfour, desire to tender their sincere thanks to Dr Clark for skillful treatment and kind attention to their late daughter, Sylvia: also to the residents of Balfour generally for many acts of sympathetic kindness during their sad bereavement and all friends for letters and telegrams of condolence."[37]

Remembering Sylvia

Sylvia's death certificate lists peritonitis as her cause of death.[38] Peritonitis is an inflammation of the peritoneum – "a silk-like membrane that lines your inner abdominal wall and covers the organs within your abdomen".[39] This inflammation is usually due to infection, possibly from a perforation in the abdomen.

Descendants have heard of Sylvia falling while being piggybacked, which may have led to this injury.[40] If untreated, it is life-threatening. Sylvia's stepmother's heartfelt words:

"She suffered a great deal of pain"[41] may confirm that Sylvia died as a result of peritonitis.

Descendants mentioned Sylvia's love of children and she often did babysitting for members of her community. It seems inevitable that she would have become a teacher if she had lived to adulthood. All three of her sisters took up teaching as their vocation.[42]

Sylvia's handsome grave was no doubt paid for by the life insurance policy on her life for 100 pounds, as listed in her will administered by the Public Trustee in Tasmania.[43] It was quite common in those years to insure the lives of young people, especially as disease was rife, and families wanted to give their loved ones a proper burial.

What became of....

Dame Durden appears in a number of references. There is the Dame Durden in the writings of Charles Dickens' *Bleak House* (1853) – a character thus named when they receive the keys to the household. But the editor of the '*Young Folks*' page appears to have selected the name Dame Durden for reasons she explains in the July 1901 edition:

> *"Every child is, I think acquainted with Dame Durden (of fairy lore), who never went anywhere or did anything without wrapping her red shawl around her shoulders, and fixing her specs, on her nose, also that she was famed for her stock of fairy tales."*[44]

The writer goes on to say the stories were told to her and she would share them with young readers, hence the nom de plume. It is unknown if there was a dedicated writer for this page or Dame Durden was the editor of *The Weekly Courier*. The column continued for the next 34 years with the last issue (available online at the time of writing this story) being June 1935. The column was then titled: *'The Children's Playground by Dame Durden'.*[45]

William McArthur, Sylvia's father, lived a long life and died on 30 December 1940 in Launceston aged 76. He was cremated and rests in Carr Villa Memorial Park, Launceston.

Stepmother Marion, died thirty years after William in 1970, aged in her early eighties. Marion also rests in Carr Villa Memorial Park, Launceston, buried in the Monumental, Section C15, 75.

Sylvia's siblings enjoyed longer lives than herself. Florence died in 1959 aged 59, Gladys died in 1979 aged 84, Alan died in 1982 aged 72,

Above: William and Marion, 1908. Source: McArthur family descendants.

Laurel 'Mavis' died in 1988 aged 86, and her beloved singing William (Willie) died in 1989 aged 80.

Balfour the township: The small but strong community of Balfour, being a town built on industry, would meet its end when the industry – copper mining – dried up. Built with little town planning other than expanding to meet the needs of the growing population, during the boom time, 1909-1914, the town was home to around 300 residents. By 1921, the industry was gone and so were the residents… 46 remained in the census count.[46]

How to find Sylvia's grave:

Fire and neglect have ravaged the small Balfour Cemetery now home to just four gravestones, including Sylvia's which lies flat on the earth next to the largest tree. The headstone reads: "In after time we'll meet her". As all Sylvia's immediate family have now since passed, they are again reunited.

Above: Graves in the cemetery at Balfour, Tasmania in 1935 before the fire, including Sylvia's.[32] Source: Circular Head Heritage Centre.

References:

1 Durden, Dame, Young Folks in *The Weekly Courier*, 11 January 1912, page 3. Libraries Tasmania. Retrieved 29 June 2021 from URL: https://stors.tas.gov.au/weeklycourier
2 Durden, Dame, Young Folks in *The Weekly Courier*, 4 January 1912, page 3. Libraries Tasmania. Retrieved 29 June 2021 from URL: https://stors.tas.gov.au/weeklycourier
3 Edie McArthur and Rob McArthur, descendants of the McArthur family. *Ancestry.com* 5 July 2021.
4 Haygarth, Nic, A tale of two headstones: pt 2, *Sylvia McArthur, Balfour correspondent*, 9 Jan 2017. Retrieved 30 June 2021: https://nichaygarth.com/index.php/2017/01/09/a-tale-of-two-headstones-part-two-sylvia-mcarthur-balfour-correspondent/#_ftnref3
5 Durden, Dame, Young Folks in *The Weekly Courier*, 18 July 1912, page 3. Libraries Tasmania. Retrieved 29 June 2021 from URL: https://stors.tas.gov.au/weeklycourier
6 Haygarth, Nick, A tale of two headstones: part two. Op.cit.
7 Dryburgh, James, *The Balfour correspondent*, 17 August 2020. Updated 3 May 2021. Retrieved 1 July 2021 from URL: https://www.fortysouth.com.au/history888/the-balfour-correspondent
8 Verrier, James, Thesis: *Development and Decline of a Mining Town: Balfour, 1906-21*. Retrieved 1 July 2021 from URL: http://www.mininghistory.asn.au/wp-content/uploads/1999.pdf
9 - 11 Email correspondence with Mr Patrick Bakes, Balfour historian. 24 August 2021
12 Durden, Dame, Young Folks in *The Weekly Courier*, 11 January 1912, page 3. Op.cit.
13 - 15 Durden, Dame, Young Folks in *The Weekly Courier*, 1 February 1912, page 3. Libraries Tasmania. Retrieved 29 June 2021 from URL: https://stors.tas.gov.au/weeklycourier
16 Durden, Dame, Young Folks in *The Weekly Courier*, 1 April 1912, page 3. Libraries Tasmania. Retrieved 29 June 2021 from URL: https://stors.tas.gov.au/weeklycourier
17 Durden, Dame, Young Folks in *The Weekly Courier*, 11 January 1912, page 3. Op.cit.
18 Haygarth, Nick, A tale of two headstones: part two. Op.cit.
19 Durden, Dame, Young Folks in *The Weekly Courier*, 13 June 1912, page 3. Op.cit.
20 Durden, Dame, Young Folks in *The Weekly Courier*, 1 February 1912, page 3. Op.cit.
21 - 22 Durden, Dame, Young Folks in *The Weekly Courier*, 18 July 1912, page 3. Op.cit.
23 Durden, Dame, Young Folks in *The Weekly Courier*, 1 April 1912, page 3. Op.cit.
24 Durden, Dame, Young Folks in *The Weekly Courier*, 13 June 1912, page 3. Op.cit.
25-26 Durden, Dame, Young Folks in *The Weekly Courier*, 18 July 1912, page 3. Op.cit.
27 Durden, Dame, Young Folks in *The Weekly Courier*, 1 April 1912, page 3. Op.cit.
28 - 29 Durden, Dame, Young Folks in *The Weekly Courier*, 13 June 1912, page 3. Op.cit.
30 Durden, Dame, Young Folks in *The Weekly Courier*, 18 July 1912, page 3. Op.cit.
31 Durden, Dame, Young Folks in *The Weekly Courier*, 3 October1912, page 3. Op.cit.
32 - 34 Durden, Dame, Young Folks in *The Weekly Courier*, 21 November 1912, page 3. Op.cit.
35 BALFOUR NEWS (1912, November 8). *Zeehan and Dundas Herald (Tas.: 1890 - 1922)*, p. 2. Retrieved June 29, 2021, from http://nla.gov.au/nla.news-article83340789
36 Deaths at Balfour. (1912, November 6). *Circular Head Chronicle (Stanley, Tas.: 1906 - 1954)*, p. 2. Retrieved July 2, 2021, from http://nla.gov.au/nla.news-article160990396
37 Bereavement notices, *Zeehan and Dundas Herald*, 9 November 1912. Retrieved 31 August 2021 from URL: https://newspaperarchive.com/zeehan-and-dundas-herald-nov-09-1912-p-2/
38 Edie McArthur and Rob McArthur, descendants of the McArthur family. *Ancestry.com* 5 July 2021.
39 Peritonitis, Patient Care & Health Information, Diseases & Conditions. *Mayo Clinic*. Retrieved 5 July 2021 from URL: https://www.mayoclinic.org/diseases-conditions/peritonitis/symptoms-causes/syc-20376247
40 Edie McArthur and Rob McArthur, descendants of the McArthur family. *Ancestry.com* 5 July 2021
41 Durden, Dame, Young Folks in The Weekly Courier, 21 November 1912, page 3. Op.cit.
42 Edie McArthur and Rob McArthur, descendants of the McArthur family. *Ancestry.com* 5 July 2021.
43 McArthur, Sylvia Tris, Will, 1913. *Public Trustee of Tasmania*. Retrieved 5 July 2021 from URL: https://stors.tas.gov.au/AD963-1-1-3$init=AD963-1-1-3_1
44 Durden, Dame, Young Folks in *The Weekly Courier*, 6 July 1901.
45 Durden, Dame, in *The Weekly Courier*, June 1935. *Libraries Tasmania*.
46 Verrier, James, Thesis: *Development and Decline of a Mining Town: Balfour, 1906-21*. Retrieved 1 July 2021 from URL: http://www.mininghistory.asn.au/wp-content/uploads/1999.pdf

Images:
- McArthur, William (photographer), Scenes on the Mount Balfour Mine Field, *The Weekly Courier*, 1 Feb 1912, p18. Launceston, Tas.: Henry Button, 1901-1935. Retrieved from URL: https://stors.tas.gov.au/ILS/SD_ILS-582993
- Sylvia's school photo: McArthur, William (photographer). Ibid.
Our grateful thanks to the McArthur family descendants, especially Edie for all her assistance and kind permission to reproduce the following photographs:
- Sylvia's grave and Sylvia as a teenager
- Sylvia (sitting on cushion) with mother, Catherine, father William, sister Florence (on Catherine's lap), and sister Gladys (standing).
- Sylvia in the mine with her father, William.
- The marriage between William McArthur and Marion May Delaney, on 19 Aug 1908 at the Roman Catholic Church.
Balfour Cemetery graves reproduced with the kind permission of the Circular Head Heritage Centre.

Up there Cazaly!
Roy Cazaly

Interred: **Roy Cazaly**, 13 January 1893 – 10 October 1963 (aged 70 years).

Location: Derwent Gardens, garden bed 29, number 629. TIP: garden bed 29 is nowhere near garden bed 27 and 28. So if you find those beds first, leave that area and continue in the area to the right of the chapel if you were facing it.

Cemetery: Cornelian Bay Cemetery and Crematorium, Queens Walk, New Town, TAS 7008.

Back in the days when footy – Australian Rules that is – was a very different game, there lived a man called Roy Cazaly, a master at the game and hero to its followers and especially those who supported the teams to which he contributed his not inadequate talents.

Born in 1893, he was the youngest of ten children of English immigrant James Cazaly and his wife Elizabeth Jemima, nee McNee. Roy's mother was a Scottish herbalist, mid-wife and contributor to the Cazaly pedigree, which was first class. James was a champion oarsman and physical instructor who trained Roy and his brothers in the family gymnasium built in their backyard. In his day, many regarded him as the best man on the Yarra River (Melbourne) whether as an oarsman or a sculler.

Like his father, the young Roy Cazaly also excelled as an oarsman but ironically it was the training given to him in the backyard gym that would take him away from the sport his father loved and onto the footy grounds of Melbourne. It would leave his father shattered… vowing never to watch his most talented son play. Apparently, he never saw Roy play football but reportedly would stand outside the footy ground gates and ask, "How's the boy doing?"[1]

A champ in the making

Like many youngsters of the era, Roy no doubt had his first contact with the game of football in the schoolyard. Many a footballer would remember the bloodied knees and injured fingers gathered as kids from kicking a heavy, rain-soaked ball and tackling opponents on the asphalt playgrounds of inner suburban schools. There were no such things as grassed ovals back then to cater for lunchtime and recess games of footy in the winter and cricket in the off-season.

Throughout his football career, Roy would always be a self-improver. At home, he had his theories about how to improve his performances by making practise times as difficult as possible. He would spend hours kicking a ball through a tyre hanging from a rope and practice his leaps by hanging a greased ball above a sandpit. Breathing at the right time was also part of Roy's routine. He believed that a quick breath at the right time when he was jumping would enhance his leap.[2]

But clearly, Roy was an all-rounder – proficient at just about anything he put his hand to. While he was still a teenager, he played cricket as a left-arm medium pacer for Port Melbourne and rowed for South Melbourne in Victorian Championship events.[3] But having been born, brought up, and educated in Albert Park and Middle Park, the call of the footy umpire's whistle was never far away. At either end of Albert Park were the two grounds where Roy would play most of his VFL (precursor to the AFL) games – Junction Oval, St Kilda's home ground is at the southernmost end, and South Melbourne's home ground, Lake Oval at the other end of Albert Park.

Making the big time

His first club after he left school was Middle Park 'Wesleys' which played in a church competition. He had four seasons there from 1906 to 1909, honing his skills and developing his fitness regime. Roy wasn't tall by today's AFL player standards, just 180cm (5ft 11 inches) and he weighed in at

VOTED BEST BY CLUBMATES

80 kilograms (12 and a half stone). Alcohol, cigarettes and fried food were definite outs, and he tapered his food and liquid intake toward the end of the week with a game coming up on the weekend. He has been called a fitness fanatic before his time.[4]

In 1910 Roy tried out at Princes Park but damaged his shoulder in a reserve grade match and, according to the South Melbourne version of events, left when he couldn't get Carlton's staff to treat his injury.[5] The next year, 1911, Cazaly turned out for St Kilda and managed his first game reasonably late in the season after some of the St Kilda regulars refused to play because of a dispute with the club over dressing sheds. He got a passing mention amongst Monday morning's *Argus* footy reports, but it was just that, a brief line about Cazaly, Hattam and Crowle being prominent defenders in St Kilda's mammoth loss. Presumably affected by the dressing shed issue the side went down 18:11 (129) to 2:3 (15).[6]

Despite that forgettable first game result at St Kilda, Roy Cazaly stayed at the club for a decade, playing 99 games, for which some sources say he was never paid.[7] Others say he was paid after two seasons.[8] Cazaly won the club's Best and Fairest in his last two seasons *(pictured opposite in the Weekly Times when voted best by clubmates)*.

While he was at St Kilda there were several significant events in Roy Cazaly's life. On 18 October 1913 he married Agnes Murtha and in 1914 their first child, Elizabeth Florence, was born. Tragically she was to die in 1916, reportedly from diphtheria. It was a hectic time for Cazaly and his growing involvement in the game took him across Victoria and throughout the suburbs, most thought just to be involved. In 1918 he coached Camberwell juniors who played in a mid-week competition on Wednesdays, likewise for 1919 when he coached in the South Melbourne District mid-week competition, and in 1921 he headed to the Western District to coach in the local Warrnambool Wednesday competition.

But why so much footy? His heavy involvement began after the death of daughter, Elizabeth, which had hit Roy hard and may have been a way for him to cope with the tragedy... or it might have been for the money, given that some said he wasn't paid by St Kilda. As time would tell, there was good money for players and coaches in the bush.

The move to the other end of the park

In 1921 Cazaly joined the 'Blood-Soaked Angels', as South Melbourne was nicknamed, according to some, after the 1918 Grand Final against Collingwood. The blood-soaked part apparently came from a catholic priest who said the mass in South Melbourne the weekend before the Grand Final saying, "I bless you blood-stained angels to win next week". And they did... by five points.[9]

Others associate the name with the violent bloodbath of the 1945 Grand Final in which Carlton defeated South Melbourne by 28 points. On the Monday after the game, the *Argus* newspaper carried the headline "Nine reported in vicious final – VFL must stop savagery."[10]

When Cazaly went to South Melbourne, he met up with two other players who would start a tradition that lives on today. Roy could take towering marks despite his lack of height, and Fred 'Skeeter' Fleiter and Mark 'Napper' Tandy would yell out simultaneously as Roy went for a mark or a ruck contest, "Up there Cazzer" which became "Up there Cazaly" and is still synonymous with Australian football.

Cazaly, Fleiter and Tandy became known as the 'terrible trio' and spent hours working with each other until they developed a sixth sense about what they might do.

It wasn't long before the crowds worked out what was happening and joined the yell for Cazaly to go for the ball... "Up there Cazaly!"

Above left to right: Mark Tandy, Fred Fleiter and Roy Cazaly, South Melbourne's ruck combination of the 1920s. Source: Wikimedia Commons.

Above: Roy Cazaly in action.
Source: Wikimedia Commons

The yell entered the Australian idiom. Infantrymen in North Africa during World War II adopted the cry and it became part of our folklore.[11] A correspondent to the *Sporting Globe* in Melbourne wrote: "In England in 1926 and 1927, while attached to the Vickers Shipbuilding Co. at Barrow in Furness, 'Up there, Cazaly' was a password with a few Aussies who worked with me."[12]

A curious move

Roy Cazaly was paid six pounds a week in his 99 games for South Melbourne which were strangely spread over two periods, 1921-24 and 1926-27. In the intervening year, 1925, when you would think Roy was at his peak, he was lured away to a tiny one-horse town in the Western District called Minyip to be captain-coach of the local team. He was paid 12 pounds a week, double what he was getting at South Melbourne.

He made the most of Minyip while there, running a fruit and confectionery business and playing mid-week footy for nearby Litchfield-Carron.[13] Even so, it was a curious move from a man who was later described as the greatest Australian Rules footballer between the two world wars, and in the time he was at South Melbourne, played in Victorian state teams 13 times.

A move to Tasmania

In 1928, Roy took his family and made the crossing of that small stretch of water to make his home in Tasmania. He was appointed coach of the 'City' club in Launceston for the season.[14] In that year City became the first northern side to win the official state premiership after it beat North Hobart by 32 points at York Park in Launceston.[15]

He had three seasons coaching City and from 1932 there followed a mixed bag of positions which included North Hobart in 1932-33, New Town, Hobart in 1934-36 and 1948-51, South Melbourne in 1937-38, Hawthorn in 1942-43, and Preston and Camberwell in the Victorian Football Association. His last professional game was with Camberwell when he was 48, but in 1951 at age 58 he played in a short veterans' match, and then a full game for New Town in which he kicked a goal.

The impact of Roy Cazaly on his newly adopted home state was to be considerably broader than just on the footy field. During his time at South Melbourne, he had studied the work of the club's doctor and masseur to satisfy his fascination with physical movement and the way muscles worked. The medicos taught him about the treatment of muscular injuries and Swedish massage.

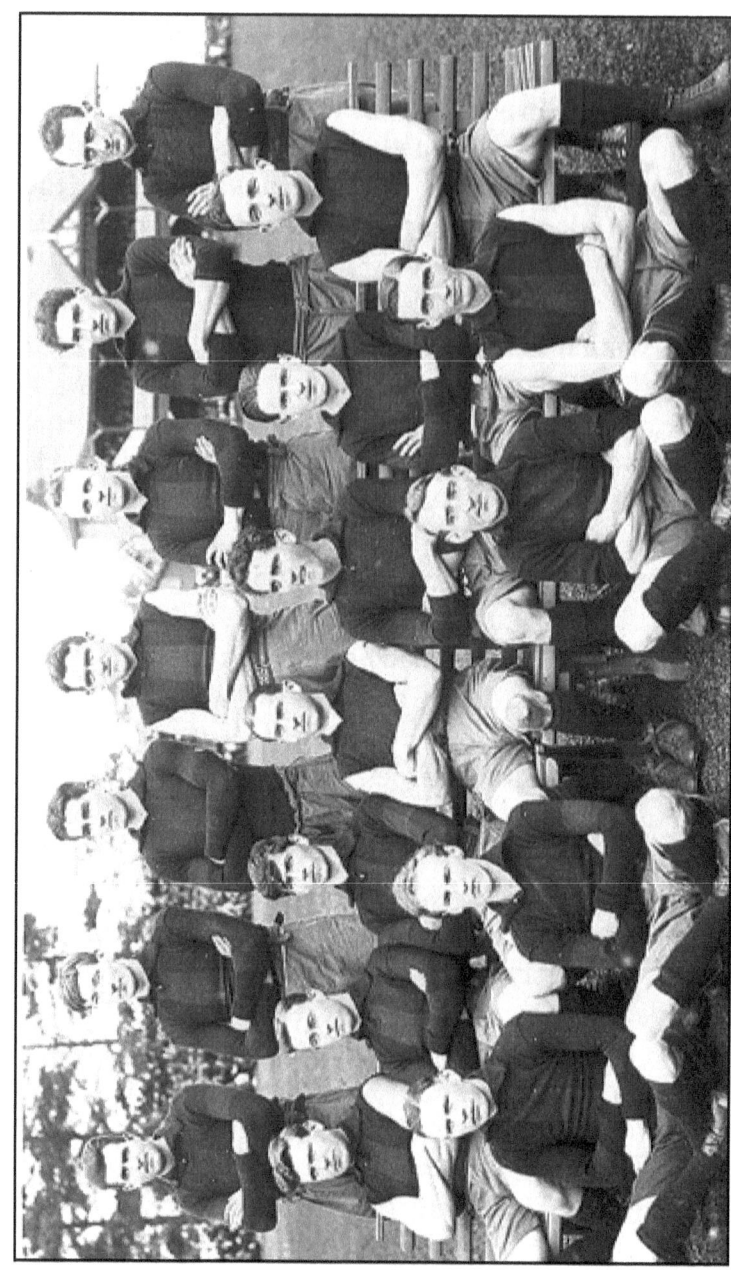

Above: 1921 North Tasmanian Football Team. Roy Cazaly, Captain and Coach seated centre middle row.
Source: Libraries Tasmania.

During the Depression of the 1930s, when times were tough, he worked on the wharves and played mid-week footy with the waterside workers. At night, he worked as a physiotherapist, treating their injuries at no cost.

An epidemic on the move

But there was a medical disaster fast approaching Tasmania – it was called polio – a potentially lethal virus that could bring on paralysis and death. During the epidemic of 1937-38 in Tasmania, it affected 421 people for every 100,000 members of the population, making it the biggest outbreak anywhere in the world. Over 2000 adults and children were affected and 81 of them died.

To avoid panic and spread of infection, the government imposed strict restrictions and called on anyone with medical training to come forward as volunteers. Cazaly had been a student of Sister Elizabeth Kenny, a self-trained bush nurse who had developed her own methods for treating polio victims… they were, however, quite controversial. He treated victims of the virus using the methods developed by Sister Kenny in a clinic he opened without charging fees. (Sister Kenny's story is in the *Great South West Queensland* volume of *Grave Tales*).

A lifetime of memories

There were many facets to the man, Roy Cazaly – fitness fanatic, footballer extraordinaire, self-trained physiotherapist, racehorse trainer, and font of knowledge about the game he loved, Aussie Rules footy. And he wasn't afraid to tell it as he saw it. Like the great rivalry that turned to violence in the State versus State footy carnivals and particularly the bitter clashes that occurred between Victoria and Western Australia – Cazaly described it: "It simmered in 1921, came to the boil in 1924, and blew the lid off in 1926," he said. "Saddles and bridles were off in the second game at Perth in 1926, and to all participants it was known as settling day. Enough happened in that game to keep the tribunals of Australia busy for weeks."[16] It was the day when Cazaly said he received his worst hit ever… the masseurs worked on him for three days to get him fit for the next game.

And the things that went on in the bush when local teams organised 'ring-ins' of city players who had the weekend off. Roy was involved in one such escapade that involved two teams, Colbinabbin and Elmore, great rivals in a local league just outside Bendigo. It was the Grasshoppers versus the Bloods, who weren't happy with the previous result between the rivals and decided to give themselves an advantage against the Grasshoppers.

Roy and several other players were smuggled aboard a train in Melbourne on Friday afternoon and it was planned that they should sneak off at a station before it got to Elmore. They did, and cars were waiting to take them to their overnight accommodation before the big game. The next day, just before the game was about to start, the 'stake money' had reached 500 pounds and Elmore was feeling very confident.

Roy says it went like this: "Uniforms complete, out we ran, regular Elmore colts prancing and preening. There was Billy Schmidt, 'Snow' Noonan, Pat Kennedy, Paddy Maloney, Mark Tandy, Jock Doherty and myself. Out ran Colbinabbin. The first player I saw was Dick Godfrey, from Hawthorn. We had played together as kids, so it was no use trying to hide anything. We smiled and knew the game was up." The Colbinabbin team had found out what was happening and organised 12 Association players as ring-ins themselves. Roy added: "In those days the game did not command the publicity it does now. Players were allowed to have a game here and there, and no notice was taken if they were playing in Wednesday games. No bar was on anyone – almost a go-as-you-please permit arrangement." [17]

Arguably, one of the lasting influences of Roy Cazaly happened in the two years he was coach of Hawthorn. When he started there the team was nicknamed the 'Mayblooms', hardly a moniker likely to strike fear in the hearts of the opposition. Apparently, the Hawthorn bush was also known as the May Tree or May Bush and flowered in the leafy eastern suburbs around Glenferrie Oval, where the club was located. Hence, the Mayblooms. But Cazaly encouraged the adoption of something a little more fearsome, like the 'mighty fighting Hawks.' He must have had enough support and in 1943 the 'Hawks' it was. [18]

The crowd's on your side [19]

While Peter Sullivan, the other half – along with Mike Brady – of the Two-Man-Band who wrote and performed the song *Up there Cazaly* was not a household name, Brady and the song were! Brady has been a regular performer at VFL and AFL Grand Finals since the song was written and first hit the airwaves in 1979. It started life as a promotional jingle for the Channel Seven footy coverage and its popularity led to the release of a full-length song version during the footy season of 1979. It became the top single by an Australian artist by sales, selling 250,000 copies. It made number one on the charts in September, the same month that Carlton won its twelfth premiership flag by defeating Collingwood by just five points.[20]

While the song is claimed to be the anthem for Australian Rules football, Channel Seven wasn't first in catching on to the popularity of Roy Cazaly and his ability to draw a crowd. One character in the play *Summer of the Seventeenth Doll*, written by Ray Lawler in 1955, had heroine 'Nance' used the phrase "Up there Cazaly" several times and after the song's release just about everyone had a go at it, including former Collingwood great turned commentator, Lou Richards. You might find it hard to believe, but in 1991, under his nickname, 'Louie the Lip', Richards actually released a hip hop version of the song. [21]

Much to do

Life was full for Roy Cazaly. He took to breeding horses on his property in Lenah Valley and won the first Tasmanian Trotting Championship in 1956 with *Master Barry*. He ran for Parliament as the Liberal Party candidate in the seat of Denison in 1950, but he was unsuccessful. [22]

His family was close. Roy played the piano and the family often had sing-songs at night. When Roy reached his mid-60s, he suffered a series of heart attacks which led to a long illness. It was eventually too much for him and on 10 October 1963, Roy died at Lenah Valley. His wife, a son and four daughters survived him.

The Australian Football Hall of Fame inducted Roy Cazaly in 1996 and immediately elevated him to AFL Legend status. His career spanned five decades, during which he played 429 senior matches, including 212 in the VFL and 32 state matches for Victoria and Tasmania.[23]

References:

1 Guerin, Andrew, *Australian Rowing History. James Cazaly*. 2013. Retrieved 6 August 2021 from URL:. https://www.rowinghistory-aus.info/rower-profiles/cazaly-james

2 Who was Roy Cazaly? *Our Footy Story*. Retrieved 6 August 2021 from URL: https://ourfootystory.com/2019/07/13/who-was-roy-cazaly/

3 Noel Counihan, 'Cazaly, Roy (1893–1963)', Australian Dictionary of Biography, National Centre of Biography, *Australian National University*. Retrieved 6 August 2021 from URL: https://adb.anu.edu.au/biography/cazaly-roy-5541/text9441

4 Early Tasmanian Football Legends. *Roy Cazaly*. Retrieved 6 August 2021 from URL: http://www.footballlegends.org/roy_cazaly.htm

5 Sydney Swans website. Our Oldest Club Champions. *Sydney Swans Media*, 2017. Retrieved 6 August 2021 from URL: https://www.sydneyswans.com.au/news/284669/our-oldest-club-champions

6 St. Kilda's New Team. (1911, July 31). *The Argus (Melbourne, Vic: 1848 - 1957)*, p. 5. Retrieved July 6, 2021, from http://nla.news-article11603993

7 Noel Counihan, 'Cazaly, Roy (1893–1963)', *Australian Dictionary of Biography*. Op.cit.

8 Darebin Heritage. *Roy Cazaly*. Retrieved 6 Aug 2021 from: https://heritage.darebinlibraries.vic.gov.au/article/72

9 Sydney Swans: Carolyn Cummins remembers... *Sydney Morning Herald*. 30 Sept 2016.

10 Nine Reported In Vicious Final, VFL Must Stop Savagery (1945, Oct 1). *The Argus (Melbourne, Vic.: 1848 - 1957)*, p. 15. Retrieved July 26, 2021, from http://nla.gov.au/nla.news-article12144645

11 Noel Counihan, 'Cazaly, Roy (1893–1963)', *Australian Dictionary of Biography*. Op.cit.

12 As Jack Rohan Sees it (1935, June 1). *Sporting Globe (Melbourne, Vic.: 1922 - 1954)*, p. 7 (Edition1). Retrieved July 27, 2021, from http://nla.gov.au/nla.news-article181691123

13 Cazaly connection subject of research, *The Weekly Advertiser*, July 1 2010. Retrieved 6 Aug 2021 from URL: http://archive.theweeklyadvertiser.com.au/2010/07/01/Cazaly-connection-subject-of-research/

14 Football Coach. (1928, January 31). *Advocate (Burnie, Tas: 1890 - 1954)*, p. 2. Retrieved July 27, 2021, from http://nla.gov.au/nla.news-article67570174

15 *Australian Football*–City South. Retrieved 6 Aug 2021: https://australianfootball.com/clubs/info/city-south/79

16 'Roy Cazaly Tells Of' (1935, May 22). *Sporting Globe (Melbourne, Vic.: 1922 - 1954)*, p. 10 (Edition2). Retrieved July 27, 2021, from http://nla.gov.au/nla.news-article181690255

17 'Roy Cazaly Tells Of' *Sporting Globe (Melbourne, Vic.: 1922 - 1954)* 1 May 1937: 8 (Edition1). Web. 27 Jul 2021 <http://nla.gov.au/nla.news-article190339964>.

18 Haby, Peter, The 1939 Mayblooms pennant, *Hawthorn Football Club*, Aug 8, 2017. Retrieved 6 Aug 2021 from URL: https://www.hawthornfc.com.au/news/469847/the-1939-mayblooms-pennant

19 'Up there Cazaly'. Two-Man-Band. 1979.

20 Australian singles charts for 1979. Up There Cazaly – Two-Man-Band. *Australian Music History*.

21 Wikipedia contributors. (2021, July 29). Up There Cazaly. In *Wikipedia, The Free Encyclopedia*. Retrieved July 30, 2021, from https://en.wikipedia.org/w/index.php?title=Up_There_Cazaly&oldid=1036016900

22 Noel Counihan, 'Cazaly, Roy (1893–1963)', *Australian Dictionary of Biography*. Op.cit.

23 Roy Cazaly Sport, *Sport Australia Hall of Fame*. Retrieved from: https://sahof.org.au/hall-of-fame-member/roy-cazaly/

Images:

-Voted Best by Clubmates (1919, July 26). *Weekly Times* (Melbourne, Vic. : 1869 - 1954), p. 18. Retrieved August 12, 2021, from http://nla.gov.au/nla.news-article222550914

-Tandy, Fleiter, Cazaly, c1920s (2018, June 9). *Wikimedia Commons*, Retrieved 2 Aug 2021 from URL:https://commons.wikimedia.org/w/index.php?title=File:Tandy_Fleiter_Cazaly.jpg&oldid=305433310.

-Roy Cazaly mark, (2016, Dec 13). *Wikimedia Commons*. Retrieved 2 Aug 2, 2021 from URL: https://commons.wikimedia.org/w/index.php?title=File:Roy_Cazaly_mark.jpg&oldid=226062066

-North Tasmania Football Team 1921. Burrow's Photo Studios, D.I.C. Photo and Barnett, photographer. (1920). Northern Tasmania Combined Football Team [picture]: collection of 15 postcards. *Libraries Tasmania*. Retrieved 7 Aug 2021 from: https://stors.tas.gov.au/AUTAS001612550002#

The last Tasmanian tiger
Mary Grant Roberts & 'Benjamin'

Interred: **Mary Grant Roberts,** 15 April 1841
            – 20 November 1921 (aged 80).

Location: Church of England, section F, number 10.

Cemetery: Cornelian Bay Cemetery and Crematorium,
            Queens Walk, New Town, TAS 7008.

Talk about a double dose of too little, too late. As the last few thylacines – Tasmanian tigers – were disappearing daily from their island home, two half-hearted efforts to slow their demise were attempted.

When the British settled Tasmania in 1803, it's estimated around 5000 Tasmanian tigers were living there.[1] This unique dog-wolf like animal with 15 to 20 distinct dark stripes across its back was largely a nocturnal animal that hunted at night and had a litter of about four. In May 1930, just 127 years later, a farmer, Wilf Batty, shot what is generally regarded as the last wild Tasmanian tiger at Mawbanna in the state's north-west after he discovered it attempting to make a meal of his chickens.

Wind forward six years to the last thylacine in captivity, which somewhere along the line had inherited the name 'Benjamin'. This tragic and isolated Tasmanian tiger in *Hobart Zoo* reportedly died of exposure after being left outside on a cold September night.

It's ironic that in July 1936, just two months before this, someone in a position of being able to do something about the demise of the native tiger decided it was time to safeguard thylacines and they were given protected status.

That, of course, did not result in more of them suddenly appearing and again someone decided all might not be right with the thylacines, asking via the *Launceston Examiner* on 10 February 1937: "Has anybody seen a Tasmanian tiger lately?" Now this enquiry was posed by a body called the Animals and Birds Protection Board and was to be circulated state-wide for: "Fears exist that this unique specimen of fauna may now be extinct."[2]

So, one attempt to do something two months before the last tiger died… and another equally useless effort five months after it died. And it's a very fair question to ask where was the Animals and Birds Protection Board in all this? It was responsible for the protection, conservation and regulation of the wild birds and animals of the state between 1929 and 1971.[3] What was it doing and why did it not see the thylacine as a species was in deep strife until after it had disappeared?

Good question!

At the time the Animals and Birds Protection Board went on its search for any evidence of the tigers' presence, it was because no-one, including a separate body, the Fauna Board, knew whether or not evidence existed. The Fauna Board wanted to: "collect any data procurable bearing on the native tiger population with a view to the reservation of an area in a suitable locality as a sanctuary to aid in the preservation of some specimens for as long as it is possible to keep them."[4]

Curiously, it was also clear from comments run by the paper that the Fauna Board's interest was not entirely altruistic as the curator of Taronga Park Zoo in Sydney was reported to have "suggested that the breeding of these animals in an enclosed area might be made quite profitable for there was an unsatisfied demand for them from zoological societies throughout the world at 50 pounds and upwards for each animal."[5] It was an idea that seemed to appeal to the boards.

Above Mary Grant Roberts. Source: Libraries Tasmania

Blame it on the Tassie tigers

It's not surprising that the collective Tasmanian bureaucratic knowledge of thylacine populations in the 1920s and 1930s amounted to zero. Ever since the place was settled and large areas of land were cleared for sheep and cattle grazing, the native tigers became easy scapegoats for the damage to stock, which was more likely caused by feral dogs and mismanagement. Bounties were handed out left, right and centre from as early as the 1830s, and they were generous.

When the government weighed into the system in 1888, the going price was one pound for an adult thylacine and 10 shillings for a juvenile. But there were other contributing factors. On top of the two thousand or so bounties handed out between 1888 and 1909, there were farmers keen to keep this sheep killer off their land. As more land was cleared, native tiger habitat destruction was widespread and diseases, like mange, took their toll. It was no wonder by the time 'Benjamin' succumbed to the freezing conditions outside his Hobart Zoo cage, there were no more left.

Tiger lady and her Beaumaris Zoo

But that doesn't mean that along the timeline of declining thylacine numbers there weren't people who at various points had, for whatever reason, tried to prolong the presence of some of Tasmania's unique fauna. One of them was a lady named Mary Grant Roberts.

Before she homed tigers of her own, Mary Grant Roberts was considered somewhat of a tiger herself. Determined, frank, active, she did work that was unseemly for a woman of her era, rebelled against the establishment, was a patriot and church attendee, and spoke out on matters of moral importance – such as disapproving of a pantomime because of the brevity of the mermaids' costumes.[6]

A girl from Hobart, at age 22 Mary lost her heart to Henry Llewelyn Roberts, and they wed on 18 August 1863 in St David's Cathedral. Henry appeared to have no passion to run a zoo – he was a clerk by trade and later established a successful wool-broking, wool sales and stock-agency company in Hobart.[7] After marriage, five children were born to occupy her time – two sons and three daughters,[8] but in 1877, now aged 36, Mary and Henry built their home, 'Beaumaris', on two acres of land in what is now a very built-up part of Battery Point – between Newcastle Street and Sandy Bay Road. Move ahead 18 years and this would become the foundation of the Beaumaris Zoo.

The zoo life

In her 26 years at the helm of the Beaumaris Zoo, later to become known as the Hobart Zoo, Mary became well known for exhibiting birds as well as thylacines. Mary purchased and sold the wild and soon-to-be extinct Tasmanian tigers to zoos in England and America.[9] It was an era when wild animals were caged, and several of the overseas species, such as the lions and tigers, were trapped and tied for transportation to the zoo and kept in concrete dens.[10]

As reported: "Between 1910 and 1919 Mrs Roberts shipped more than a dozen Tasmanian tigers and a similar number of devils to London, New York, and other places...

Above: Tasmanian tigers at Beaumaris Zoo. Source: Wikimedia.
Below: All that remains of the gates to the zoo site, 1983. Source: Wikimedia.

In 1910 Mrs Roberts paid the country dealers £8 each for tigers, but as they became scarcer the price gradually rose, to reach £20 by 1919. She made a good profit, as cheques received from overseas were up to £40 each."[11] Given that the average male salary in 1915 was £52,[12] Mary made over half a year's income (less the country dealers' fee) from the sale to cover her expenses of feeding and maintaining her zoo animals.

She was praised for her focus on the wildlife, flora and fauna of Tasmania and her attention and care for every animal in her zoo.[13] When a visitor said: "A very nice hobby of yours, Mrs Roberts", Mary retorted indignantly, "Hobby indeed", as she regarded it as her life's work, devoting most of the day to tending her animals.[14]

The zoo included monkeys, kangaroos, wallabies, wombats, Chinese pheasants, the tigers and devils, which Mary said were her "first favourites"[15] and when asked if she feared any of her collection, she responded that she "was on the best of terms with all except the bronze-breasted Burmese peacock, a most savage brute!"[16]

In 1910, a *Sydney Morning Herald* reporter wrote of Mary's zoo: "The habits and natural surroundings of every creature are studied; and, as far as possible, they are housed accordingly, and no one need hesitate to take a child to see the collection. Indeed, it is probable that many Tasmanian children will never see some of their rarer animals and birds except in Mrs Roberts's garden, for many forms are rapidly disappearing, and as no public effort is being made to preserve even the most interesting."[17]

Aged 80, Mary Roberts died in Hobart on 27 November 1921, survived by all her children. Her husband had passed away two years prior. She left her zoo to her daughter, Ida, who gifted it to the Hobart City Council.[18] And it was relocated to Queen's Domain. The Council took over the maintenance and were granted an annual subsidy from the government of £250. After only 18 months, the grant was discontinued.[19] In 1922 the zoo collection was audited and totalled 48 animals and 100 birds. One of these animals was 'Benjamin' the last Tasmanian tiger. As we know, this poor creature succumbed to the freezing conditions outside his Hobart Zoo cage in 1936. The zoo was closed in 1937 when the lack of visitors and maintenance costs made it unsustainable.[20]

Nothing, including the Tasmanian tiger, remained.

But are there any more?

Since the death of 'Benjamin,' there have been many expeditions aimed at capturing native Tasmanian tigers for zoos and museums – none have ever been found. Many say they have seen Tasmanian tigers in the wild, some have even taken moving pictures of the 'suspects'. Some of those who have filmed them will argue that they are the 'genuine article' but when pressed, admit the chances of the sightings being genuine are a long shot. The animal was officially declared extinct in 1986.

A story that was broadcast on the ABC in 2020 said that as of late 2018, according to the Australian government, "The details of eight supposed sightings of the animal, also known as the thylacine, in recent years were released by the Department of Primary Industries, Parks, Water and Environment in Tasmania."[21] The reported sightings don't appear to have been followed up by the government or the ABC.

However, *New Scientist* magazine reported on a mathematical study from the University of California, Berkley, that suggests: "the chances of Tasmanian tigers being alive in 2017 are virtually zero – the probability is as little as 1.6 trillion to one.[22]

So, if Tasmanian tigers are extinct, why do people keep seeing them? Well one good reason may have been identified by Christopher French, the founder of a psychology research unit at the University of London. He says: "Many people who go looking for such enigmatic creatures have an emotional investment in identifying them." In their minds, they are convinced the creatures are already out there. That makes it easier to "begin seeing quarry in every shadow and rustle of brush... or in photographs that don't offer a clear look at the animal in question. It can also cause people to genuinely miss details that might contradict their preferred hypothesis."[23] In short, thylacine seekers see them because they want to see them.

De-extinction of the Tasmanian tiger

Today, many years after the last known Tasmanian tiger died, the animal is a potential candidate for 'de-extinction' and scientists are working on research that could lead to the cloning of native tigers. A bioscience researcher from the University of Melbourne, Professor Andrew Pask, says the mapping of the animal's DNA, which his team achieved in 2019, could allow for breeding programs. The professor says, "It is no longer science fiction. We have all the tools to do it," but, he added, "if attempted now it would take decades and billions of dollars; money and time which would be better spent preserving populations of living marsupials."[24] Given that in 2018, the Red List of Threatened Species named Australia as the fourth worst nation on earth for animal extinctions, the professor seems to be on the right track.

References:

1 *National Museum Australia.* Extinction of thylacine. https://www.nma.gov.au/defining-moments/resources/extinction-of-thylacine

2 Are They Extinct? (1937, February 10). *Examiner (Launceston, Tas: 1900 - 1954)*, p. 8 (DAILY). Retrieved August 6, 2021, from http://nla.gov.au/nla.news-article52123602

3 *Libraries Tasmania.* Knowledge Base-Thylacine. https://libraries.tas.gov.au/get-help/knowledge-base/Pages/kb-thylacine.aspx

4 - 5 Are They Extinct? (1937, February 10). Op.cit.

6 - 8 Guiler, Eric, Roberts, Mary Grant (1841–1921), Australian Dictionary of Biography, *Australian National University.* Retrieved 27 July 2021 from: https://adb.anu.edu.au/biography/roberts-mary-grant-8228/text14403

9 Honour roll of women, Mary Grant Roberts, *Tas Government.* Retrieved 27 July 20201 from: https://www.communities.tas.gov.au/csr/programs_and_services/tasmanian_honour_roll_of_women/inductees/2006/mary_grant_roberts

10 - 11 "Tigers" (1967, May 10). *The Australian Women's Weekly (1933 - 1982)*, p. 12. Retrieved July 28, 2021, from http://nla.gov.au/nla.news-article48078602

12 Australian Wages. (1915, April 1). *The Register (Adelaide, SA: 1901 - 1929)*, p. 6. Retrieved July 28, 2021, from http://nla.gov.au/nla.news-article60749958

13 A Woman's Zoological Garden. (1910, April 20). *The Sydney Morning Herald (NSW: 1842 - 1954)*, p. 5. Retrieved July 28, 2021, from http://nla.gov.au/nla.news-article15119767

14 Woman Zoologist. (1912, August 11). *The Sun (Sydney, NSW: 1910 - 1954)*, p. 20. Retrieved July 28, 2021, from http://nla.gov.au/nla.news-article228816804

15 - 16 Mitchell, Josh, The metal gate shouts Beaumaris Zoo to passers-by, but who stops anymore ...? *tasmaniatimes.com* 30 January 2019. Retrieved 27 July 2021 from URL: https://www.tasmaniatimes.com/2019/01/the-metal-gate-shouts-beaumaris-zoo-to-passers-by-but-who-stops-anymore/

17 A Woman's Zoological Garden. (1910, April 20). Op.cit.

18 "Tigers" (1967, May 10). The Australian Women's Weekly. Op.cit.

19 Beaumaris Zoo (1936, February 25). *Examiner (Launceston, Tas. : 1900 - 1954)*, p. 5 (daily). Retrieved July 28, 2021, from http://nla.gov.au/nla.news-article51999538

20 *Centre for Tasmanian Historical Studies,* Zoos, the companion to Tasmanian History, 2006. Retrieved 27 July 2021 from URL: https://www.utas.edu.au/library/companion_to_tasmanian_history/Z/Zoos.htm

21 Jacobo, Julia, Sightings of Tasmanian tiger, thought to be extinct for 80 years, *ABC News,* 18 October 2019. Retrieved from URL: https://abcnews.go.com/International/sightings-tasmanian-tiger-thought-extinct-80-years-reported/story?id=66345508

22 Klein, Alice, Odds that Tasmanian tigers are still alive are 1 in 1.6 trillion. *NewScientist,* 18 April 2017. Retrieved from URL: https://www.newscientist.com/article/2128077-odds-that-tasmanian-tigers-are-still-alive-are-1-in-1-6-trillion/

23 Elbein, Asher, Tasmanian Tigers Are Extinct.... *The New York Times,* 10 March 2021. Retrieved from URL: https://www.nytimes.com/2021/03/10/science/thylacines-tasmanian-tigers-sightings.html

24 Powell, Sandy. *The Canberra Times.* 21 January, 2021. University of Melbourne professor Andrew Pask says... https://www.canberratimes.com.au/story/7093524/de-extincting-tasmanian-tigers-no-longer-science-fiction/

Images:

- Mary Grant Roberts. *Libraries Tasmania.* Retrieved 27 July 2021 from: https://stors.tas.gov.au/NS823-1-69#

- Tasmanian tigers at Beaumaris. *Wikimedia.* Public Domain. Retrieved 28 July 2021 from URL: https://commons.wikimedia.org/w/index.php?curid=4384747

- Gates to the old Beaumaris Zoo (Hobart Zoo) site. Photograph by MagicFlute1983, *Wikimedia.* Retrieved 28 July 2021 from URL: https://commons.wikimedia.org/w/index.php?curid=3375649

- Thylacine with three cubs, Hobart Zoo, 1909. Image in the public domain *(right).*

Above: Graves on King Island. Below: A monument to the Neva victims on King Island. Reproduced with the kind permission of Arthur Garland and sourced via Monuments Australia.

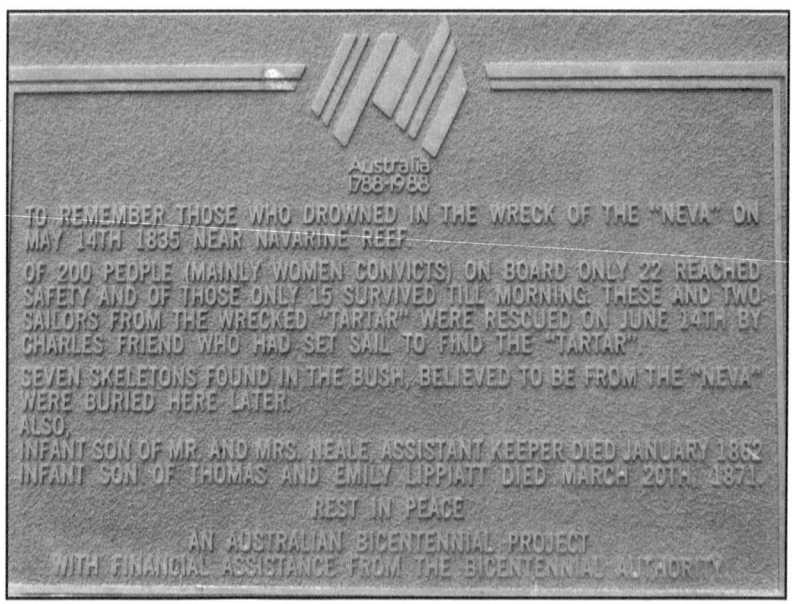

Australia
1788-1988

TO REMEMBER THOSE WHO DROWNED IN THE WRECK OF THE "NEVA" ON MAY 14TH 1835 NEAR NAVARINE REEF.

OF 200 PEOPLE (MAINLY WOMEN CONVICTS) ON BOARD ONLY 22 REACHED SAFETY AND OF THOSE ONLY 15 SURVIVED TILL MORNING. THESE AND TWO SAILORS FROM THE WRECKED "TARTAR" WERE RESCUED ON JUNE 14TH BY CHARLES FRIEND WHO HAD SET SAIL TO FIND THE "TARTAR".

SEVEN SKELETONS FOUND IN THE BUSH, BELIEVED TO BE FROM THE "NEVA" WERE BURIED HERE LATER.
ALSO;
INFANT SON OF MR. AND MRS. NEALE ASSISTANT KEEPER DIED JANUARY 1862
INFANT SON OF THOMAS AND EMILY LIPPIATT DIED MARCH 20TH. 1871.

REST IN PEACE

AN AUSTRALIAN BICENTENNIAL PROJECT
WITH FINANCIAL ASSISTANCE FROM THE BICENTENNIAL AUTHORITY.

Women and children on board
The *Neva* female convict ship

Memorial: A plaque dedicated to the *Neva* and its victims – Tasmanian Seafarers' Memorial.

Location: Triabunna, east coast, TAS 7190.

Graves: King Island grave and memorial.

Location: King Island, off the north-west coast of Tasmania, Australia, 7256.

T here was no throwing of streamers or celebration on Thursday 8 January 1835 when the three-masted barque, the *Neva*, departed from the docks and sailed from Cork in Ireland bound for Australia. Under the command of Captain B. H. Peck, on board were 150 female convicts, 55 children, mainly babies and toddlers, nine free female emigrants including wives of banished Irishmen who were making the journey to be reunited, the daughter or two of an impoverished family surrendered with a view of securing a new life on a free pass[1], and the balance made up of a male crew to number 241 passengers.[2]

While there were a few hardened criminals amongst the ladies on board, many of the women were convicted for petty crimes but received harsh sentences, including transportation to the penal colony, in this case, New South Wales, Australia. And so, they set sail on a long and arduous journey to the other side of the earth, not knowing what their destinies would be.

Tough sentences for petty deeds

You could be forgiven for thinking that the British court of the day sentencing Irish citizens wanted to reduce its lower-class population, given the number of their people they sentenced to deportation for the most trivial of crimes. On board being deported for seven years for their crimes were Jane McIlvenna, 33, who stole a hat, Mary Cassidy, 19, for the theft of a handkerchief, Catherine Connor, 24, who stole a sheet, and Ellen Magennis, 23, for stealing shoes.[3] If seven years seemed hard, spare a thought for Anne Cullen, 21, who was on board with a life sentence for possessing a stolen cow and Louise Mellefont, 47, sentenced to life for forgery.[4]

With passengers living together in close surrounds, the *Neva* sailed for over four months. During the journey, three people died and a child was born.[5] There was also, according to reports, a good time had by some – rum aplenty and stories of the women and the crew liaising abound. This was not allowed but with four months at sea, plenty of young women aboard and a small crew of men, who is to say what company they sought.[6] After four months, with land finally in sight, tragedy struck.

Above: An illustration of the Neva. Source: The World's News, 9 June 1937.

Women and children last

The lookout for land began at noon on Wednesday 13 May 1835, when the ship was 90 miles from King Island, at the entrance to Bass Strait.[7] In the quiet of the early hours of the morning, about two o'clock, land was spotted. The captain was on deck at the time and gave orders to tack[8] but the ship struck rock and the passengers heard the horrendous sound of grating and tearing. The reef the *Neva* hit was described in the day's newspaper as "not correctly laid down in any chart."[9]

The *Neva,* now so close to land, was smashed. Imagine the panic below deck of the caged women at the mercy of the rising waters. But the force of the pounding sea opened the bars and freed any women who were imprisoned, although an account by one of the female prisoners, Ellen Galvin, attributes their release to the captain: "On the ship striking, the captain immediately came down, unlocked the door and released all the women prisoners, as well as those in the black hole and desired us all to come on deck."[10]

It was every person for themselves and the pinnace (a small ship) was lowered with four of the crew on board, including the captain, and Surgeon-Superintendent.[11]

The adage of 'women and children' first was not maritime law and did not come into common use until 17 years later in 1852, when the paddle-wheeled steam transport *Birkenhead* sank carrying 480 soldiers, crew, and about 26 women and children. As the *Birkenhead* went down, "Colonel Seton called on the soldiers to 'Stand fast!' If they jumped overboard, they might endanger the boats, which were still close by. Instead, they kept ranks and went down with the ship in shark-infested waters. All received their orders and carried them out as if they were embarking instead of going to the bottom. There were only 193 survivors out of 638 passengers and crew, but all the women and children were saved. The disaster gave rise to the *Birkenhead Drill* meaning 'women and children first' as a standard procedure during any sinking."[12]

But this heroism was not practised on board the *Neva* in 1835 and with so many on board, would not have been achievable. The women and children rushed to the boats which were swamped. The pinnace was also swamped by women trying to get on board, and several of the crew were drowned.[13] The captain and two surviving sailors from the pinnace were now back on board and the crew launched the long boat – the only remaining boat – but the sea soon tossed it as well. It is impossible to imagine the panic and fear as over 200 people – mothers, young women, children, and male crew, tried to scramble to safety when none was to be found.

The Truth newspaper well described the moment: "When the vessel struck the rock in the relentless breakers she divided into four parts, each of which was covered with terror-stricken female convicts, screaming for help in the most piteous manner. This was indeed a moment of terror, which would have appalled the boldest."[14]

The rough sea, the screams, the panic was frightful and soon all that remained were 22 people – crew and women convicts – clinging pitifully to whatever they could find until the sea took them ashore on King Island almost eight hours after they were first submerged in the freezing May waters.[15]

One of those female convicts was Rose Ann Hyland, who told of the ordeal: "When the ship struck, I was in bed in the black hole that night… the captain ordered the ladder to be hauled up, and that we, who had been in the black hole, were to be kept down, but myself and other two succeeded in getting on deck. Most of the other women, who had been in the main prison, had got on deck and into the Cuddy where they were drinking, and some of them were so drunk as to be unable to help themselves.

"I was on the poop [stern deck where the wheel is located] when the ship opened, and… I stuck to this part of the wreck and went some part of the way on shore upon it. When we came close to another part of the wreck, one of the sailors caught hold of me and pulled me upon it. I fell off and was a second time caught hold of by the same man, and placed again upon the wreck. When we got near the shore, this man [Thomas Sharp] jumped off the wreck and carried a boy on shore; he returned for me, and then for another woman."[16]

The dramatic illustration of the sinking Neva.
Source: The Capricornian, 26 May 1927.

The rescue of those who remained

To have escaped the wreck and made it to shore was no guarantee of survival. Seven of the ladies died soon after from exhaustion. The remaining 15 survivors were challenged once again – they set up shelters, scrounged provisions, finding a cask of beef, flour, and some spirits[17] and lived on the bare minimum for the next two weeks. On day 15, the sight of a small boat – the *Tartar* – also wrecked, was most fortunate for the *Neva* survivors.

Owned by Captain Charles Friend, the *Tartar* crew followed the trail of *Neva* debris and found, to their surprise, the small group of survivors.[18] Mr Friend was passing the island with another crew in the *Sarah Ann*, heading to Portland Bay, when he digressed to help the survivors despite the risk to himself and his crew. The survivors of both wrecks were taken on board, but not before more than 100 of the women and children's bodies were buried, under the guidance of Mr Friend, in their new and permanent home, King Island.[19]

One can only imagine the relief of leaving the island and the despair of knowing that they were still

Above: King Island and its proximity to landmarks. Source: The Age, 1939.

to be imprisoned, and on 27 May 1835, the remaining party arrived in Launceston including Captain B.H. Peck and crew members – Joseph Bennett, Thomas Sharpe, John Wilson, Edward Calthorpe, Thomas Hines and Robert Bullard. The female convicts who survived were Ellen Galvin, Mary Slattery, Ann Cullen, Rose Ann Hyland, and Rose Ann Dunn. Three remained on King Island – crew members, John Robinson and William Kidney, plus Margaret Drury, to be collected by the cutter, *Shamrock,* along with any provisions that had floated ashore (clothing and rum namely).[20] Eventually, the female prisoners were forwarded to Port Jackson.[21]

It was the third convict ship in two years lost to the seas off Australia – the first was the female convict ship, *Amphitrite*, two years prior with 170 lives lost; the second was *George the Third*, claiming 134 lives in 1834 and now the *Neva* in 1835 with 224 lives lost.[22] Ten years later, the loss of 400 lives with the sinking of the British barque, *Cataraqui*, on 4 August 1845 saw a call for lighthouses to stop the carnage and the Cape Otway lighthouse was constructed.

But now with the *Neva* sunk, a board of enquiry was established and reviewed the *Neva* evidence on hand, resulting in the board offering congratulations to *Neva*'s officers "on their humanity".[23] They attributed the cause of the disaster to the conditions, and congratulated the rescuer, Mr Charles Friend, awarding him £75 in recognition of his efforts. Not an inconsiderable sum in 1835.[24]

What became of…

The ladies previously mentioned – **Jane, 33**, who stole a hat, **Mary, 19**, theft of a handkerchief, **Catherine, 24**, who stole a sheet, **Ellen [Magennis], 23**, stole shoes, and **Louise, 47,** the forger, all perished. **Anne 21**, who possessed a stolen cow, survived and married William Howard in Launceston in 1844, nine years after the shipwreck. Anne had a daughter, Mary, who was placed in an orphanage for five years before being discharged.[25]

Captain Peck sailed from Launceston to Sydney on the *Nimrod* in August and left our shores for England on the *Andromeda* as a passenger in September 1835.[26]

Thomas Sharpe, the crewman who rescued Rose Ann Hyland and another young boy, survived. Along with the five fellow surviving seamen, Thomas eventually took up positions on other ships.[27]

DEPARTURES.

September 10.—Sophia Jane and Tamar (steamers), for Newcastle.

September 13.—Andromeda (brig), Gales, for London ; passengers, Captain Peck, Mrs. Parrot, and Miss Brown.

Above: The captain's departure listed in The Colonist, September, 1835.

The remaining surviving women:

Margaret Drury, 24, a little woman at 155 cm (5ft1) with dark hair, who initially remained behind on King Island with crew member **John (Peter James) Robinson** married him the year after. She was released in 1840. They had two children and Margaret lived another thirty years, dying aged 53 in 1865 in Tasmania. John died in Victoria about 15 years later.[28] Margaret was sent to Australia for stealing money and a watch from her aunt and uncle.[29]

Ellen Galvin who received seven years for vagrancy, lost her mother and sister on the *Neva*. Three years after the sinking, in 1838, she married William Lawrence while still imprisoned, and was released in 1841.[30] **Rose Ann Hyland** convicted for larceny, married Thomas Dorkins (Dorking) while imprisoned in 1836 and was freed in 1841.[31] **Mary Slattery** who was sentenced to seven years for larceny, died three years after the shipwreck, in 1838.[32] **Rose Ann Dunn** was also sentenced to seven years for vagrancy in 1832. Rose Ann married William Mears in 1835 and was freed in 1849.[33]

How to pay your respects:

You can visit the Tasmanian Seafarers' Memorial – where all seafarers and locals who lost their lives at sea are remembered, dating back to 1803 – at Triabunna on the east coast of Tasmania (86 kilometres or 53 miles north-east of Hobart). The plaque commemorating the *Neva* passengers and crew reads:

Convict Transport Barque of 327 tons sailed from Cork, Ireland on 8.1.1835. Captain Peck with 26 officers and crew, 150 female convicts with 33 children, 9 free women and 22 children bound for Sydney. 13.5.1835 struck Harbinger Reef north of King Island with 239 aboard. 22 made landfall where 7 later died. – Tasmania's second worst shipwreck –[34]

You can also visit the graves on King Island where a plaque commemorating those who died was unveiled in 1988, Australia`s bicentennial year. There is also a small gravesite where seven bodies that were found in the bush and believed to have been passengers from the *Neva*, are buried.

References:

1 Wallace, Arminta, Worst shipwreck you've never heard of, *The Irish Times*, 27 April 2013. Retrieved 8 August 2021 from URL: https://www.irishtimes.com/life-and-style/people/worst-shipwreck-you-ve-never-heard-of-1.1373988

2 Melancholy Shipwreck. (1835, July 2). *Launceston Advertiser (Tas. : 1829 - 1846)*, p. 4. Retrieved August 8, 2021, from http://nla.gov.au/nla.news-article84777543

3 - 4 Wallace, Arminta, Worst shipwreck you've never heard of, *The Irish Times*. Op.cit.

5 Melancholy Shipwreck. (1835, July 2). *Launceston Advertiser*. Op. cit.

6 Wallace, Arminta, Worst shipwreck you've never heard of, *The Irish Times*. Op.cit.

7 - 8 Melancholy Shipwreck. (1835, July 2). *Launceston Advertiser*. Op. cit.

9 Colonial Times (1835, June 30). *Colonial Times (Hobart, Tas. : 1828 - 1857)*, p. 4. Retrieved August 8, 2021, from http://nla.gov.au/nla.news-article8648270

10 Todd, Kevin, Locating the Neva, *Exterior Worlds, Hidden Stories*, Issue 13, 2010. University of the Sunshine Coast. Retrieved 10 August 2021 from URL: http://www.doubledialogues.com/article/locating-the-neva-art-and-history/

11 Melancholy Shipwreck. (1835, July 2). *Launceston Advertiser*. Op. cit.

12 National Army Museum, *Women and Children First*, United Kingdom. Retrieved 9 August 2021 from URL: https://www.nam.ac.uk/explore/birkenhead-sinking

13 - 14 The Tragedy of the Female Convict Ship "NEVA" (1923, August 26). *Truth (Brisbane, Qld. : 1900 - 1954)*, p. 12. Retrieved August 10, 2021, from http://nla.gov.au/nla.news-article203907330

15 Melancholy Shipwreck. (1835, July 2). *Launceston Advertiser*. Op. cit.

16 Robinson, Ann, The Convict Ship Neva | An Irish Maritime Tragedy on Australian Shores, *Coast Monkey*, 13 May 2021. Retrieved 9 August 2021 from URL: https://coastmonkey.ie/neva-convict-ship-irish-maritime-tragedy-australia/

17 Old Shipping Disaster (1926, April 28). *Examiner (Launceston, Tas. : 1900 - 1954)*, p. 5 (DAILY). Retrieved August 9, 2021, from http://nla.gov.au/nla.news-article91609229

18 - 20 Melancholy Shipwreck. (1835, July 2). *Launceston Advertiser*. Op. cit.

21 Old Shipping Disaster (1926, April 28). *Examiner (Launceston, Tas. : 1900 - 1954)*, p. 6 (DAILY). Retrieved August 9, 2021, from http://nla.gov.au/nla.news-article91609229

22 Melancholy Shipwreck. (1835, July 2). *Launceston Advertiser*. Op. cit.

23 - 24 Old Shipping Disaster (1926, April 28). *Examiner*. Op.cit.

25 Todd, Kevin (artist), *Transportation Memorial* – https://toddartist.com/ Retrieved 10 Aug 2021 from URL: http://www.toddartist.com/catalogues/Neva%20Survivors.pdf

26 Departures. (1835, September 17). *The Colonist* (Sydney, NSW : 1835 - 1840), p. 7. Retrieved August 9, 2021, from http://nla.gov.au/nla.news-article31716975

27 Old Shipping Disaster (1926, April 28). *Examiner*. Op.cit.

28 David Robinson family tree, *Ancestry*. Retrieved 9/8/21 from ancestry.com.au

29 David Robinson, Margaret (Drury) Robinson (abt. 1812 - abt. 1865), *Wikitree*, created 28 May 2020. Retrieved 9 August 2021 from URL: https://www.wikitree.com/wiki/Drury-2532

30 - 33 Todd, Kevin (artist), *Transportation Memorial*, Op.cit.

34 Wikipedia contributors. (19 Jan 2021). Neva (1813 ship). In *Wikipedia*. Retrieved 10 Aug 2021, from URL: https://en.wikipedia.org/w/index.php?title=Neva_(1813_ship)&oldid=1001415145

Images:

- Garland, Arthur (photographer), "Neva" graves and monument on King Island. *Monuments Australia*. Reproduced with the kind permission of Arthur Garland and sourced via Monuments Australia. Retrieved 10 August 2021 from URL: https://www.monumentaustralia.org.au/themes/disaster/maritime/display/110242-%22neva%22

- Illustration of the Neva. Australiana (1937, June 9). *The World's News* (Sydney, NSW : 1901 - 1955), p. 18. Retrieved August 16, 2021, from http://nla.gov.au/nla.news-article131464550

- Map of King Island proximity: BASS STRAIT'S MARINE (7 Jan 1939). *The Age* (Melbourne, Vic. : 1854 - 1954), p. 8. Retrieved August 10, 2021, from http://nla.gov.au/nla.news-article205955726

- Illustration of the sinking Neva (26 May 1927). *The Capricornian (Rockhampton, Qld.: 1875 - 1929)*, p52. Retrieved 10 Aug 2021, from http://nla.gov.au/nla.news-article70647404

- The captain departs: DEPARTURES. (1835, September 17). *The Colonist (Sydney, NSW : 1835 - 1840)*, p. 7. Retrieved August 10, 2021, from http://nla.gov.au/nla.news-article31716975

Above: Scottsdale Memorial Board.
Photo kindly supplied by Tony Sweeney.

Sweeney's fate
Private John Joseph Sweeney

Memorial: John Joseph Sweeney, 2 April 1879 – 2 October 1916, (aged 37)

Location: Scottsdale RSL, 30 George St, Scottsdale, TAS 7260.

Of all the terrible concepts developed by armies in many battles over many years, surely there has been no greater horror conceived than sending men scratching their way down rat-hole like tunnels to place massive caches of high explosives under one's enemies, intending to blow them off the face of the planet.

By the beginning of 1917, largely because of refinements during World War I, the planting of underground mines had become an essential tool in the Allied arsenal and its generals planned to use it in their attempts to regain positions that had been a German stronghold since being captured from the French in December 1914.

The Messines Ridge, located south of Ypres in Belgium, had been a thorn in the side of the Allies. It gave the Germans a dominant position overlooking the Ypres salient and after years of suffering heavy losses, the Allies planned a breakout with the first objective being to capture the Messines Ridge.

The man in charge of that operation, General Sir Herbert Plumer, had ordered that over 20 mines be placed under German lines at Messines and over the next five months more than eight kilometres of tunnels were dug and between 450 and 600 tons (410 and 545 tonnes) of explosive was left underground until it was called upon to do its deadly deed.

At 3.10am on 7 June 1917, the mines were detonated simultaneously. The blast killed an estimated 10,000 German personnel and was audible in Dublin and heard by British Prime Minister, Lloyd George, in his office at 10 Downing Street, London.[1]

Addressing senior staff on the eve of the explosions, British General, Charles Harington, is reported to have said: "Gentlemen, we may not make history tomorrow, but we shall certainly change the geography."[2]

The biggest bang

But this was the result of years of tunnelling now refined to achieve the most diabolical results. To give an idea of how perfect the process had become, it's believed "The 1917 Messines mines detonation was probably the largest planned explosion in history prior to the Trinity atomic weapon test in July 1945 and the largest non-nuclear planned explosion before the British explosive efforts on the Heligoland Islands in April 1947."[3]

But it wasn't always that way.

Tunnelling to undermine enemies has been around for at least 4000 years, with Assyrian carvings showing units of its army tunnelling under the walls of enemy cities and archaeological diggings from Troy show a number of underground passages running beneath the city walls. Roman sieges were often accompanied by tunnelling and also used by them to defend their own settlements.

Fountain of horror

After falling out of favour for some time, the tactic re-emerged during the American Civil War with tunnel bombs being planted under entrenched soldiers at the siege of Vicksburg, Mississippi, in 1863. In 1864 at the siege of Petersburg, soldiers of Major General Ambrose Burnside bored a tunnel that was 150 metres (500 feet) long and 6.1 metres (20 feet) below the surface of the earth. They then loaded it with 3700 kilograms (8000 pounds) of gunpowder and when Union troops exploded their device, 352 Confederate soldiers died in the resulting blast.

A local journalist recorded the horror of what had just transpired and wrote: "Clods of earth weighing at least a ton, and cannon, and human forms, and gun-carriages, and small arms were all distinctly seen shooting upward in that fountain of horror."[4] The vast crater that was left was 40 metres (130 feet) long, 18 metres (60 feet) wide, and nine metres (30 feet) deep.[5]

Military mining, and its associated horrors, was back.

John Sweeney's days

During World War I almost 420,000 Australians put their hands up to volunteer in the Australian Imperial Force for overseas service. What is important to remember is they were not enlisting in the regular Army but a special force raised for the duration of WWI and every one of them was a volunteer… a fact that would be brought home in a devastating way for one Tasmanian man and his family.

John Joseph Sweeney grew up on the north-west coast of Tasmania and went to school in Ulverstone. It is believed he then went to work in the west coast mines and for the railways. In 1903, when the North Lyell Mine smelters closed and consequently the port, his family moved to Lietinna in the north-east and John Sweeney settled in nearby Scottsdale.

In October 1904 he married Amy Ion but the union only lasted until December of that year. Even so, John and Amy had a daughter, Doris Sweeney, who was born after the marriage split. In all probability John then returned to his parents' home in Lietinna, taking on work as a bushman and miner, before heading overseas.

In 1914, the year of the beginning of the so-called 'War to end all wars', John was in New Zealand working as the head of several gangs clearing an area now known as the Aorangi Forest Park, about 50 kilometres south-east of the capital, Wellington.

John Sweeney's timber getters were known as the 'Tasmanian Gang', hard-working and hard-drinking but respected and in demand. His three brothers, Bernard, Harold and Edward, along with their brother-in-law, John (Jack) Adams, also ventured across the Tasman… after all, there was a healthy 'quid' to be made. The 323 hectares (800 acres) of the forest they felled became known as 'Sweeneys' Paddock'.

So, if things were travelling so well for the 'Tasmanian Gang' why did its leader down tools and join the New Zealand Army to do battle against Germany, Austria-Hungary, the Ottoman Empire and Bulgaria – the so-called Central Powers or Quadruple Alliance?

Getting in on the action!

In the early days, the sentiment in New Zealand was akin to that of its southern hemisphere neighbour and British colony, Australia. Many joined up to avoid missing out on the adventure that was shaping up on the other side of the world and they needed to be quick, as everyone was saying the war would be over in days… surely by Christmas 1914.

NEW ZEALAND EXPEDITIONARY FORCE.

ATTESTATION OF

No. _____ Name: *Sweeney John Joseph* Regiment or Unit: *Wmk*

Questions to be put to the recruit before enlistment.

1. What is your name? — *John Joseph Sweeney*
2. Where were you born? — *Stanley — Tasmania*
3. Are you a British subject? — *Yes*
4. What is the date of your birth? — *2nd April 1879*
5. What is your trade or calling? — *Bushman*
6. Are you an indentured apprentice? If so, where, and to whom? — *No*
7. What was the address at which you last resided? — *Pirinoa, Via Featherst...*
8. Have you passed the Fourth Educational Standard or its equivalent? — *Yes*
9. What is the name and address of your present or last employer? — *Payne & Sutherland, Pirinoa*
10. Are you married? — *No*
11. Have you ever been sentenced to imprisonment by the Civil power? If so, when and where? — *No*
12. Do you now belong to any military or naval force? If so, to what corps? — *No*
13. Have you ever served in any military or naval force? If so, state which and cause of discharge. — *No*
14. Have you truly stated the whole (if any) of your previous service? — *Yes*
15. Have you been registered for compulsory military training under the Defence Act, 1909? If so, where? — *No*
16. Have you ever been rejected as unfit for the military or naval forces of the Crown? If so, on what grounds? — *No*
17. Are you willing to be vaccinated or revaccinated? — *Yes*
18. Are you willing to serve in the Expeditionary Force in or beyond the Dominion of New Zealand under the following conditions, provided your services should so long be required: For the term of the present European war and for such further period as is necessary to bring the Expeditionary Force back to New Zealand and to disband it? — *Yes*

Note.—Your discharge will not be granted before your return to New Zealand unless permission for discharge elsewhere be obtained from the G.O.C. the New Zealand Expeditionary Force.

I, *John Joseph Sweeney*, do solemnly declare that the above answers made by me to the above questions are true, and that I am willing to fulfil the engagement made.

Signature of Recruit: *J. Sweeney*

Signature of Witness: *N. B. Morrison*

Oath to be taken by recruit on attestation.

I, *John Joseph Sweeney*, do sincerely promise and swear that I will be faithful and bear true allegiance to our Sovereign Lord the King, his Heirs and Successors, and that I will faithfully serve in the New Zealand Military Forces, according to my liability under the Defence Act, and that I will observe and obey all orders of His Majesty, his Heirs and Successors, and of the Generals and Officers set over me, until I shall be lawfully discharged. So help me, God!

Certificate of Magistrate or Attesting Officer.

The above questions were read to the above-named recruit in my presence. I have taken care that he understands each question, and that his answer to each question has been duly entered as replied to, and the said recruit has made and signed the declaration and taken the oath before me, at *Trentham*, N.Z., on this 25th day of *October* 1914.

Signature of Attesting Officer: _____

Above: John Sweeney's enlistment paper.
Kindly supplied by Tony Sweeney from NZ Military Archives.

On 21 October of that year, 35-year-old John Joseph Sweeney enlisted. Despite being a proud Australian he was in New Zealand at the time so his first placement was with the Wellington Mounted Rifles, then the Otago Infantry Regiment. It certainly wasn't all new to him as he had spent time in the Tasmanian militia.

Above: The Wellington Mounted Rifles Regiment at Awapuni Camp, prior to embarkation. Source: A. H. Wilkie, 1924.

But what was coming would not only be new to John, but perilous, potentially terrifying and carried with it the ability to shatter the spirit of a man. It would also leave John Sweeney as a loner and show him to not always be a model soldier. While in transit from New Zealand to Egypt, where troops would undergo further training before being posted, John Sweeney went AWOL – absent without leave.

As the ship transporting his unit from New Zealand to the Middle East was passing through Hobart in October 1914,[6] John probably thought they should have given him leave to visit his family there. They didn't but he went regardless. It cost him six days' pay but worst of all, it left a black mark against his name.

And this wasn't to be the only occasion when he took it into his own hands to take leave. Before his unit was posted, it happened again – this cost him eight hours' detention.

Roll out the changes

In the meantime, two tumultuous events occurred, which changed John's life forever. First, he was posted to Gallipoli on 9 April 1915 and so became an original ANZAC. Shortly afterwards, because of his experience as a miner working underground and handling explosives, he was transferred out of his battalion and into the Tunnelling Division.

The role of a Gallipoli tunneller was extremely hazardous, nerve-wracking, not to mention back-breaking. In many places, those assigned to the cramped tunnelling duties became known as 'Clay Kickers' for the methods they developed for extracting the soil from tunnels they were burrowing or trenches they were digging. Teams comprised a 'kicker' who, using his kicking iron, would shuffle the lumps of soil back to a 'trammer' who passed it along and out of the tunnel. Others used a system called 'working the cross' which involved a digger who sat, supported with his back on a wooden beam (the cross), and scooped out the soil in front of him which was worked back down the tunnel.

And all this while Turkish tunnellers were actively searching out their workings. Discovery could lead to a hand-to-hand fight five metres under the ground in an area less than a metre square – the weapons were usually razor-sharp knives, the options, kill or be killed!

Whichever way you looked at it, there was very little upside to tunnelling for John Sweeney and the other Gallipoli tunnellers. This would be terrifying work even if the Turks weren't doing it as well. Everything had to be managed in absolute silence in spaces too small for a man to turn around and, in most cases, in darkness, with almost no fresh air. The rule was "if a candle would burn, the air was good enough to work in. If it went out, it was time to get out". [7]

And yet one of those who assessed the work of the New Zealand tunnellers concluded that their efforts at Quinn's Post, the most advanced ANZAC post, "in a large measure… saved ANZAC to the British."[8] The task had been to create a sap (covered trench) from Quinn's Post to Courtney's Post. It took from April to November, 24 hours a day for eight months. Part of the incessant danger at Quinn's lay in the fact that enemy positions oversaw it on three sides and to raise one's head here above the parapet of the trench was to invite instant death from every watchful Turkish rifleman. Until mid-June, the fighting at Quinn's was of a ferocity and intensity unequalled on any other part of the line.

Here death was waiting above and below the ground.

Paying the price

The plain brutality of life in Gallipoli and on the line at Quinn's Post was taking its full toll physically on Private Sweeney. He was hospitalised in Cairo in August 1915 with an attack of colitis, a nagging, painful inflammation of the large intestine. When John recovered, the military dispatched him back to the Dardanelles, but it wasn't long before he was back in a Cairo hospital, this time after a nerve gas attack. So, back to Gallipoli again, only to be injured and sent back to Cairo three more times.

The physical price being paid by John was also having a psychological effect on him. In those days it was called 'shell shock' – the impact of constant shelling or pressure from the continual fighting – no rest at any turn. Today we call what soldiers in battle suffer, Post Traumatic Stress Disorder, and it is recognised as an ailment characterised by failure to recover after experiencing or witnessing a terrifying event. It had John Joseph Sweeney in its grasp.

The hard man is broken

New Zealand military historian, Christopher Pugsley, is well-known for his writings on NZ military discipline and says "Sweeney was one of those brave men who worked as a tunneller in the narrow drives under the front line at Quinn's and Courtney's Posts. It was enough to break the bravest man, and it broke Sweeney. He had survived but it had broken him. He was a hard man, a tunneller, who liked a drink and thought he could take anything. But of course, he couldn't."

Then, on 9 January 1916, John embarked with his unit for Egypt. After being hospitalised again in Egypt, Private Sweeney officially re-joined the 1st Otagos at Armentieres, in France, on 10 July 1916. He was immediately sent on eight days leave in England because he was a Gallipoli veteran. On his return from England, John was detailed for guard duty in the quarters. On 25 July he was found to be absent and declared a deserter on 19 August.

After wandering behind the lines for several weeks,[9] there were reports he had been to a café near Armentieres for a meal, but having no money, he left his pay book with the proprietor. When apprehended, it was said that John tried to pass himself off as an Australian tunneller attached to a New Zealand tunnelling unit.

Subsequently, he said he had no intention of deserting and was simply trying to join up with the second tunnelling company until he found his comrades. When questioned about where he was going, he said he was looking for the 12th Australian Battalion and when asked who they were replied, "South Australians and Tasmanians."

John also said that he had permission to be where he was and referred the arresting officers to Sergeant Stevens who was apparently at an ammunition dump some distance away. It was also noted in John's paperwork that when arrested, he was not wearing any badges on his uniform.

Later it was revealed that there was no effort ever made to contact Sergeant Stevens and there was no record of John ever having been issued with any badges. In July 1916, he was court-martialled for desertion and sentenced to death by firing squad at dawn.[10]

The harshest penalty

At his court-martial, John Sweeney pleaded "Not Guilty", but no-one from the 'Otagos' spoke up for him as he was a stranger. He had never been in the lines or served with them because he had been transferred to the tunnelling unit as soon as he arrived at ANZAC Cove. Nothing was said in his defence and they emphasised his past misdemeanours, all minor. John's Gallipoli service in the treacherous tunnels was ignored as were his lengthy hospitalisations. He was found guilty and sentenced to "suffer death by being shot".[11]

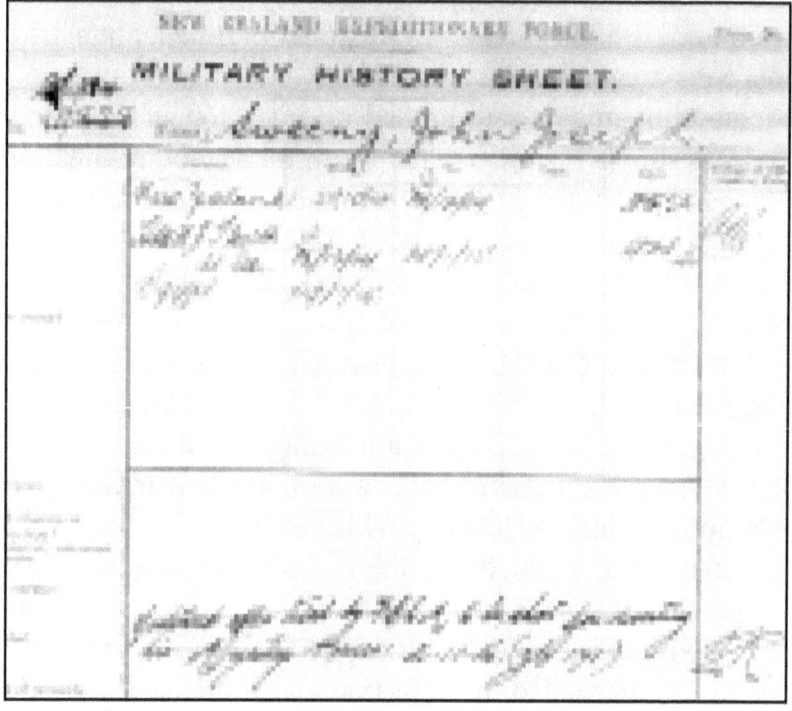

Above: Military personnel files for John Joseph Sweeney.
Source: New Zealand Defence Force.

Some senior army officers regarded the court-martial evidence as unsatisfactory. Private Sweeney was not represented at the trial and there appeared to have been serious irregularities. Legal procedures were ignored, and the evidence presented was conflicting and incomplete. The only questions put to the prosecution were by the defendant. His medical history and courageous service in Gallipoli were not considered because "conduct sheets were lost".[12]

Private John Joseph Sweeney's execution was carried out in Meaulte, France at 5.44am on 2 October 1916. He was 37 years old. A witness to the execution, Sergeant A.E.M. Rhind, noted in his diary: "A deserter twice over and yet he went out to be shot without showing fear".[13] He was buried in Dartmoor Cemetery near Becordel, France.

Crime and punishment

But did the punishment match his crimes? We know of his Hobart AWOL – penalty, six days' pay. He went AWOL twice the following February before being posted to Gallipoli. In the first instance, the penalty was six days' pay; on the second occasion, the penalty was eight hours' detention. After Gallipoli, but before France, there was another drunken AWOL episode with the loss of two more days' pay. John was then caught drunk in the canteen after hours. That earned him ten days' confinement to barracks. He also had several other offences recorded against him.

Penalties went from a few days' pay lost and confinement, to being shot at dawn. Was the massive escalation deserved or did John fail to realise (was he of sound mind) that repercussions of his continuing reckless, but relatively minor, misconduct could be as serious as they ultimately proved?

Above: John Sweeney's grave in France. Source: Wikitree.

Christopher Pugsley accurately summed up the contemporary mindset of the presiding officials: "it seems that the court was more conscious of the battle to be fought than Sweeney's fate". The final decision rested with the British commander-in-chief, Douglas Haig, who sent him to execution, not on the circumstances of the case, but the perceived need for a deterrent. They made John Sweeney an example to his fellow comrades to maintain discipline and stiffen morale – the firing party was made up of men from his own battalion.[14]

Had he been a member of an Australian unit this could not have happened – the Australian Army did not allow its troops to be executed, after the public outcry that followed 'Breaker' Morant's execution during the Boer War.

Cruel letter

A further blow to the grieving Sweeney family was the diabolical treatment of John Sweeney's father, Bernard. He had been advised of his son's fate in early October 1916, but it was not until 38 days later that he was told his son had been the subject of an execution. The conveyer of this dreadful news was New Zealand general, A.W. Robin. In December 1916, Bernard Sweeney wrote to Brigadier General Robin:

"I must say it is a great blow to me to hear of my son's death in that way. He was the last I would have thought do such a thing. Would you kindly let me know if there is any chance of ever hearing any more of the case and if he left anything to come to me or his mother? The smallest article would be of comfort to us. Thanking you for your letter."[15]

John Sweeney's estranged wife, Amy, predeceased him, dying in 1910, so in his will, John left his effects to his mother. The New Zealand Army did not give his parents anything of comfort, also denying them access to his records which remained sealed until 1987. Although John Joseph Sweeney had not provided for his daughter in his will, his father Bernard was able to arrange for the New Zealand Army pension to be paid to Amy Sweeney's aunt, Mrs Maria Wilson, who had the care of Amy and John's young daughter, Doris, aged 11 at the time of her father's death.

Gallipoli hero recognised

There was a degree of recognition of John's heroic actions and it came from, of all people, British General Sir William Birdwood and reported in the local Scottsdale paper, the *North Eastern Advertiser* on 2 March 1920: "Residents of Lietinna and West Scottsdale on Saturday the 21st, gathered at the cross roads, Lietinna, to welcome General Sir William Birdwood and party. The corner was decorated with flags and laurel-wreaths. General Birdwood stayed to present gold medals to the next-of-kin of our fallen soldiers. With a few feeling words he pinned on to each of the bereaved ones the much-prized medal, the design being a cross and crown, with the name of the hero."[16] Amongst those names was that of John Joseph Sweeney.

The presentation of the commemorative medal to a representative of John Joseph Sweeney's family meant much in terms of restoring him to his rightful place as a Gallipoli hero. It was made more meaningful by its being presented by the commanding officer recognised as "the spirit of ANZAC".[17]

According to family descendants, when Private Sweeney's files were finally released in 1987, the New Zealand Defence Department still refused access to the court-martial file. That file was not released until September 1988 and then only after negotiations through the Ombudsman by the New Zealand newspaper, the *Wairarapa Times-Age*. Ross Annabell, the *Times-Age* reporter, was permitted to view the file at the National Archives. He received the file in an envelope. The door was closed and even the staff of the National Archives could not enter.

Military historian, Christopher Pugsley's analysis was that the New Zealand Commanders failed in their responsibilities. There were mitigating circumstances in Sweeney's case. His service in Gallipoli and his lengthy periods in hospital were ignored during the sentencing procedure. In the judgment of British military historian, Julian Putkowski, the execution was "military judicial murder".[18]

Pardoned

In September 2000, eighty-four years after Private Sweeney's execution, the New Zealand Parliament officially granted Australians John Joseph Sweeney and John King, along with three New Zealanders, posthumous pardons under the Pardon for Soldiers of the Great War Bill. These pardons came after a long campaign in Britain and a similar campaign in New Zealand led by Invercargill MP, Mark Peck. The campaigns were given much media attention in Australia and several national TV documentaries were produced.

The Parliament recognised that they were heroes who fought in horrific battles and were most probably suffering from a post-traumatic stress disorder. An important aspect of the pardon was the restoration of memory. This was in terms of public memory, but it also had the important effect of restoring the soldier to his family by withdrawing the veil of silence that had been drawn over their fate. Notably, the Scottsdale RSL had already added John's name to their honour roll about two years before his pardon.

Perhaps the most poignant legacy of John Joseph Sweeney is that in the Turanganui valley in New Zealand, for some years after World War I, the locals talked of Flanders Poppies springing up in the area cleared by John Joseph Sweeney and his Tasmanian team. After burning, the land had been re-sown with imported grass seed from France or Belgium and the poppies grew wild amongst the grasses.

Lest we forget

You can visit the memorial featuring John Sweeney's name at the Scottsdale RSL. No photo exists of John Sweeney.

Sincere thanks to Mr Tony Sweeney:

The material relating to the life and movements of John Joseph Sweeney contained in this story was taken from the writings of Tasmanian, Tony Sweeney, from his articles written for the RSL, *Sweeney's War.* They traced the movements and events as they related to Tony's father, Syd, along with Syd's two brothers, Dan and Ted, and their cousin, John Joseph Sweeney. Tony said: "In *Sweeney's War"* I endeavoured to give voice to some of what my father found almost impossible to speak about." [19] Our sincere thanks to Tony for all his work on this story. The writer, Chris Adams, is a cousin of Tony Sweeney.

References:

1 The battle of Messines – 1917, *firstworldwar.com*. Retrieved 11 January 2022 from URL: https://www.firstworldwar.com/battles/messines.htm

2 Australian National Memorial France. Hill 60, Ypres: the peak of Military Mining. *Sir John Monash Centre*. Retrieved 11 January 2022 from URL: https://sjmc.gov.au/hill-60-the-peak-of-mine-warfare/

3 Spencer, John. The Return of the Tunnel Bomb: A Medieval Tactic on the Modern Battlefield. *Modern War Institute at West Point*. Retrieved 11 January 2022 from URL: https://mwi.usma.edu/return-tunnel-bomb-medieval-tactic-modern-battlefield/

4 Adams, Simon. *Britannica*. Battle of the Crater American Civil War [1864]. Retrieved 11 January 2022 from URL: https://www.britannica.com/event/Battle-of-the-Crater-1864

5 Defeat of Grant at Petersburg. (1864, October 27). *The Mercury (Hobart, Tas: 1860 - 1954)*, p. 3. Retrieved December 9, 2021, from http://nla.gov.au/nla.news-article8829147

6 Mounted Rifles units, Page 8 – Wellington Mounted Rifles timeline 1914-19, *New Zealand at War*. Retrieved 11 January 2022 from URL: https://nzhistory.govt.nz/war/wellington-mounted-rifles/1914

7 How a clay kicking team works, *BBC NEWS*, 1 July 2016. Retrieved 11 January 2022 from URL: https://www.bbc.com/news/av/magazine-36688479

8 Waite, Major Fred, The New Zealanders at Gallipoli (1919).

9 The Great War John Joseph Sweeney, *The Wartime memories project*. Retrieved 11 January 2022 from URL: https://wartimememoriesproject.com/greatwar/view.php?uid=217650

10 John Joseph Sweeney (1879-1916), *WikiTree*. Retrieved 11 January 2022 from URL: https://www.wikitree.com/wiki/Sweeney-370#Court_Martial

11 Sweeney, Tony. *Sweeneys' War*. Articles written for the RSL.

12 Ibid.

13 Ibid.

14 Flanagan, Martin, Tale of tunneler Sweeney highlights terrible darkness of war, *The Sydney Morning Herald.*, 24 April 2014. Retrieved 11 January 2022 from URL: https://www.smh.com.au/national/tale-of-tunneler-sweeney-highlights-terrible-darkness-of-war-20140424-zqyib.html

15 Sweeney, Tony. *Sweeneys' War*. Op.cit.

16 APA citation Lietinna (1920, March 2). *North-Eastern Advertiser (Scottsdale, Tas: 1909 - 1954)*, p. 3. Retrieved January 4, 2022, from http://nla.gov.au/nla.news-article151270806

17 Birdwood, William, *Australian War Memorial*. Retrieved 11 January 2022 from URL: https://www.awm.gov.au/visit/exhibitions/dawn/legend/birdwood

18 Sweeney, Tony, John Joseph Sweeney, Coward or Hero? The sad tale of a Tasmanian soldier's WW1 experiences whilst serving with the New Zealand forces. *Diggers and Nurses of Dorset Municipality, Tasmania*, Facebook page, 3 February 2018. Retrieved 11 January 2022 from URL: https://www.facebook.com/1555679018051227/posts/the-sad-story-of-a-local-ww1-soldier-who-lived-in-scottsdale-before-the-war-the-/2028877040731420/

19 Sweeney, Tony. *Sweeneys' War*. Op.cit.

Images:

- Scottsdale Memorial Board: photo kindly supplied by Tony Sweeney.

- Enlistment papers kindly supplied by Tony Sweeney from the NZ Military Archives.

- The Wellington Mounted Rifles Regiment, under Lieutenant Colonel W. Meldrum, at Awapuni Camp, prior to embarkation. Source: Wilkie, A. H., *Official War History of the Wellington Mounted Rifles Regiment 1914-1919*, Whitcombe and Tombs Limited, 1924, Auckland. Public domain.

- Military personnel files for SWEENEY, John Joseph - WW1 8/1384 - Army; Record no: 0111302; R no: R7823257; Series: 18805.

- John Sweeney's grave in France: John Joseph Sweeney (1879 - 1916), Wikitree. Retrieved 11 January 2022 from URL: https://www.wikitree.com/wiki/Sweeney-370#Court_Martial

Left: William Peacock's grave. Right: Sir Henry Jones' grave. Both in Cornelian Bay Cemetery, Hobart.

The Apple Isle & the jam fleet

George Peacock, William Peacock, Henry Jones & William Shoobridge

Interred:	**William Davidson Peacock,** 1847 – 16 November 1921 (aged 74).
Location:	Wesley, section H, site 46.
Interred:	**Sir Henry Jones,** 19 July 1862 – 29 October 1926 (aged 64).
Location:	Church of England, section Z, site 23.
Cemetery:	Cornelian Bay Cemetery and Crematorium, Queens Walk, New Town, TAS 7008.

There are apparently two main reasons why Tasmania is sometimes called the "Apple Isle". The first is that once upon a time a lot of apples were grown there and it is the state where exporting apples got its start. In fact, so much product was being shipped from its shores that the ships became known as the 'jam fleet'. The second reason is considerably less likely, and that is, if one should look at a map of Tasmania, it is very much shaped like an apple.[1]

So, to get to the origin of the prominence of apples in Tasmania's history we need to go back a bit. The name William Bligh will be familiar to anyone seeking even the sketchiest understanding of Australia's early days – he was the infamous captain whose crew, led by acting-Lieutenant Fletcher Christian, mutinied on the ship, the *Bounty*.

Above: Robert Dodd's painting of the mutineers turning Lt. Bligh and crew adrift. Source: State Library of New South Wales.

To review this bit of history, four movies tell the story, each with sterling casts. Featuring in the role of Fletcher Christian are Errol Flynn (1933), Clark Gable (1935), Marlon Brando (1962) and Mel Gibson (1984). Of the latter three, the Mel Gibson version is the most historically accurate, according to Professor Douglas O. Linder of an American based school of law.[2]

But in August 1788, the year before Lt. William Bligh lost his ship because of the *Bounty* mutiny of April 1789, Lt. Bligh and his crew landed on Bruny Island's Adventure Bay. Their goal primarily was to replenish firewood and fresh water, but while they were there, they contributed in a small way to the future of Tasmania as an apple-growing region. Bligh had been there eleven years earlier in 1777, when he was Master of *HMS Resolution*, commanded by James Cook. Bligh was then 22, and it was said: "to be appointed sailing master on a major research vessel was a great tribute to his skill and connections."[3] Perhaps then he saw the place as a grand location for an orchard. And so, on his return visit the seed was sown.

The planting of trees

Now on board Bligh's ship, *HMS Bounty,* was a collection of fruit trees which he had acquired at the Cape of Good Hope. On Bruny Island, he and his on board botanist, David Nelson, sowed a veritable garden of everything from plums, peaches and apricots to vines and corn. Among the fruit trees were three fine young apple trees, the first to be introduced into Tasmania. Sadly, on Bligh's return in 1792, he found all his plants had been burnt out… except for one apple tree that survived.

This was not the tree that heralded generations of apple growing, and fortunately, the Tasmanian apple industry did not have to rely on Bligh's efforts for its foundation, but it recognised that the region was marked as ideal for fruit and crop growing. What followed was almost a backyard DIY movement from the labour of settlers that led to the growth of the industry.

Above: Lt.-Gov David Collins.
Source: Tasmanian Archives:
LMSS754/1/30.

In 1803 the settlement that John Bowen had established at Risdon Cove was deemed vulnerable to changing tides and poor water supply and it certainly did not impress the man who would take over, Lieutenant-Governor David Collins *(pictured)*. That decision might have been a bit hasty given its climate was very similar to that of England and most suited to growing apples, pears and crops that grew in the 'old country.'[4]

Nevertheless, after three trips across the Derwent River to view viable alternatives, Lt.-Gov Collins relocated the settlement eight kilometres (5 miles) downriver, on the opposite shore. They landed at Sullivans Cove on 21 February 1804 and created the settlement that was to become Hobart, making it the second-oldest-established colony in Australia.[5]

Land grants were handed out as early as 1804 to hard-working settlers, military personnel, and convicts who had completed their sentences. In all, over 2000 acres of land bordering Hobart was granted, and convict labour saw to its clearing – ripe, so to speak for cropping to be established.[6]

A major pest

Of course, there is always a pest or two that causes havoc – think rabbits, grasshoppers and cane toads – but in the apple's case, it was the codling moth. This small, brown moth requires fruit to survive, and as early as 1861, the *Launceston Examiner* was bemoaning "the immense destruction this year occasioned by the grub in apples" and offering tips so it may be "extirpated",[7] that is, eradicated or destroyed completely.

Above: the trouble-making codling moth. Source: Wikipedia.

In 1879 the codling moth was still causing destruction and when Parliament's House of Assembly met on Friday 26 September 1879, the speaker worked through the notices of motions including one from Dr E. L. Crowther "to move that the select committee appointed by this House last session, re codling moths, be again appointed, in order to enquire into the destruction of fruit by the codling moth, and if possible to suggest some means for limiting the spread of the pest."[8] The motion that was agreed to, but regardless, the codling moth settled in and remained a pest.

Fast forward seven decades to the 1950s and the problem continued with the Burnie *Advocate* reporting: "Moth lure traps maintained by the Department of Agriculture in various fruit districts continued to indicate that light brown apple moths were particularly active in most orchards throughout the State in the past week."[9]

Regardless, the apples of Van Diemen's Land, later renamed Tasmania (1856), became a commercial enterprise of significance. Towards the end of the 19th century, the apple industry was burgeoning, and new engineering and irrigation techniques, and commercial ventures to export apples to the mainland and overseas were started.

The four enterprising gentlemen who took up this mantle were George Peacock, William Peacock, Henry Jones and William Shoobridge. Not only were apples in demand especially in European markets, but there was much to gain from the by-products of apples including jams, cider and dried fruit.[10]

The apple and jam men

Of great impact in the burgeoning industry was agriculturalist and industrial innovator **William Ebenezer Shoobridge** *(pictured)*, whose knowledge and study of hydrostatics and engineering saw the development of new irrigation techniques, in particular, for apples. At his family's estate, the irrigation system which he developed "overcame the dryness of  the deep porous soil",[11] resulting in the crop increasing sevenfold between 1866-79, and his techniques for pruning changed the industry and saw him in much demand.

While William Shoobridge worked on the crop, significant work was being done on the by-products and canning of goods.

Businessman **George Peacock** was born in Bath, England, and arrived in 1850 and got to work – marrying and opening a grocery and fruit shop in his new home of Hobart Town. By 1867 the fruit part of his business took precedence and George became one of the first manufacturers of canned jam in the colonies, using copper pans, and boilers to create the steam for canning.[12]

Regarded as a hard worker and disciplinarian by his workers[13] (there was, however, no mutiny), George Peacock led his employees in prayers at the start of each workday,

Top: 1851, George Peacock's magnum bonum plum jam. Below: the jam factory in Victoria c1925-1945. Source: State Library Victoria.

allowed no swearing and sacked anyone who drank and smelled of liquor. Soon his nephew, William, 22, who had emigrated to Australia, joined him in the business. Oddly, given George's displeasure of his staff imbibing, William was sacked for refusing to manage a jam factory attached to a distillery – he was a man of temperance as well.

So, while his nephew, William, went and opened his own jam factory,[14] George Peacock continued to run his business, his son and stepson assisting, and expanded across the mainland to Sydney. His stepson, H. J. Pryde, who managed his Sydney store, was instrumental in changing the company name to the Australasian Jam Co.

George also experimented with fish, canning it, and sending it off to every capital to see how it fared. He retired in 1891, leaving the management of his business to his son, Ernest, along with Mr Achalen Palfreyman, and his foreman, Henry Jones, who would become a tour de force in the industry. George died in 1900 leaving a wife and eleven children and was buried in Waverley Cemetery, Sydney.

The next generation

George Peacock's 'dismissed' nephew, **William Davidson Peacock**, continued in the industry with great aplomb. Shipping was such a major part of the business's success and William successfully exported fruit to Europe in 1895. Cleverly, and ahead of his time, he guaranteed full cargo space to induce European ships to take on fruit in Tasmanian ports, whereas previously exporters like himself, had to ship their fruit for export to the mainland first.[15] By 1898 William, 51, was sharing this strategy with his uncle's foreman, Henry Jones, and between them, their two companies dominated the Tasmanian fruit export industry.

William died a very wealthy man in 1921, aged 74, owning property and shares in Henry's company – part of his former business which Henry took over. After providing for his widow and adopted daughter, William bequeathed his house and estate in Swan Street, Hobart, to his wife for the rest of her life, and thereafter, it was to be used as a government hospital or home for the incurable.[16] To this day the house contributes as William had hoped, as part of the Hobart & Southern Districts Adult Community Mental Health Services and is known as the Peacock Centre. In 2016, the heritage building was partially destroyed by fire but was redeveloped.

Above: William's label. Source: Libraries Tasmania.

Henry Jones was an astute and ambitious businessman, born in Tasmania and married to Alice who bore him twelve children.[17] As a young man in his thirties, Henry, working closely with George Peacock's son, Ernest, and Achalen Palfreyman, expanded the business in areas that supported their needs – distribution, hop growing, financing fruit growers and sailing vessels which guaranteed them cargo space. Hence, the 'jam fleet', and it led to Jones & Co becoming the agent for many British shipping agencies and insurance companies.[18] Soon more factories followed on the mainland, and overseas. By 1902, the business became a large public company named Henry Jones Co-operative Limited, with Henry as its chairman.

Left: William Peacock. Source: Tasmanian Archives NS738/1/2020.
Right: Henry Jones. Source: State Library Victoria.

Above: Workers at the IXL factory, 1927. Source: State Library of Victoria.

With fingers in many pies or fruit, Henry stepped up, taking a controlling share in William's company in 1910 and taking over the company outright nine years later when William retired. You will know this company which is an iconic part of our history to this day and bears the motto Henry lived by: *I excel in everything I do*'... IXL.[19] While Henry Jones enjoyed much business success, he was also brave and there were projects he tried that failed, but that did not tarnish his ambitions and success. In 1919, he was knighted;[20] Sir Henry Jones it was.

Henry died aged 64, on 29 October 1926 in Melbourne. He was in a negotiation at the time when a blood clot in his heart caused a heart attack. His wife and children survived him and with the fortune amassed, wanted for nothing.

The Apple Isle

Today, Tasmania is Australia's second-largest apple producer after Victoria. In 2020/21 over 41 thousand tonnes of apples were produced and enjoyed.[21] Who first coined the phrase 'The Apple Isle' appears to be a mystery. The first reference to it in the newspapers of Tasmania is in 1903 when Mr G.H. Reid in a short verse states: "In the Apple Isle you'll find me."[22]

While tourism marketing is not apple-flavoured these days, the contribution of the trailblazing farmers, engineers, and industrialists who put the Apple Isle on the map and created work for generations cannot be overestimated. Their inventiveness, ambition, perseverance, failures and victories paved the way and as the saying goes, allowed descendants to stand on the shoulders of giants.

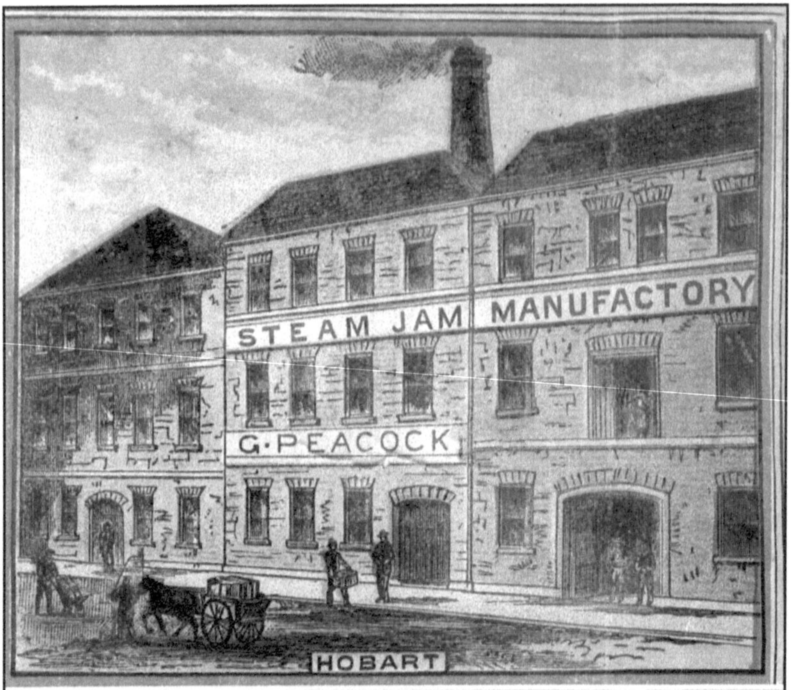

Above: The IXL factory in 1851. Source: State Library, Victoria.
Below: today, it is the Henry Jones Art Hotel. Book a room and visit!

References:

1 15 awesome facts about Tasmania, *Life's an adventure*. Retrieved 28 March 2022 from URL: https://www.lifesanadventure.com.au/15-awesome-facts-tasmania/

2 Linder, Douglas, O., Famous Trials, *UMKC School of Law*. Retrieved 25 March 2022 from URL: https://www.famous-trials.com/bounty/398-movies

3 Exploration: William Bligh, *Our Tasmania*. Retrieved 28 March 2022 from URL: https://www.ourtasmania.com.au/exploration-bligh.html

4 Hall, Beth. 15 Oct 2014. Apples of the Huon – Part 1, https://tasmaniangeographic.com/apples-of-the-huon-part-one/

5 Currey, John. The companion to Tasmanian History. David Collins. https://www.utas.edu.au/library/companion_to_tasmanian_history/C/David%20Collins.htm

6 Hall, Beth. October 15, 2014. Op.cit.

7 Apple Grub. (1861, February 21). *Launceston Examiner (Tas.: 1842 - 1899)*, p. 3 (MORNING). Retrieved March 25, 2022, from http://nla.gov.au/nla.news-article38757926

8 Parliament of Tasmania. (1879, September 27). *The Mercury (Hobart, Tas.: 1860 - 1954)*, p. 2. Retrieved March 25, 2022, from http://nla.gov.au/nla.news-article8981684

9 Apple moth busy in orchards (1953, Dec). *Advocate*, p. 3. http://nla.gov.au/nla.news-article69499908

10 Servant, Nathalie, Apple Industry. Centre for Tasmanian Historical Studies, 2006, *University of Tasmania*. Retrieved 25 March 2022 from URL: https://www.utas.edu.au/library/companion_to_tasmanian_history/A/Apple%20industry.htm

11 Chapman, Peter, 'Shoobridge, William Ebenezer (1846–1940)', Aust Dictionary of Biography, *Australian National University*, https://adb.anu.edu.au/biography/shoobridge-william-ebenezer-906/text14799

12 - 14 Peacock, George (1824–1900)', Aust Dictionary of Biography, *Australian National University*. Retrieved 25 March 2022 from: https://adb.anu.edu.au/biography/peacock-george-4378/text7125

15 Brown, Bruce, Peacock, William Davidson (1847- 921). Centre for Tasmanian Historical Studies (2005); *University of Tasmania*. Retrieved 23 March 2022 from URL: https://www.utas.edu.au/library/companion_to_tasmanian_history/P/Peacock.htm

16 The Late W.D. Peacock. (1922, April 12). *The Mercury (Hobart, Tas.: 1860 - 1954)*, p. 6. Retrieved March 25, 2022, from http://nla.gov.au/nla.news-article23561080

17 - 18 Brown, Bruce, Henry Jones. Centre for Tasmanian Historical Studies (2005); *University of Tasmania*. Retrieved 23 March 2022 from URL: https://www.utas.edu.au/library/companion_to_tasmanian_history/J/Jones%20Henry.htm

19 Brown, Bruce, Peacock, William Davidson. Op.cit.

20 Reynolds, John, 'Jones, Sir Henry (1862–1926)', Aust Dictionary of Biography, *Australian National University*. Retrieved 25 Mar 2022 from: https://adb.anu.edu.au/biography/jones-sir-henry-6874/text11911

21 Hickey, Sean, The Big Apples of Australia, 10 Jan 2022. *Rural Bank*. Retrieved 25 Mar 2022 from: https://www.ruralbank.com.au/blog/knowledge-and-insights/the-big-apples-of-australia/

22 The Courting of "Tassy." (1903, April 12). *The Sunday Sun (Sydney, NSW: 1903 - 1910)*, p. 7. Retrieved March 28, 2022, from http://nla.gov.au/nla.news-article230029524

Images:

- Dodd, R. (2). The Mutineers. *State Library of New South Wales*. Retrieved 28 March 2022 from URL: https://search.sl.nsw.gov.au/permalink/f/1cvjue2/ADLIB110162811

- LMSS754/1/30 Photograph/Portrait/Sketch-Colonel David Collins, Lt Governor 1804-10. [photographer J. W. Beattie; Copy made from "The Governors of Tasmania : from 1804 to 1896"] Tasmanian Archive and Heritage Office. *Libraries Tasmania*. Retrieved 28 Mar 2022 from: https://stors.tas.gov.au/AI/LMSS754-1-30

- Winkley, Simon & Walker, Ken [photographers], Codling mother, Museum Victoria. *Wikipedia*, Retrieved 28 March 2022, from: https://en.wikipedia.org/w/index.php?title=Codling_moth&oldid=1078826601

- William Shoobridge, *Parliament Tasmania, http://www.parliament.tas.gov.au/history/tasparl/shoobridgew344.htm

- Gilks. (1851). Peacock's magnum bonum plum jam & factory. Kronheim & Co.; *State Library Victoria*. Retrieved 28 March 2022 from URL: http://search.slv.vic.gov.au/permalink/f/1cl35st/SLV_ROSETTAIE1495423

- Henry Jones IXL collection of photographs, ca.1925-1945 from: http://handle.slv.vic.gov.au/10381/464457

- W. D. Peacock & Co. (Tas.) Fancy Apples, *Libraries Tasmania*. Retrieved 28 March 2022 from URL: https://stors.tas.gov.au/TASIMAGES$init=AUTAS001126188630W800

- NS738/1/2020 Photograph - Mr W. D. Peacock, Tasmanian Exhibition, 1894-5, Season Ticket Holder - Lefroy Street. Tasmanian Archive and Heritage Office. *Libraries Tasmania*. Retrieved 28 March 2022 from: https://stors.tas.gov.au/NS738-1-2020

- Portrait of Henry Jones, *Stonnington Library*, Ref. No.: PH1671.3. Retrieved 28 March 2022 from: https://stonnington.spydus.com/cgi-bin/spydus.exe/FULL/WPAC/ARCENQ/26762551/22935776,1?FMT=IMG

- (1927). Henry Jones IXL collection of photographs. State Library of Victoria. Retrieved 28 March 2022 from URL: http://search.slv.vic.gov.au/permalink/f/1fe7t3h/SLV_VOYAGER2356721

123

Above: North Mount Lyell disaster memorial at Queenstown Lyell Cemetery. Photograph by Arthur Garland, Monument Australia.

The North Mount Lyell mine disaster

42 men

Interred: Memorial to the victims of the North Mount Lyell mine disaster.

Cemetery: Queenstown Lyell Cemetery, Cemetery Road off Conlan Street, Queenstown, TAS 7467.

On Saturday morning, 12 October 1912, life in and around the North Mount Lyell mine at Queenstown in western Tasmania was probably fairly normal – that is, tense because of safety issues that miners had been constantly warning about – but a tightknit, friendly and committed community of workers who toiled under normal circumstances up to 335m (1100 feet) underground.[1]

Like most days of the week, that morning around 170 miners went down the single shaft of the mine to various levels where they worked to extract copper ore, which was crushed underground before being taken to the surface on a conveyor belt. But somewhere between 11.15am and 11.30am on this morning, tragedy was about to strike after a fire was reported in the pump house on the 700-foot level (213m). It led to one of Australia's most terrible mining disasters. Of the 170 men who went down the mine that day, 42 would not return alive. Only 73 emerged that day and the battle to save a further 55 men trapped below produced some remarkable rescue efforts and acts of sheer bravery.

The appropriate word to describe the scene at the Mt Lyell mine was 'chaotic'. Outside the mine, uncertainty surrounded the status of the fire and the number of miners remaining inside. Smoke quickly filled the mine both above and below the 700-foot (213m) level making initial rescue attempts difficult and repeated attempts to enter the mine impossible.

News of the fire on the 700-foot level was spread throughout the mine by men whose only resort was to run along drives and levels calling out to the working men, warning them of the dire situation facing them. There was no warning system in the labyrinth of tunnels and mined out stopes and of course, that meant many men, especially those deeper in the mine, got the news far too late to save themselves or be rescued by someone else.[2]

The rescue plan

Despite the desperate situation that faced the trapped miners, there was a rescue plan. It revolved around bringing breathing equipment from one of the Victorian mining operations to Queenstown by way of ship to Burnie and rail to Queenstown. Whatever the plan, speed was of the essence… the equipment not only had to reach Tasmania but then be transported to the Mt Lyell mine in time to make a difference.

Above: Families at the scene of the disaster . Source: Weekly Times.

Meanwhile, a maritime diving suit that was located in Burnie was rushed to the mine. One brave soul volunteered to go down the mine in the suit and actually made it down as far as the 850-foot level (260m). Unfortunately the suit was of no help and the bold volunteer was hauled to the surface almost immediately, after the weight of the suit and confines of the underground prevented most movement and it was impossible to bend while wearing it.

Now the rescue equipment on its way from Victoria seemed like it would offer the best chance of locating any miners who may have survived in the bowels of the mine. The SS *Loongana*, a Bass Strait passenger ship, was pressed into service for the Tasmanian dash and made the trip from Melbourne to Burnie in 12 hours 46 minutes, averaging 22 knots. It was a time not beaten for many years.[3] Also, the travel time of the train carrying the rescue gear between Burnie and Queenstown was apparently never bettered.

Hope and an anguishing decision

Once the equipment and trained fire-fighters were on the scene and managed to make their way down to the 700-foot level the immensity of the tragedy was there for them all to see. The rescue party discovered a group of deceased miners who were victims of the carbon monoxide that swept through the mine from the fire. There was no hope for any of them but one man, Joe McCarthy, had pinned a note to a timber stanchion. It was addressed to his wife and published in *The Zeehan and Dundas Herald* five days after the fire.

"Seven hundred level. North Lyell mine, 12-10-12. If anyone should find this note convey to my wife.

Dear Agnes. – I will say good-bye.

Sure I will not see you again any more.

I am pleased to have made a little provision for you and poor little Lorna. Be good to our little darling. My mate, Len Burke, is done, and poor old V. and Driver too. Good-bye, with love to all.

Your loving husband, Joe McCarthy."[4]

Above: People standing in the street reading news of the disaster. Source: National Library Australia.

It was just one of the touching attempts at communication from men who appeared to be doomed, but not all were quite so fatalistic. One read:

"Well and cheerful. J. Ryan growing weaker. The air at the 1,000ft level is good."[5]

As the rescuers found survivors in the mine, a plan of escape from the bottom of the shaft was put into practice on the Wednesday afternoon. *The Zeehan and Dundas Herald* reported it appeared to be easy for some, for others not so… "North Lyell, Wednesday, 1 p.m. The entombed men who will be rescued from the No. 40 stope at the 1,000ft level will be brought along the drive to the main shaft, and from there to the winze (a shaft or inclined passage). They will be pulled from there on the cage to the 700ft level, climb 300ft through passes and sets of timber, and then 200ft in buckets. Thence they will be brought to the mouth of No. 2 tunnel."[6]

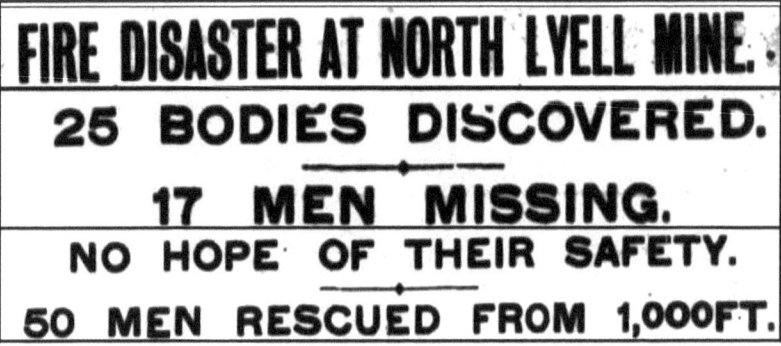

Above: Newpaper headlines on 17 October 1912.
Source: The Zeehan and Dundas Herald.

Above: Ryan, the Shift Boss, emerging after being 100 hours below.
Source: University of Tasmania Library Special and Rare Collections.

Above: Funeral procession with photographers on the hill. Source: Tasmanian Archive & Heritage Office.

The men had now spent over four days – 109 hours – underground in wet and cold surroundings and there was no food. Fifty five miners were rescued but 42 miners had perished at the beginning of the rescue operations and attempts to recover their bodies had failed.

The fire continued to burn and after 10 days and with 18 miners still missing it was decided to seal the mine. Five months later those men were located and their bodies were brought to the surface. They were placed in coffins and for the second time, Queenstown witnessed a mass funeral with railway flat trucks draped in black crepe for the solemn procession to the Queenstown Cemetery.

Above: Miner 'Linnell' being rescued from 1000 feet level.
Source: University of Tasmania Library Special and Rare Collections.

Unsung heroes

Mr W. Bolton and Mr Thomas Gays, 22, *(pictured)* will never be forgotten for their bravery. While the process of extracting those who had now been found alive continued, quietly and not wishing to be noticed were numbers of miners who could have escaped, but rather went back to save their mates. *The Australasian Mine Safety Journal* reports that there were many deeds of heroism and courage from miners who were at the bottom of the mine while the cage was still operating. Once it had jammed and blocked the only shaft, there was no way out.

In one case miners who could have been rescued were awaiting the cage, "but that they saw a number of men staggering in the smoke almost overcome, and instead of saving themselves they calmly returned to succor (sic) as best they might those who were in a bad plight. Mr Bolton was up to No. 2 drive twice but returned to look for his mates. Mr Gays rose to the height of absolute heroism. The cage was ready to come up when he saw a married man on the plat (platform). He calmly stepped out of the cage into the blinding smoke and sent it up the shaft. That was the last cage that left."[7] He was an only son.

Paying the price

Without wishing to disparage what were remarkable efforts by many who went to great lengths, probably even risking their lives to save others, there is one man who stands out amongst this band of heroes. His name is Albert Mansfield Gadd, a miner who had been elected as one of the Union safety inspectors. A memorial to him stands at Miner's Siding in Queenstown.

Albert had no thought for his own well-being. Once he had escaped the terror of what was happening down the shaft of the Mt Lyell mine fire, he went back down the shaft several times, hoping to rescue some of his mates and bring them to safety. Eventually, the fumes, the carbon monoxide, was too much for him and he had to stop. But the damage was done and several months later without fuss or publicity, he went to a Launceston private hospital where he died.

The *Hobart Mercury* said of him: "He died as he lived, quietly and without ostentation, poisoned by the gas which slew those whom he had tried to rescue.[8]

Albert Gadd died on 20 February 1913. He was 32 years old and is generally regarded as the 43rd victim of the disaster. Tragically, his wife gave birth to a son two months after his death. Albert Gadd was awarded the Clark Gold Medal by the Royal Humane Society and is still remembered in Tasmania. On the centenary of the disaster the people of Queenstown put these simple words on a memorial to mark the disaster: 'To the Memory of ALBERT MANSFIELD GADD, a brave miner. He died from mon-oxide poisoning.

Gassed while rescuing his mates in the North Lyell mine disaster. He died on 20th Feb. 1913 aged 32 years. Greater love hath no man than this that he gave up his life for his mates.'

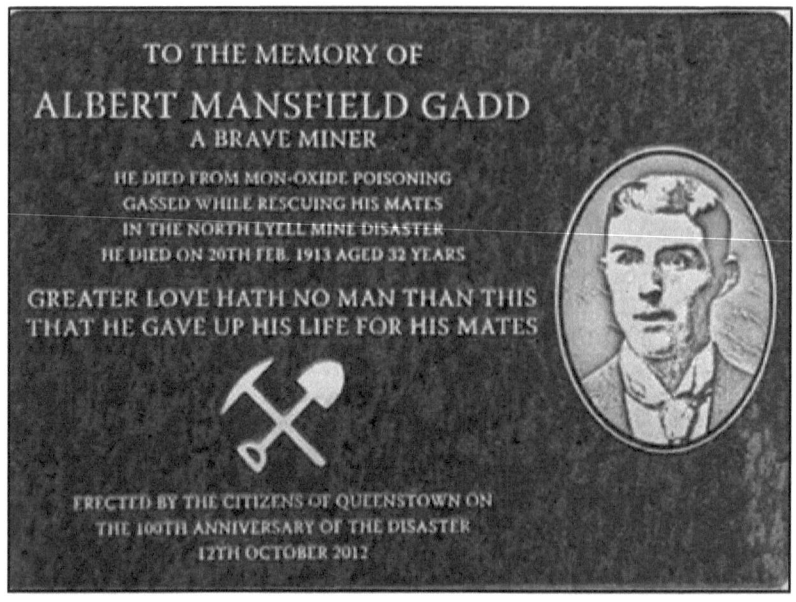

Above: The monument erected by the people of Queenstown, 100 years after Albert's death, to remember the hero.
Source: Reproduced with the kind permission of Monument Australia.

On Sunday morning, after the disaster, the townsfolk must have been about as despondent as it was possible to get in Queenstown. There were few developments overnight and they gathered around the mine entrance wanting to be the first to hear any news. There were around 100 women at the tunnel mouth who had been at the mine all night... some with accompanying children. Coal fires burned all night to keep them warm but when the bleak morning arrived, there was little for them to do except stare at the shaft entrance and speculate amongst themselves on the chances of their loved one, be it husband, father or brother's chances of survival.[9]

Seeking answers

The Royal Commission into the fire returned an open finding however the mine owners claimed a disgruntled employee and unionist who wanted to discredit the mine started the fire. Electrical engineer and former parliamentarian, Peter Shultze[10], who has written a book on the disaster, points out that the mine owners had already suppressed evidence of a number of electrical fires that had occurred at the underground pump site. There were no fuses in the control circuits and on two previous occasions where there had been fires, they had to switch off the power to be able to put the fires out.

There was no question that the conditions under which Mount Lyell's miners worked were less than ideal and probably extremely unsafe. *The Mercury* ran a story just two weeks before the disaster occurred in which miners questioned the conditions and told of circumstances they believed would lead to an immense collapse.[11] Even by the poor standard of the day, Mt Lyell did not have a reputation for high safety standards. The mine had also registered accidents with multiple fatalities in 1902, 1903 and 1908. A safety record of this kind would immediately close a mine site today, however in the early part of the 20th-century conditions such as these were, sadly, all too common.[12]

After the tragedy, the mine continued to operate and those who lost loved ones in the disaster of 1912 continued to grieve, reminding all of the price of taking riches from the ground. Mrs Agnes McCarthy had twin girls four months after her husband, Joseph, died.[13] On the 1st, 2nd and 3rd anniversary of his death, Mrs McCarthy paid tribute to her husband, who had left a note for her by his body, with a notice in the paper:

McCarthy – in sad and loving memory of my dear husband, Joseph, who met his death so bravely on the 12 October, 1912 in the Mount Lyell disaster.
Little I thought when you bade me good-bye, left me to die;
You had left me for ever, left me to die;
Not even thy dear lifeless face did I see,
But as long as life lasts, I'll remember thee.
Inserted by his loving wife, Agnes McCarthy.[14]

The victims:

John Bawden, single, 25
John (Jack) Bolton, single, 38
William Henry Bowker, married, 42 (died 1919)
Louis Burke, married, 43
James Davey, married, 37
George Gard, single, 21
Charles Green, single, 22
James Thomas Hall, married, 32
William Horne, married, 45
Henry Jones, single, 22
Zephaniah Lewis, married, 41
Joseph McCarthy, married, 40
Edmund Michael McCullagh, single, 49
Bernard McLoughlin, married, 35
Herbert John Mitchell, single, 23
Cornelius O'Keefe, single, 26
Christopher Quake, single, 50
Francis John Rolfe, married, 31
Thomas Saunderson, married, 37
James William Smith, single, 19
James Tregonning, single, 18
Richard John Treverton, married, 34

Valentine Bianchini, single, 48
John Bourke, single, 24
Samson Bray, married, 33
John Creeden, married, 46
Albert Gadd, married, 32
Thomas Gays, single, 22
Francis Guy, married, 27
Eden Hills, single, 21
John Jenkins, married, 28
John M. Leeman, single, 27
Thomas Maher, married, 31
Eugene McCasland, single, 27
James McGowan, single, 23
Arthur McMaster, married, 27
Peter Moore, single, 48
James Robert Park, married, 37
Patrick Reiley, widower, 46
James Roland Rolfe, single, 22
Leonard Sydney Scott, married, 22
John Studwell, single, 20
William Tregonning, single, 20
Henry Wright, married, 54.

References:

1 Wikipedia contributors. (2021, September 2). North Mount Lyell disaster. In *Wikipedia, The Free Encyclopedia*. Retrieved 04:55, February 11, 2022, from https://en.wikipedia.org/w/index.php?title=North_Mount_Lyell_disaster&oldid=1041957601

2 Devonport, Mining on the West Coast – 1912 Mt Lyell disaster. *Bass Strait Marine Centre*. Retrieved 29 March 2022 from URL: https://www.bassstraitmaritimecentre.com.au/mining-on-the-west-coast-1912-mt-lyell-disaster/

3 Conolly, Pauline. Loongana to the rescue, *Pauline Connolly*. Retrieved 29 March 2022 from URL: https://paulineconolly.com/2020/loongana-to-the-rescue-a-mercy-trip-after-a-tasmanian-mine-disaster/

4 - 6 Fire Disaster at North Lyell Mine. (1912, October 17). *Zeehan and Dundas Herald (Tas.: 1890 - 1922)*, p. 2. Retrieved February 20, 2022, from http://nla.gov.au/nla.news-article83338545

7 A Tasmanian Tragedy – Disaster at Mt Lyell. A Tasmanian Tragedy - Disaster at Mt Lyell - Mining Safety News, 30 April, 2015, *Australasian Mine Safety Journal*. (amsj.com.au)

8 Albert Gadd. (1913, February 25). *The Mercury (Hobart, Tas.: 1860 - 1954)*, p. 4. Retrieved February 20, 2022, from http://nla.gov.au/nla.news-article10275833

9 Devonport, Mining on the West Coast – 1912 Mt Lyell disaster. *Bass Strait Marine Centre*. Retrieved 29 March 2022 from URL: https://www.bassstraitmaritimecentre.com.au/mining-on-the-west-coast-1912-mt-lyell-disaster/

10 A Tasmanian Tragedy - Mining Safety News. Op.cit.

11 The Mt. Lyell Agreement. (1912, September 30). *The Mercury (Hobart, Tas.: 1860 - 1954)*, p. 5. Retrieved February 22, 2022, from http://nla.gov.au/nla.news-article10250809

12 A Tasmanian Tragedy - Mining Safety News. Op.cit.

13 GENERAL TELEGRAMS. (1913, February 22). *The Mercury* (Hobart, Tas. : 1860 - 1954), p. 3. Retrieved March 29, 2022, from http://nla.gov.au/nla.news-article10275519

14 Family Notices (1913, October 11). *The Age (Melbourne, Vic.: 1854 - 1954)*, p. 5. Retrieved February 28, 2022, from http://nla.gov.au/nla.news-article196230257

15 Victims North Mount Lyell disaster. *Wikipedia, The Free Encyclopedia*. Retrieved 29 March 29 2022 from URL: https://en.wikipedia.org/w/index.php?title=North_Mount_Lyell_disaster&oldid=1041957601

Images:

Garland, Arthur [photographer] North Mount Lyell disaster memorial. Reproduced with the kind permission of Mr Garland and Monument Australia. https://monumentaustralia.org.au/themes/disaster/industrial/display/99633-north-lyell-mine-disaster-

The Disaster at the North Lyell Mine, Tasmania. (1912, October 26). *Weekly Times* (Melbourne, Vic.: 1869 - 1954), p. 28. Retrieved March 23, 2022, from http://nla.gov.au/nla.news-article222599850

People standing in the street reading news of the North Mount Lyell mine disaster, Queenstown, Tasmania, 1912. *National Library Australia*. Retrieved 23 March 2022, from http://nla.gov.au/nla.obj-153091836

Newpaper headlines: Fire Disater at North Lyell Mine. (1912, October 17). *Zeehan and Dundas Herald* (Tas.: 1890 - 1922), p. 2. Retrieved March 23, 2022, from http://nla.gov.au/nla.news-article83338545

Colin Dennison (Curator) (1912). Images of West Coast Tasmania, *University of Tasmania Library Special and Rare Collections*. Retrieved 23 March 2022. Images as follow:

• North Lyell - Ryan, the Shift Boss, emerging after being 100 hours below. https://sparc.utas.edu.au/north-lyell-ryan-the-shift-boss

• North Lyell - Miner 'Linnell' being rescued from 1000 feet level. https://sparc.utas.edu.au/7

Queenstown - Mt Lyell Mine - funeral procession drawn by Mt Lyell train (1912), *Tasmanian Archive and Heritage Office*. Sourced: *Wikimedia* 23 March 2022 from URL: https://commons.wikimedia.org/w/index.php?curid=65671684

Thomas Gays: North Lyell Heroes. (1912, November 10). *The Sun* (Sydney, NSW: 1910 - 1954), p. 7. Retrieved March 23, 2022, from http://nla.gov.au/nla.news-article228836335

Ladies on the pitch
Lily Poulett-Harris

Interred: (Harriet) Lily Poulett-Harris, 2 September 1873 – 15 August 1897 (aged 23).

Location: Church of England, section J, number 80.

Cemetery: Cornelian Bay Cemetery and Crematorium, Queens Walk, New Town, TAS 7008.

Above: Lily Poulett-Harris. Source: Wikipedia.

Like most ladies of the Victorian era, Lily Poulett-Harris sang charmingly and played violin and piano most proficiently. Unlike most ladies of the era, Lily also played cricket and did a capital job of it. But she was not just talented with a bat, Lily, at age 20, was the founder and captain of the first women's cricket team in Australia. While some may debate this, given the occasional game was played prior, Lily formed a competitive club and her women's team in Tasmania – the Oyster Cove Ladies' Cricket Club – was extremely successful. The year was 1894 and the team, captained by Lily, initially played their first-ever ladies' competition cricket matches against North Bruny,[1] the rival team sailing in for the game.

A family affair

Cricket and teaching were both family affairs. And with four brothers and seven sisters, Lily had enough siblings to make up a cricket team. However, sadly, they did not all survive or come to live on Australian shores.

Long before Lily was born, her father, Richard Poulett-Harris, married Catherine Prior Hall in 1844, and they had two sons and four daughters. Catherine died 12 years later, and Richard sailed from Gravesend in the U.K., to Hobart with his two sons and daughter, Charlotte, leaving three daughters behind. Richard married again in 1858 and his bride, Elizabeth, gave birth to two sons and four daughters, including Lily and her twin sister, Louisa, in September 1873. Tragically, her half-brother, Richard, had died of severe burns in 1859, and Charlotte was institutionalised in an asylum the year before Lily was born.[2]

*Above: Lily (left) and her twin, Louisa, c.1880s. Source: Wikipedia.
Below left: Lily's father, Richard. Source: Tasmanian Archive and Heritage
Office. Middle: Lily's brother Henry. Source: Wikimedia. Right: Lily's sister the
actress, Miss Mary Milward (stage name), 1905. Source: Punch.*

Closer to her own age, there was big sister, Eleanor, 12 years Lily's senior, Henry, eight years older, Anna, four years older, and her twin, Louisa.[3]

It is no surprise that Lily grew up to become a teacher given her father was rector and head of the Hobart Boys' High School[4] and Lily's twin sister, Louisa, taught at the Ladies Grammar, in Hobart. Lily would teach at both her father's and her sister's schools.[5]

She was a bright star, and a practical thinker who did not shy away from a challenge. Lily had proven herself academically as well. One can only image her parents' pride when in 1884, at the age of 11, she sat for an exam at her father's school for the prestigious Newcastle Scholarship. Lily came second but knew she could not have accepted it as she was not eligible. It was termed a "trial of strength".[6]

The year after, aged 12, she saved her mother, Elizabeth, from serious burns and possible death when her mother accidentally caught fire trying to burn off some brushwood and dry grass which she thought might harbour snakes. Her dress caught ablaze, but Lily had the presence of mind to wrap her wet swimsuit around her mother, extinguishing the flames.[7]

But it was her love of cricket that would put her on the map. After all, cricket ran in the family. Her father was a trustee of the Southern Tasmanian Cricket Association and her older brother, Henry Vere Poulett-Harris, toured New Zealand with a Tasmanian cricket team in the 1880s[8] and played five first-class cricket matches for the Tasmania and Western Australia cricket teams between 1883 and 1899.[9]

Ladies on the pitch

Lily wasn't the only lady who liked a game of cricket. By the end of the 1894 season, two more teams joined in – Hobart with Huonville – and not long after, Ranelagh and Green Ponds donned their whites and joined in.[10]

While considered in some reports to be the first women's cricket team in Australia, eight years prior on 8 March 1886, the Fernleas Women's Cricket Team took on the Siroccos at what is now known as the Sydney Cricket Ground. This was a charity match with Nellie Gregory as captain of Fernleas and Nellie's sister, Lily, at the helm of the Siroccos. It did not result in a regular fixture of women's games, but it meant Australia spawned a women's cricket side before the White Heather Club of Britain was formed in 1887.[11]

But, as for Lily's achievement, getting the first regular competitive team sport of women's cricket off the ground would indeed make her the founder of women's cricket in Australia, and the first women's cricket captain. Lily either opened the batting or took the third-order batswoman position.

Unlike the men in their whites, the women played in summer dresses, which had their limitations.[12] Certainly, the long dresses meant some LBWs were difficult to call, but they snagged some balls as well, so all was fair in love and cricket.

Early in December 1894, Lily's Oyster Cove team took on Hobart's Atalanta ladies, winning by 17 runs. The visiting team sailed to the match, arriving on the SS *Nubeena*, declaring they were "delighted by the trip and the welcome given them by the Oyster Cove ladies."[13] Lily made a respectable 20 and "bowled well"[14] to obtain wickets. In bowling, Miss E. Holmwood was the star of the match with 10 wickets for 21 runs, and a fine left-hand catch![15]

As Lily's Oyster Cove team had sailed to Bruny Island by yacht earlier in the 1894 season when they took victory by 36 runs,[16] the North Bruny team sailed to take on Oyster Cove in the last match of their first season in 1894. The sportswriter of Hobart's *The Mercury* applauded the "plucky" North Bruny team for undertaking the trip from Bruny, "as a stiff westerly gale was blowing, against which they had to beat across. Many of the ladies were considerably upset by the rough passage, and this no doubt had something to do with their defeat."[17]

Yet, despite the stoicism of the North Bruny team, the match was won by the home team by an innings and 41 runs. On this day, Lily's Oyster Cove team batted first and made a total of 91, for which Lily (captain) was said to be mainly responsible with "a prettily played innings of 40."[18] Miss R. Jackson was also said to have made a splendid catch from her own bowling.

Not to be outdone were the North Bruny bowlers with "Misses Denne (captain) five wickets for 25 runs, V. Davis three for 17, and G. Young one for 14."[19]

At the start of the new year, January 1895, the Oyster Cove Ladies' Cricket Club met the Heather Ladies' Cricket Team for a friendly match and again Lily's team won, this time by an innings and 27 runs. *The Mercury* newspaper commented: "The bowling for Oyster Cove was very good, indeed – Misses L. Poulett-Harris, two for 1; O. Jackson, four for 4; R. Jackson, seven for 19."[20]

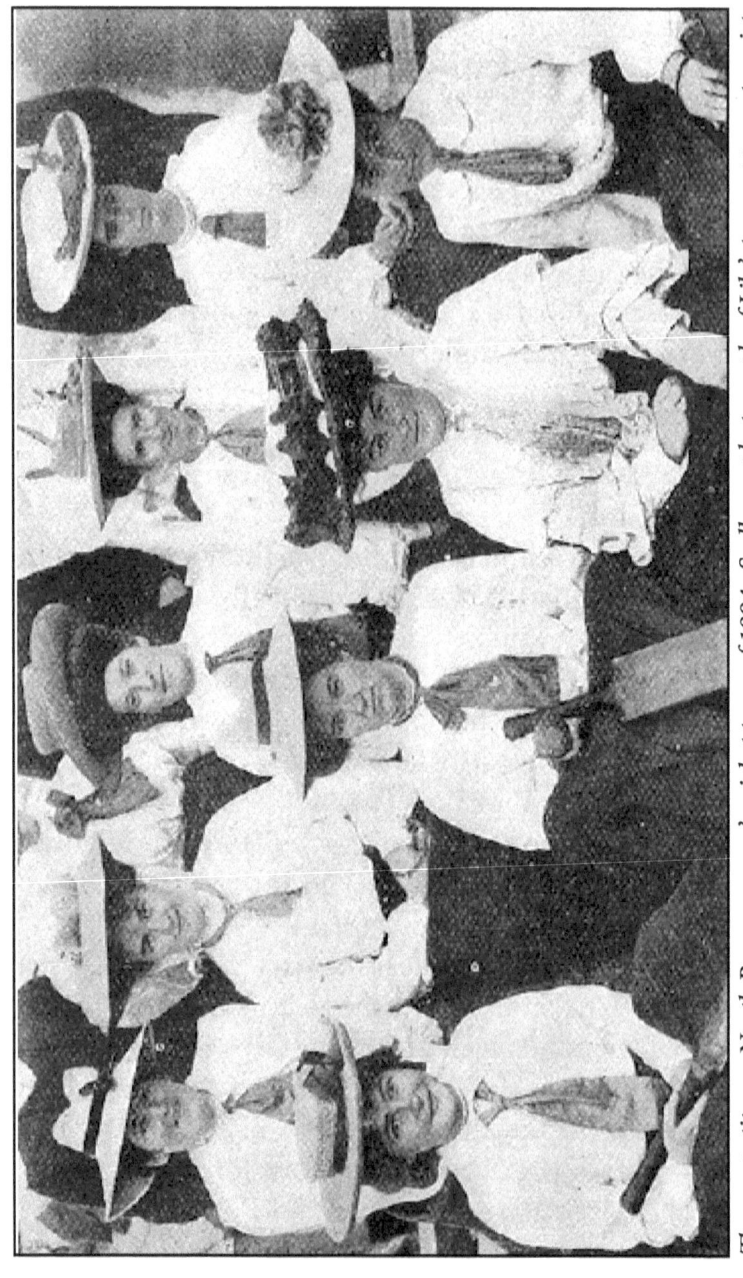

The competitors – North Bruny women's cricket team of 1894. Sadly, no photograph of Lily's team appears to exist. Reproduced with the kind permission of the Channel Museum.

A bright flame extinguished

Lily played cricket in the competition she established for three years until, in 1897, ill health forced her retirement, and tuberculosis peritonitis racked her body. Aged 23, Lily died – a bright flame extinguished all too soon.

Lily's twin sister, Louisa, outlived her twin by 44 years. Louisa took to the stage and achieved fame and respect on the Australian theatre circuit using the stage name Mary Milward and appearing with The Brough-Flemming Company of Sydney. One reviewer noted of her performance: "The principal ladies, including Miss Milward, received numerous handsome bouquets of flowers."[21]

On returning to Hobart with the theatre company for a performance at the Theatre Royal in 1906, *The Mercury* reported: "It may not be generally known that Miss Mary Milward (nom d' theatre) who comes to Hobart with the Brough-Flemming Comedy Company is a daughter of the late Rev R. D. Poulett-Harris of the High School. Miss Milward has been a member of the Company since its inauguration. Her many friends will doubtless give her a hearty welcome to her native city."[22] When she stopped treading the boards, Louisa went on to teach music and elocution, dying on 29 December 1941, aged 68.[23] She was cremated.

Lily's was a brief life but in her moment in history, she inspired women to take up the sport, which continues to this day. A tribute from a colleague described her as having a "mirthful and happy disposition, ever endeavouring to make those with whom she came in contact – and those not a few – cheerful and happy."[24] The writer added: "Fear, it is said, was a thing unknown to her."[25]

How to pay your respects:

Lily is buried in Plot J-80, Cornelian Bay Cemetery, Hobart. In 1899, one year before the new century and two years after her death, Lily's father passed away and was buried in the same grave. There is a memorial plaque remembering Lily on the rear wall of All Saints Church, Macquarie Street, South Hobart. Play on, ladies.

LADIES' CRICKET MATCH.

OYSTER COVE V. NORTH BRUNY.

A cricket match which has excited a considerable amount of interest was played on the North Bruny ground on Saturday, 6th inst., between eleven members of the Oyster Cove Ladies' Cricket Club, and a like number of the North Bruny ladies, which, after a good match, was won by the Oyster Cove team by 31 runs. The visitors were kindly conveyed to and from Barnes' Bay in Mr. R. Hughes' yacht by the owner and Mr. G. E. Hughes. The play on both sides was really good, especially considering the little practice which many of the players had prior to the match. The feature of the match was undoubtedly the fine not out innings of Miss L. Poulett-Harris, captain of the winning team, who, going in first, carried her bat right through the innings for 64 runs, including four 4's and three 3's.

Above: Player of the match... the Mercury reports, 9 January 1894.

References:

1 Tasmanian Honour Roll of Women, Harriet (Lily) Poulett-Harris, *Tasmanian Government*. Retrieved 23 August 2021 from URL: https://www.communities.tas.gov.au/csr/programs-and-services/tasmanian_honour_roll_of_women/inductees/2021/harriet-lily-poulett-harris

2 French, E. L., 'Harris, Richard Deodatus Poulett (1817–1899)', *Australian Dictionary of Biography*, National Centre of Biography, *Australian National University*. Retrieved 25 Aug 2021 from URL: https://adb.anu.edu.au/biography/harris-richard-deodatus-poulett-3726/text5855

3 Harriet (Lily) Poulett-Harris, *Ancestry*, ancestry.com.au

4 Trinity Church (1933, June 1). *The Mercury (Hobart, Tas. : 1860 - 1954)*, p. 10. Retrieved August 25, 2021, from http://nla.gov.au/nla.news-article24898471

5 Tasmanian Honour Roll of Women. Op.cit.

6 Our Cable News. (1884, June 9). *Launceston Examiner (Tas. : 1842 - 1899)*, p. 2. Retrieved August 24, 2021, from http://nla.gov.au/nla.news-article90546235

7 The Mercury. (1885, November 5). *The Mercury (Hobart, Tas. : 1860 - 1954)*, p. 2. Retrieved August 27, 2021, from http://nla.gov.au/nla.news-article9112883

8 Lennon, Troy, The Southern Stars owe..., *The Daily Telegraph*. Retrieved 23 Aug 2021 from: https://www.dailytelegraph.com.au/news/the-southern-stars-owe-a-huge-debt-to-the-tasmanian-schoolteacher-who-became-australias-first-female-cricket-star/news-story/2e77497d4f93b455516cf7c5ca70b0bb

9 Cricket Archive. Retrieved via *Wikipedia* 26 August 2021 from URL: https://www.espncricinfo.com/player/henry-harris-5585

10 Tasmanian Honour Roll of Women. Op.cit.

11 - 12. Lennon, Troy. Op.cit.

13, 14, 15. Ladies' Cricket Match. (1894, December 10). *The Mercury (Hobart, Tas. : 1860 - 1954)*, p. 4. Retrieved August 26, 2021, from http://nla.gov.au/nla.news-article9311056

16 Burgess, Georgie, Women's cricket in Australia started in late 1800s in southern Tasmania, *ABC Radio* Hobart, 31 May 2020 from URL: https://www.abc.net.au/news/2020-05-31/womens-cricket-in-australia-started-in-southern-tasmania/12282814

17, 18, 19. Ladies' Cricket Match. (1894, May 8). *The Mercury (Hobart, Tas. : 1860 - 1954)*, p. 2. Retrieved August 24, 2021, from http://nla.gov.au/nla.news-article13270268

20 LADIES' CRICKET MATCH. (1895, January 2). *The Mercury (Hobart, Tas. : 1860 - 1954)*, p. 3. Retrieved August 26, 2021, from http://nla.gov.au/nla.news-article9309649

21 Amusements Theatre Royal. (1906, October 23). *The Mercury (Hobart, Tas. : 1860 - 1954)*, p. 8. Retrieved August 27, 2021, from http://nla.gov.au/nla.news-article12818679

22 Music And Drama. (1906, October 2). *The Mercury (Hobart, Tas. : 1860 - 1954)*, p. 7. Retrieved August 27, 2021, from http://nla.gov.au/nla.news-article12829570

23 Case, Roy, *The Pebble in My Shoe: An Anthology of Women's Cricket*. Published by AuthorHouseUK, 5 November, 2018.

24, 25. Woodbridge. (1897, August 27). *The Mercury (Hobart, Tas. : 1860 - 1954)*, p. 3. Retrieved August 24, 2021, from http://nla.gov.au/nla.news-article9403855

Images:

- Baily, H.H. (photographer) Lily Poulett-Harris, c1890s, *Wikipedia*. Retrieved 24 August 2021 from URL: https://commons.wikimedia.org/w/index.php?curid=32648716

- Lily Poulett-Harris (left) and her twin sister, circa early 1880s. Tasmanian archives, *Wikipedia*. Retrieved 24 Aug 2021 from URL: https://commons.wikimedia.org/w/index.php?curid=32869647

- Richard Poulett-Harris, Allport Library and Museum of Fine Arts, *Tasmanian Archive and Heritage Office*. Retrieved 25 Aug 2021 from: https://stors.tas.gov.au/ILS/SD_ILS-612468

- Henry Vere Poulett-Harris. *Wikimedia Commons*. Retrieved 24 Aug 2021 from: https://commons.wikimedia.org/w/index.php?title=File:Henry_Vere_Poulett-Harris.jpg&oldid=550445233.

- Miss Mary Milward, (1905, September 28). *Punch* (Melbourne, Vic. : 1900 - 1918; 1925), p. 32. Retrieved August 27, 2021, from http://nla.gov.au/nla.news-article175413061

- The North Bruny women's cricket team of 1894. Reproduced with the kind permission of the Channel Museum – https://channelmuseum.org/

- Cricket. (1894, January 9). *The Mercury* (Hobart, Tas. : 1860 - 1954), p. 3. Retrieved September 23, 2021, from http://nla.gov.au/nla.news-article13276183

The caricaturist
Thomas Midwood

Interred: **Thomas Claude Wade Midwood,**
22 September 1854 – 11 September 1912
(aged 57).

Cemetery: Saint Luke's Anglican Cemetery, 6 Wellington
Street, Richmond, TAS, 7025.

Above: A young Thomas Midwood.
Reprinted with the kind permission of Libraries Tasmania.

Thomas Midwood had a sensible job. Like many of his era, no doubt he was encouraged to knuckle down, get a job, and Thomas had secured work as a clerk at the Hobart Post Office. Born in Hobart, Tom was a child of the Establishment – he descended from conservative parents and grandparents, born to serve and given to duty.

But there was a rebellious and creative side to the public servant. With an eye for the quirky and a dab hand with a pen, Thomas Midwood had a gift, and in the years from 1870 to the 1890s, perhaps the rebel came out in Tom when he abandoned his sensible job and went to sea.[1] He worked as an able seaman and lived to tell the tale after being wrecked on the Queensland coast.[2] Tom was an accomplished musician on the piano and several stringed instruments – mastering the banjo and mandolin,[3] and he toured with a musical company in the United States.[4] During this time, he married his beloved Beatrice Hewitt in 1883, and brought into the world two sons and two daughters.[5]

But it would be his gift for caricature that would immortalise Thomas Midwood. On his return from his overseas adventures, he put his drawing skills to good use in a paid occupation – working as a draughtsman in the Public Works Department. Here he stayed for over two decades.[6] On the side, he captured some of Tasmania's most interesting people and characters with his pen.

Tasmania's first cartoonist

Not one for idleness, Tom produced caricatures prolifically, predominantly male subjects, along with a unique set carved in Huon pine. He contributed to the periodical, the *Critic* (published between 1907 and 1924) which was described as "not overly political, but it did have a strong populist strain, telling much of the history of Hobart's half-world"[7] and it's here that Tom's work found a home. The Southern Tasmanian Photographic Society's President, Nat Oldham, in 1928 described Tom as "Hobart's one and only cartoonist of that period, and he pictured every character in the city that was worth handing on to posterity, from poor old 'Nobby' Dickson, who sold a cigar and a light, to the Judges on the Supreme Court Bench. Clergymen, barristers, musicians, public servants, businessmen, publicans, as well as sinners, all came under the spell of his magic pencil and brush."[8]

Tom drew both for pleasure and for commercial businesses such as "*The Illustrated Directory of Hobart: containing the names of the principal business houses of Hobart*" (1893, *Libraries Tasmania*). To this day, the commercial art drawings created by Tom preserve many of the local businesses of the era, now long gone.

Tom's characters

Town folk and colleagues from the public service were not immune to Tom's creative interpretation.

Henry Higgins, the butcher who provided his wares to the good people of Hobart was believed to have one of the first shops in Hobart to use electric power. Of note too were Higgins' three sons – Arthur, Ernest and Tasman – who founded Higgins Bros Cinematographers in 1913 and became a significant part of the early Australian film industry.[9]

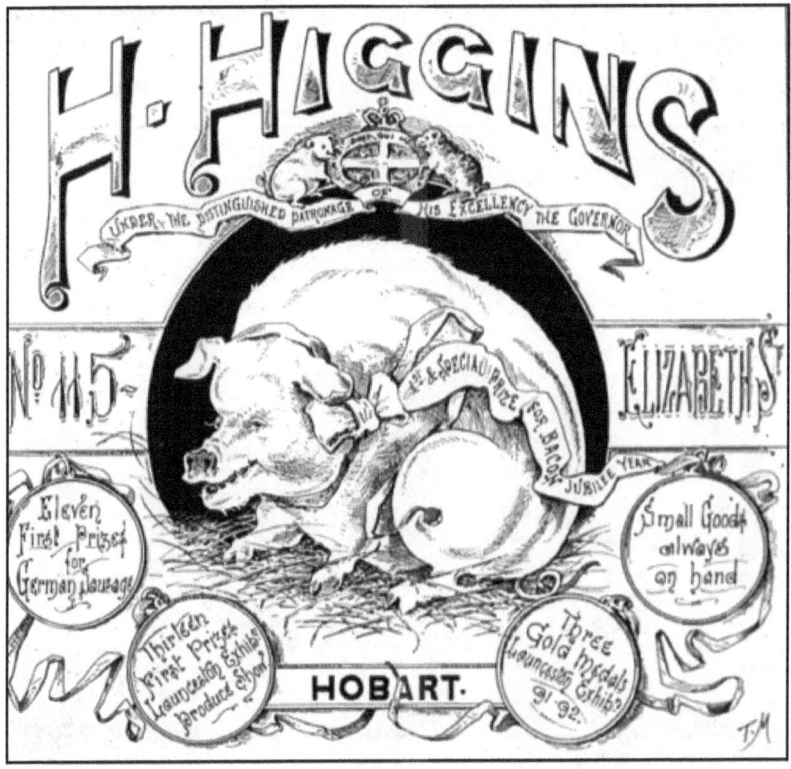

Above: The caricature of Henry Higgins might be missing these days, but the advertisement created by Tom remains. Source: Libraries Tasmania.

In 1900, Higgins' butcher shop would come in handy – Ernest set up a projector on the shop's balcony with a screen on a building across the street.[10] Ernest, a bioscope operator at a Hobart theatre, shot more than fifteen films, including the Tommy Burns versus Jack Johnson fight which became a 1908 documentary film. Some footage of the 14th round of the fight exists today.[11] Second son, Arthur, was also a prolific cinematographer and worked on *The Sentimental Bloke* (1919), *On Our Selection* (1920), and had a shot at directing too. Tasman, the youngest, worked on *Jewelled Nights* (1925) and *In the Wake of the Bounty* (1933), which starred Errol Flynn.[12] But Errol Flynn aside, let's not forget, it was Higgins senior, the butcher, who was captured in ink by Tom.

The Higgins butchery. A photo by the Anson Bros to serve as a centrepiece of an advertisement for Henry Higgins, family butcher.
Source: W.L. Crowther Library, Tasmanian Archive and Heritage Office.

Captain Harold – did not escape Tom's pen. A retired Indian Army Officer and somewhat of an eccentric with a mania for water tanks, sadly, Captain Harold ended his life by drowning himself in one.

Above: Captain Harold [caricature]. Source: University of Tasmania Library.

Yorkie – was a colleague of Tom's in the public service who hailed from Yorkshire and loved to row. Tom captured him at his rowing practice. When 'Yorkie' left, he took the illustration with him to his next destination, Kalgoorlie. The drawing was said to be "one of the great solaces of his life when the heat and dust were almost unbearable, to gaze at this picture of himself, and think of his friends on the Derwent, in cool, pleasant Tasmania."[13]

Bruce Wood – a member of the Hobart Amateur Operatic Society, was a subject of Tom's pen. Bruce was keen for the opportunity to sing, with performances from Gilbert and Sullivan, to lending his voice to a fundraising concert for the girl guides.[14]

Tom Jennings – might Mr Jennings have been a paid model... paid in suits, that is? Tom captured Mr Jennings modelling for the "awkward figure" in

the catalogue advertisement for John R. Johnston & Co., Hobart, tailors and mercers. The late Mr Jennings weighed 206 kilograms (32.5 stone) and cut a resplendent figure in a suit "fitted perfectly" and accessorised by a fob watch.

Above: Bruce Wood [caricature]. Source: University of Tasmania Library. Right: Modelling for the 'awkward figure', Tom Jennings. Source: Libraries Tasmania.

THE LATE TOM JENNINGS. Weight, 32½ stone.

FIRST CLASS MATERIAL AND TRIMMINGS.
THE BEST WORKMANSHIP.
THE MOST AWKWARD FIGURE FITTED PERFECTLY.
VERY MODERATE CHARGES.

Above: A mature Thomas Midwood with his banjo.
Reprinted with the kind permission of Libraries Tasmania.

Last days

During his life, Tom and his work touched many people. After an illness of three months, he died in 1912, aged 57, at his residence on the corner of Duke and High Streets, Sandy Bay.[15] Beatrice survived her husband, dying thirty years later on 22 January 1942. All four of the children – Edwin, Estelle, Reginald and Gladys – survived Tom, but not Beatrice, who buried her two youngest after her husband.[16]

The tributes that poured in for Tom, his talent, and his character spoke volumes about the unassuming artist.

The Daily Post noted he "had a happy knack of depicting idiosyncrasies which appealed very strongly to those who knew the man whom he portrayed."[17] The 1928 edition of *The Mercury* concurred: "He had a merry wit, and saw the humour of things at once, but he was seldom harsh or caustic. He could, however, if occasion required it, produce the most ridiculous and fantastic of caricatures."[18]

A friend paid his respects in *The Mercury* saying in some respects Tom "was as old as a thousand years, in others he was one of the most generous-hearted souls that ever drew the breath of life."[19]

Of his skills, it was said an English artist looking at some of Tom's work proclaimed: "He is simply an artistic genius and a marvel… and quite good enough for *London Punch*."[20]

But it was Tom who said: "I like to run with the crowd… once I tail out from this I will be noticed, and then trouble comes in."[21] Unassuming was another one of his fine traits.

Above: Tom's range of characters. Source: Allport Library and Museum of Fine Arts, Tasmanian Archive and Heritage Office.

References:

1 Biography, Thomas Midwood 1854-1912, *University of Tasmania*, August 2009. Retrieved 18 October 2021 from URL: https://www.utas.edu.au/library/exhibitions/midwood/biography.html

2 MEN AND WOMEN. (1912, September 13). *Daily Post (Hobart, Tas.: 1908 - 1918)*, p. 6. Retrieved October 18, 2021, from http://nla.gov.au/nla.news-article189096508

3 PHOTOGRAPHIC SOCIETY (1928, May 3). *The Mercury* (Hobart, Tas.: 1860 - 1954), p. 10. Retrieved October 18, 2021, from http://nla.gov.au/nla.news-article29790442
MLA citation

4 Biography, Thomas Midwood 1854-1912, *University of Tasmania*, Op.cit.

5 & 6 Ibid.

7 Thomas Midwood - Professor Emeritus Michael Roe (notes from his speech launching the Thomas Midwood exhibition at the Morris Miller Library). University of Tasmania, 26 May 2008. Retrieved 18 October 2021 from URL: https://www.utas.edu.au/library/exhibitions/midwood/biography.html

8 PHOTOGRAPHIC SOCIETY (1928, May 3). Op.cit.

9 Thomas Midwood - Professor Emeritus Michael Roe. Op.cit.

10 Wikipedia contributors. (2020, July 15). Arthur Higgins. In *Wikipedia*, The Free Encyclopedia. Retrieved 04:09, October 19, 2021, from https://en.wikipedia.org/w/index.php?title=Arthur_Higgins&oldid=967780573

11 Wikipedia contributors. (2021, May 15). The Burns-Johnson Fight. In *Wikipedia*, The Free Encyclopedia. Retrieved 03:57, October 19, 2021, from https://en.wikipedia.org/w/index.php?title=The_Burns-Johnson_Fight&oldid=1023260781

12 Jones, Callum, J., Cinema & Television, Tasmania's Film History, 1 June, 2021. The Tasmanian Landscape in Films, *tasmaniantimes.com* Retrieved 19 October 2021 from URL: https://tasmaniantimes.com/2021/06/tasmanias-film-history/

13 PHOTOGRAPHIC SOCIETY (1928, May 3). Op.cit.

14 AMUSEMENTS. (1910, December 7). *The Mercury (Hobart, Tas.: 1860 - 1954)*, p. 3. Retrieved October 18, 2021, from http://nla.gov.au/nla.news-article10084538

15 MEN AND WOMEN. (1912, September 13). *Daily Post (Hobart, Tas.: 1908 - 1918)*, p. 6. Retrieved October 18, 2021, from http://nla.gov.au/nla.news-article189096508

16 Lydiate family tree, *Ancestry*. Retrieved 18 October 2021 from URL: https://www.ancestry.com/family-tree/person/tree/12949235/person/12039568387/facts

17 MEN AND WOMEN. (1912, September 13). Op.cit.

18 PHOTOGRAPHIC SOCIETY (1928, May 3). Op.cit.

19 Ibid.

20 NOTES BY THE WAY. (1912, September 20). *Critic (Hobart, Tas.: 1907 - 1924)*, p. 2. Retrieved October 18, 2021, from http://nla.gov.au/nla.news-article162299855

21 Ibid.

Images:

- Tom Midwood In: Album of Thomas Midwood. Comprises illustrations, family photographs, general photographs including ship-board scenes, poems. *Libraries Tasmania*, Tasmania Archives NS6759/1/1. Retrieved 28 October 2021 from URL: https://stors.tas.gov.au/NS6759-1-1$init=NS6759-1-1_009

- Midwood, Thomas Claude Wade, [illustrator], The illustrated directory of Hobart containing the names &c. [i.e. etc.] of the principal business houses in the city / designed and drawn by T. Midwood. Mercury, [1893?]. *Libraries Tasmania*. Retrieved 19 October 2021 from URL: https://stors.tas.gov.au/ILS/SD_ILS-684309

- H. Higgins, No. 115 Elizabeth St., Hobart [drawn by T. Midwood], *Libraries Tasmania*, Archive and Heritage Office. Retrieved 19 October 2021 from URL: https://stors.tas.gov.au/TASIMAGES $init=AUTAS001126250737W800

- [Hobart]: Anson, [1888?], Grafton House photographed by the Anson Bros. W.L. Crowther Library, Tasmanian Archive and Heritage Office. Retrieved 19 October 2021 from URL: https://stors.tas.gov.au/ILS/SD_ILS-197134

- Midwood, Thomas Claude Wade, Captain Harold - retired Indian Army Officer, eccentric, lived in Bellerive, had a mania for water tanks and ended his life by drowning himself in one [caricature] 1854-1912. *University of Tasmania Library*, UTAS SPARC M7-8. Retrieved 18 October 2021 from URL: https://sparc.utas.edu.au/index.php/captain-harold

- Midwood, Thomas Claude Wade, Bruce Hood - very fond of singing songs at parties, his favourite being 'Egypt' - Could not stop him once he began [caricature] 1854-1912. *University of Tasmania Library*, UTAS SPARC M7-19. Retrieved 18 October 2021 from URL: https://sparc.utas.edu.au/index.php/bruce-hood

- Midwood, Thomas Claude Wade, [illustrator], 1854-1912, John R. Johnston & Co., 37 Murray St., Hobart, tailors & mercers &c [i.e. etc.] The Mercury [1893?]. *Libraries Tasmania, Tasmanian Archive and Heritage Office*. Retrieved 19 October 2021 from URL: https://stors.tas.gov.au/ILS/SD_ILS-685305

- Midwood, Thomas Claude Wade [Photograph], Banjo players on board ship - shows Tom Midwood [R] Midwood In: Album of Thomas Midwood. Comprises illustrations, family photographs, general photographs including ship-board scenes, poems. *Libraries Tasmania*, Tasmania Archives NS6759/1/1. Retrieved 28 October 2021 from URL: https://eprints.utas.edu.au/6925/

- Midwood, Thomas Claude Wade [illustrator], Well known citizens of southern Tasmania / T. Midwood. *Allport Library and Museum of Fine Arts, Tasmanian Archive and Heritage Office*. Retrieved 19 October 2021 from URL: https://stors.tas.gov.au/ILS/SD_ILS-99267

Above: Miss Marjorie Williams' grave at Campania Cemetery. Photo supplied and reproduced with the kind permission of Linda McKenzie.

The crash of the DC-3
The passenger in seat 6

Interred: **Marjorie May Williams** (nee Howlett), 13 February 1917 – 10 March 1946 (aged 29).

Cemetery: Campania Cemetery, Lee Street, Campania, TAS 7026.[1]

Interred:

Elsie May Buckman, 1892 – 10 March 1946 (aged 54);

Gustavus Walton Knight, 1880 – 10 March 1946 (aged 66);

Joan Sommers Ogilvie, 1927 – 10 March 1946 (aged 19);

Cyril P. Schaedel, 16 July 1889 – 10 March 1946 (aged 56);

Uta Ida Smith, 1918 – 10 March 1946 (aged 28);

Thomas W. Spence, 14 January 1916 – 10 March 1946 (aged 30);

Edward Joseph Tudor, 1888 – 10 March 1946 (aged 58).

Cemetery: Cornelian Bay Cemetery and Crematorium, Queens Walk, New Town, TAS 7008.

Interred: **Leila Joynson**, 1914 est.– 10 March 1946 (aged 32).

Cemetery: Saltwater River Cemetery, 128 Saltwater River Road, Premaydena, TAS 7185.

Marjorie Williams, 29, hadn't seen her husband, Private Ron Williams, for four years. He had been on war service[2] and arrived in Melbourne on Saturday 9 March 1946 from Darwin. Marjorie was flying there to meet him for a long-awaited reunion. Her ticket was for seat six on the flight departing from Cambridge, Hobart for Melbourne on Sunday 10 March 1946. But Marjorie wasn't on the bus to the airport, and as Mr Alfred Carbines was desperate to get to Melbourne, he got permission to take her seat on the bus. If she should not arrive at the airport in time, he would be on hand to take seat six.

When the bus arrived, Mr Carbines was sorely disappointed – of course Marjorie was at the airport eager to see her husband – she had driven there by private car. Resigned to the wait, he booked a flight for Monday. Mr Carbines did not know then that it was his lucky day. Marjorie caught the plane; her husband Ron waited all night at the Essendon aerodrome to meet her. Marjorie never arrived.[3]

Edward Tudor, 58, was keen to get on the flight taking him to his son, Graham's wedding in Melbourne. He was no doubt proud of his 'boys' – Graham was a student at Melbourne University and had played football for Carlton. Now he was to be wed. His other son, David, was a Tasmanian Rhodes Scholar in 1940.[4]

Correll Allison, 37, and Leila Joynson, 32, were returning from holidaying at Premaydena in the southeast of Tasmania. Also on a holiday visit were Thomas and Patricia Ryan who had been staying at Heathorn's Hotel, Hobart, and Cyril Schaedel, 56, who once lived in Hobart but had moved to Melbourne. He was back in his old territory catching up with family, friends and colleagues.[5]

On Sunday 10 March 1946, their lives intersected for a short while as they boarded a DC-3 aircraft (Douglas C-47-DL) with 18 other passengers and crew on board.

Plane down

At 8.45pm the DC-3 took to the air, on its way from Cambridge, Tasmania, to Essendon, Melbourne, with 25 people on board. Poor weather had delayed it earlier in Melbourne and now, running four hours late, the flight was given the all-clear to depart from Tasmania.[6] The passengers were finally on their way, but only ten minutes after take-off the plane took a death dive into the sea just off Seven Mile Beach, in Frederick Henry Bay. The Air Traffic Controller received no distress call.[7]

Eyewitnesses claimed that when the plane approached a bridge near the aerodrome, it was still flying at tree-top level and it was not going to making the clearance height.[8]

"The plane was flying very low – less than 100 ft. up. It seemed that she was losing height fast and a few seconds later I heard a loud crash,"[9] Mr J. H. Wilson, a young returned soldier and resident of Seven Mile Beach, said. "There was a crash as it dived into the sea about 200 yards from the shore in shallow water."[10]

Mr Reynolds, also of Seven Mile Beach, heard the plane fly over his house: "The engine seemed to be running properly", he said. But a few seconds later, Mr Reynolds heard the engine stop and within seconds, the sound of the plane hitting the sea. A "glow from the beach of both exhaust stacks" told him the engines were still running.[11] Another resident, Mr Vernon, agreed "both engines were still running as the plane crashed."[12]

Captain Thomas Spence   Third Officer Austin Gibson   Miss Correll Allison

Mr Cyril Schaedel   Miss Pauline Trimmer (air hostess)   Mr E. Tudor

Miss Uta Smith   Mr James O'Donnell   Mrs Valerie Ringrose

Above: Some of the victims aboard the DC-3 plane that crashed at Seven Mile Beach. Sources: please refer to references at the end of the story.

Family and friends waiting in Melbourne to collect their loved ones were told it was overdue and were sent home. An official statement was issued after midnight.[13] Newspapers reported there was "little hope that any persons survived as it is believed the plane went to the bottom in a few seconds."[14]

Doctors, a mine-sweeper, and small boats with police and trained water rescuers onboard tried to reach the spot, but the ferocious sea forced them back to shore.[15] All night in the freezing cold, rescuers worked and stood vigil.

Bodies washed up

The next morning, Monday 11 March, seven bodies of victims washed up on Seven Mile Beach, approximately 180 metres (short of 200 yards)[16] from where the plane went

Above: What remained. The DC-3 plane on Seven Mile Beach: Source: Australian Film and Sound Archive, Tasmania, 1946.

Above: The Argus newspaper front page:.
Source: National Library of Australia, 12 March 1946.

down into the sea. The captain was able to be identified, but other passengers were not initially – reports claimed they were terribly injured from the impact as "the plane crashed at great speed headfirst into the sea."[17]

The plane remained where it fell, the weather too rough for its recovery and meanwhile, the police and citizens of the region manned the area. Mr B. Hayes, an ambulance driver, was praised for staying on duty continuously for over 24 hours without taking meals, a compassionate gesture for families waiting and hoping for their loved ones to be recovered.[18]

Around the beach, washed ashore, were suitcases and personal belongings of the ill-fated passengers – wallets, briefcases, even tennis racquets,[19] memories from the recent holiday. The air hostess's chair was also washed ashore.[20]

Two days later, two more bodies described as "shockingly mutilated"[21] were washed up and identified as retired school teacher, Mr Gustavus Knight, and another passenger, Mr Brian Davis who was in Hobart to see his father.[22]

The head of a woman believed to be Mrs Elizabeth Ringrose, of Melbourne, was found about 3.2 kilometres (2 miles) from the main wreckage.[23] Mrs Ringrose was married and the mother of six adult sons. She had been travelling with her daughter-in-law, Valerie, who also perished, leaving behind a husband, son and daughter.[24]

Nine days later, the body of Miss Leila Joynson washed ashore on Seven Mile Beach.[25] She was engaged to be married to Mr E. Noye,[26] but was not brought back to Victoria, instead buried at the Saltwater River Cemetery, Premaydena, Tasman Peninsula, and survived by her sister, Hazel.[27] That her travelling friend, Miss Correll Allison's body was recovered, is assumed as she was buried in Brighton Cemetery, Victoria. However, her name appeared in the list of unidentified victims after the accident.[28] Both Leila and Correll's parents pre-deceased them.[29]

Except for one body that was found over three kilometres away (in a two miles radius of the crash site), twenty bodies were found within 1.6 kilometres or a one-mile radius.[30] Four bodies were never recovered. At the inquest the four remaining unidentified were: David Collum (crew member), Robert Black – seat 2, Correll Allison – seat 4, and Charles Grant – seat 18.[31]

SCENE OF THE CRASH

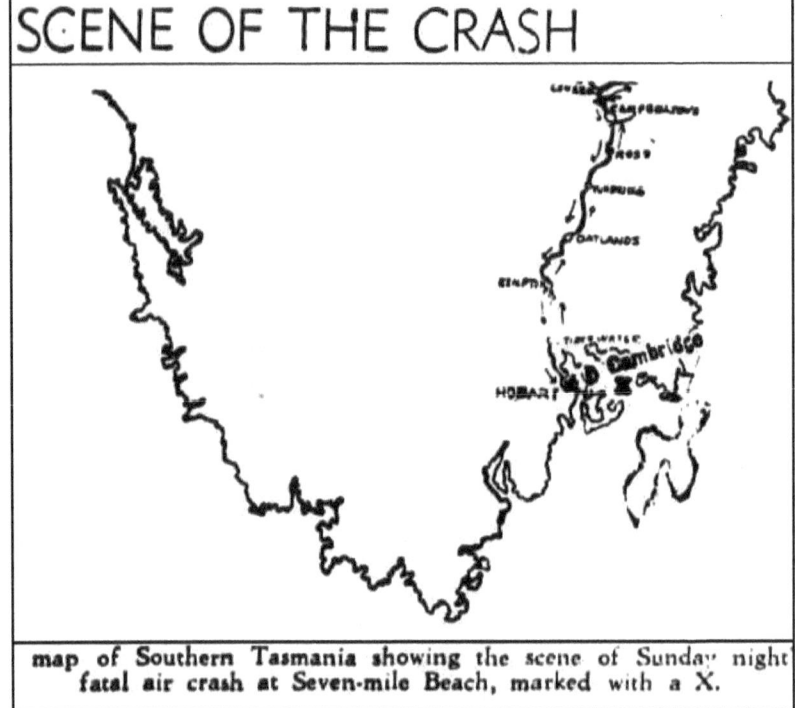

map of Southern Tasmania showing the scene of Sunday night fatal air crash at Seven-mile Beach, marked with a X.

Above source: Advocate, 11 March 1946.

The aftermath

Considered one of Australia's worst civil aviation accidents in the 20th century,[32] Australian National Airways (ANA) officials were at pains to understand why it happened, especially as the weather on take-off was favourable, and so the inquiry began.

An ornithologist spoke of finding a large gannet dead on Seven Mile Beach and believed the bird, given its mutilated condition suggesting a fast-moving object hit it, might have impacted with the captain's cabin and been the cause of the accident.[33]

But Civil Aviation Department Officers undertook elaborate tests, drew up numerous scenarios highlighting the angle of climb and descent, and studied eyewitness statements, to discover the cause. After a process of elimination, they believed there was an error in the cockpit and that the automatic pilot was inadvertently engaged shortly after take-off while the gyroscope was caged.[34]

How could this happen? Two controls approximately the same size and distance apart were positioned at the foot of the instrument panel. One was for the cross feed to enable both engines to draw on each other's fuel source; the other turned the automatic pilot on and off. In error, the pilot under-instruction may have turned on the automatic pilot that in seven seconds took them head-on into the sea. It was recommended that the controls be re-designed so that a mix-up would never happen again.[35]

The spotlight was put on the Captain, Thomas William Spence, 30, an experienced former RAAF pilot. It was revealed he had been discharged as medically unfit almost five years earlier, in 1941, because he was a diabetic.[36] He applied for a civil licence and while the list of illnesses on the application form did not include diabetes, Thomas did not include it when asked if he had any serious illnesses.[37] Authorities believe his illness may have contributed to the crash. The cause of death of the passengers was multiple fractures and injuries.[38]

Mr Justice Simpson of the Supreme Court of the Australian Capital Territory, who conduct an inquiry into the accident, stated he was satisfied that "the accident to the A.N.A. airliner, which crashed off Seven Mile Beach, Hobart, on March 10, resulting in the death of 25 persons, was not due to any major structural failure in the machine nor with its engines."[39]

The lost and the left behind

Sadly, as with all tragedies, the loss could never be compensated, but a recent airline policy change, enacted only a week before the tragedy ensured all passengers on ANA flights were insured with the purchase of their airline ticket. The next of kin of the DC-3 tragedy victims each received a 2000 pound insurance payout.[40]

The passengers and crew on board were a diverse group. Captain Thomas Spence was highly regarded, had an impressive flying career and was considered by the company to be "one of their most promising young pilots" according to fellow Captain, Bob Jackson. Hailing from Queensland, Thomas was a single man, survived by two brothers.[41]

The co-pilot, David J. Collum, 21, from East Kew, Victoria, had about 1,400 hours of flying experience.[42] His body was never found but his wallet was washed ashore and remained in the possession of his daughter, Sandra, for the remainder of her life. She was 13 months old at the time of his death.[43]

It was the first ANA flight for third officer, Austin Gibson, 37, from South Australia, only recently discharged from the RAAF. During his service, he was a flight lieutenant and commended for his war service. For five years, he served as a flight instructor.[44] Austin Gibson was married with four children.

Air hostess, Pauline Trimmer, 20, was an only child and had started training to be a hostess only one month earlier. She had 31 hours of flying experience notched up.[45]

Miss Iris Thompson was 19 and a middle child with two sisters. She was gainfully employed at Lewisham Hospital, and before that, at His Master's Voice. Iris's mother heard of the accident from a girl working at a store nearby and thought of Iris, but did not believe it was her flight; the police informed her two hours later.[46]

Hailing from Western Australia, Mr James O'Donnell, 37, had only been in Tasmania a short while working as Assistant Conservator of Forests. He was married and a father to three.[47] Mr Brian Davis had flown to Tasmania to see his sick father. His wife thought he had missed the plane, but her landlady broke the news to her the next morning.[48]

Miss Joan Ogilvie, 19, was a trainee nurse who had missed her flight several days earlier and was rescheduled onto the ill-fated DC-3.[49] Four nurses acted as her pallbearers at her funeral two days after.[50]

Miss Uta Ida Smith, 28, was on her way to Melbourne for a holiday. She was the only daughter of Alfred and Ida, and had been active in the land army. Her body was recovered the day after the accident.[51]

Mr Kenneth Wootton, 54, was in Hobart as a delegate at the Metal Trades conference. He was keen to get home and had his flight arrangement messed up and delayed. His wife, Grace, and 17-year-old son, Jim, waited until midnight in the waiting lounge at the airport before returning home, only to receive the call later telling them of Kenneth's fate. Jim took over his father's accountancy business for two decades, and for the rest of his long life was a frequent visitor to Tasmania.[52]

Mr Gustavus Walton Knight was a retired Hobart school teacher and former headmaster of several schools including Elliott, Sorell, Lindisfarne and the Huonville School.[53] Mr Cyril Schaedel, who had moved from Hobart to Melbourne, was renowned in Victorian racing circles and was meant to fly home earlier in the week, but stayed to attend the Hobart Turf Club Cup meeting.[54]

Mr Robert Black was well-known in the Melbourne automobile industry. Mrs Elsie Buckman, 54, from Sydney was visiting her sister. Elsie was a senior packer at the Dazzle Manufacturing Co., in Leichhardt. She was remembered for her tireless work for disabled soldiers in Sydney, especially at the Callan Park Mental Hospital[55] and for the Red Cross. Elsie was buried in Tasmania.

Marjorie, 29, of seat six, and her soldier husband, Ron, were never reunited. Her funeral left her father, Fred's residence in Campania, on the Thursday after the crash, for the Campania Cemetery. Mr Alfred Carbines who coveted her seat, we believe lived a long life.

Courting superstition, ironically the plane did not have a seat numbered 13.[56]

Form 4   C O P Y   AUSTRALIAN NATIONAL AIRWAYS PTY. LTD.

VH- AET

PASSENGER WAYBILL

Date 10th March

| From | HOBART | To | ESSENDON | Via | | Depart 4.50 p.m. A.M. P.M |
| Captain | SPENCE | | F/Officer COLLUM/GIBSON | | Hostess | TRIMMER |

SEAT	TICKET No.	NAME	WEIGHT PASS.	LUG.	FROM	TO	FARE	PRIOR- ITY	LUGGAGE CHECK	REMARKS
1	11298	Mr. Tudor	206	27	H	M			19596	
2	50934	Mr. R. Black	190	} 98	H	M			97	7007
3	50935	Mrs. Black	168		H	M			98	
4	27505	Miss Allison	141	} 97	H	M			99	
5	27606	Miss Joynson	137		H	M			600	
6	28711	Mrs. R. Williams	150	35	H	M			19627	
7	40876	Mrs. V. Ringrose	187	50	H	M			28	
8	27396	Mr. C. G. Knight	169	47	H	M			29	7010
9	29474	Mrs. Ringrose	145	20	H	M			31	
10	28791	Mr. J. Wise	157	27	H	M			32122	
11	40390	Mr. B. J. Davis	142	26	H	M			7132	
12	51223	Mr. Wootton	168	24	H	M			19622	
14	29795	Mr. J. O'Donnell	178	18	H	M			33	
15	30014	Mrs. McDonald	225	48	H	M			25	32008
16	50818	Mr. T. Ryan	184	} 61	H	M			44626	
17	50813	Mrs. Ryan	138		H	M			19626	
18	50770	Mr. Grant	182	30	H	M			32126	
19	27748	Mr. Schaedel	189	75	H	M			7115	1508/7008
20	51241	Miss J. Ogilvie	149	39	H	M			7116	
21	27404	Miss H. Smith	114	28	H	M			17	
22	27746	Mrs. Buckman	134	29	H	M			18	44508
23			3,453	779						

LOAD SUMMARY

DESTINATION	Melb.							TOTALS	THROUGH WEI
PASSENGERS	3,453							3,453	
LUGGAGE	779							779	
P.M.G. MAIL	---								
SAFE HAND & DIRECT MAIL	---								
FREIGHT									
TOTAL	4,232							4,232	

Above: the fateful passenger list, 10 March 1946.
Source: National Archives of Australia.

References:

1 Funerals Of Four Victims Of Airliner Tragedy (1946, March 15). *The Mercury (Hobart, Tas.: 1860 - 1954)*, p. 13. Retrieved 1 Jan 2022, from http://nla.gov.au/nla.news-article26175558
2 Going To Husband (1946, March 12). *The Mercury (Hobart, Tas. : 1860 - 1954)*, p. 4. Retrieved January 1, 2022, from http://nla.gov.au/nla.news-article26174965
3 25 Believed Killed in Plane Crash (1946, March 11). *Goulburn Evening Post (NSW: 1940 - 1954)*, p. 3. Retrieved 8 Dec 2021, from http://nla.gov.au/nla.news-article103302737
4 Crash Victim Was Flying to Son's Wedding (1946, March 11). *The Herald (Melbourne, Vic.: 1861 - 1954)*, p. 3. Retrieved 30 Dec 2021, from http://nla.gov.au/nla.news-article245392012
5 Crash Victims' Bodies on Beach (1946, March 11). *The Herald (Melbourne, Vic.: 1861 - 1954)*, p. 1. Retrieved 8 Dec 2021, from http://nla.gov.au/nla.news-article245392074
6 & 7 -25 Lose Lives When DC3 Airliner Crashes... (1946, March 11). *Advocate (Burnie, Tas.: 1890 - 1954)*, p. 5. Retrieved 8 Dec 2021, from http://nla.gov.au/nla.news-article68966207
8 Crash Victims' Bodies on Beach (1946, March 11). *The Herald.* Op.cit.
9 Bodies Of Seven Washed Up from Airliner Wreck (11 Mar 1946). *The Telegraph (Bris, Qld.: 1872 - 1947)*, p. 1. Retrieved 1 Jan 2022, from http://nla.gov.au/nla.news-article188444031
10 Hobart Air Liner Crash (1946, March 12). *Daily Examiner (Grafton, NSW: 1915 - 1954)*, p. 1. Retrieved 31 Dec 2021, from http://nla.gov.au/nla.news-article194920227
11 List of Victims. (1946, March 12). *Cairns Post (Qld.: 1909 - 1954)*, p. 1. Retrieved December 31, 2021, from http://nla.gov.au/nla.news-article42486327
12 Bodies Of Seven Washed Up... *The Telegraph,* 11 March 1946. Op.cit.
13 25 Lose Lives When DC3 Airliner Crashes...*Advocate*, p. 5. Op.cit.
14 Bodies Of Seven Washed Up... *The Telegraph,* 11 March 1946. Op.cit.
15 & 16 Crash Victims' Bodies on Beach (1946, March 11). *The Herald.* Op.cit.
17 25 Believed Killed in Plane Crash (11 Mar 1946). *Goulburn Evening Post (NSW: 1940 - 1954)*, p. 3. Retrieved 8 Dec 2021 from http://nla.gov.au/nla.news-article103302737
18 Converted C47s Not Being Grounded... (1946, March 13). *The Mercury (Hobart, Tas.: 1860 - 1954)*, p. 4. Retrieved Dec 31, 2021, from http://nla.gov.au/nla.news-article26175200
19 Crash Victims' Bodies on Beach (1946, March 11). *The Herald.* Op.cit.
20 25 Believed Killed in... 11 March 1946. *Goulburn Evening Post.* Op.cit.
21, 22, 23 Plane Tragedy (1946, March 13). *Kalgoorlie Miner (WA: 1895 - 1954)*, p. 4. Retrieved December 8, 2021, from http://nla.gov.au/nla.news-article95580664
24 Going To Husband (1946, March 12). *The Mercury.* Op.cit.
25 Body Recovered (1946, March 20). *Daily Examiner (Grafton, NSW: 1915 - 1954)*, p. 1. Retrieved 31 Dec, 2021, from http://nla.gov.au/nla.news-article194929116
26 Tombstone and Memorial inscriptions of Tasmania, 2nd ed. 1999. *Genealogical Society of Tasmania Inc.,* Index 2694. Retrieved 1 Jan 2022 from Ancestry.com.au
27 Family Notices (1946, March 22). *The Mercury (Hobart, Tas.: 1860 - 1954)*, p. 10. Retrieved January 1, 2022, from http://nla.gov.au/nla.news-article26176861
28 Inquest On Air Crash Victims (1946, July 23). *Advocate (Burnie, Tas. : 1890 - 1954)*, p. 2. Retrieved January 1, 2022, from http://nla.gov.au/nla.news-article69050329
29 *Ancestry.* Retrieved 1 January 2022 from *Ancesty.com.au*
30 List of Victims. (1946, March 12). *Cairns Post.* Op.cit.
31 Inquest On Air Crash Victims (1946, July 23). *Advocate.* Op.cit.
32 Piggott, Michael, Disasters. Commonwealth Government Records, Tasmania. *National Archives of Australia,* 2013. Retrieved 30 Dec 2021 from URL: https://www.naa.gov.au/sites/default/files/2020-06/research-guide-commonwealth-government-records-about-tas.pdf
33 Bird May Have Caused Plane Crash (1946, May 2). *Daily Examiner (Grafton, NSW: 1915 - 1954)*, p. 3. Retrieved 8 Dec 2021, from http://nla.gov.au/nla.news-article194917093
34 1946 Australian National Airways DC-3 crash explained. *Everything Explained Today.* Retrieved 30 Dec 2021 from URL: https://everything.explained.today/1946_Australian_National_Airways_DC-3_crash/
35 Elaborate Tests Told Story of Air Tragedy (1946, June 17). *The Sun (NSW: 1910 - 1954)*, p. 2. Retrieved Dec 30, 2021, from http://nla.gov.au/nla.news-article229455287
36 & 37 Pilot Of Crashed Plane Was a Diabetic (1946, May 8). *Weekly Times (Melb, Vic.: 1869 - 1954)*, p. 2. Retrieved 30 Dec 2021, from http://nla.gov.au/nla.news-article224420558
38 Jones, Callum, J., Tas That Was... *TasmanianTimes.com,* 7 April 2021 Retrieved 30 Dec 2021 from URL: https://tasmaniantimes.com/2021/04/tas-that-was-the-1946-australian-national-airways-dc-3-crash/

39 Finding In Hobart Air Crash (1946, June 12). *The Canberra Times (ACT: 1926 - 1995)*, p. 4. Retrieved Dec 30, 2021, from http://nla.gov.au/nla.news-article2686329

40 Crash Victims' Bodies on Beach (1946, March 11). *The Herald.* Op.cit.

41 List Of Victims. (1946, March 12). *Cairns Post.* Op.cit.

42 Job, Macarthur (1992). Air Crash Vol. 2, Chapter 3. *Aerospace Publications Pty. Ltd.* Fyshwick, Australia. *Wikipedia* (2021, April 20). Retrieved Dec 30, 2021, from https://en.wikipedia.org/w/index.php?title=1946_Australian_National_Airways_DC-3_crash&oldid=1018818143

43 Beniuk, David, just one trace of dad..., *The Mercury* - Sunday Tasmania, 13 March, 2016. Retrieved from: https://www.themercury.com.au/news/tasmania/just-one-trace-of-dad-70-years-after-plane-crash-tragedy-at-seven-mile-beach/news-story/b189c73e9c4cdbcdac1261ae31a17df7

44 2 Sth. Australians In Hobart Crash (1946, March 11). *News (Adelaide, SA: 1923 - 1954)*, p. 1. Retrieved 8 Dec 2021, from http://nla.gov.au/nla.news-article128349798

45 2 Sth. Australians In Hobart Crash (1946, March 11). *News (Adelaide, SA: 1923 - 1954)*, p. 1. Retrieved 8 Dec, 2021, from http://nla.gov.au/nla.news-article128349798

46 Local Victim of Plane Tragedy. (1946, Feb 6). *The Cumberland Argus and Fruitgrowers Advocate (Parramatta, NSW: 1888-1950)*, p3. Retrieved 8 Dec 2021 from http://nla.gov.au/nla.news-article105742982

47 WA Forestry Man Among Crash Victims (1946, March 11). *The Daily News (Perth, WA: 1882 - 1955)*, p. 1. Retrieved 8 Dec, 2021, from http://nla.gov.au/nla.news-article78246401

48 & 49 Personal Stories of Plane Tragedy (1946, March 13). *Weekly Times (Melbourne, Vic.: 1869 - 1954)*, p. 5. Retrieved 8 Dec 2021 from http://nla.gov.au/nla.news-article224424826

50 Converted C47s Not Being Grounded... (13 Mar 1946. *The Mercury.* Op.cit.

51 Family Notices (1946, March 12). *The Mercury* (Hobart, Tas. : 1860 - 1954), p. 12. Retrieved 4 Jan 2022, from http://nla.gov.au/nla.news-article26174896

52 Kenneth's feeling still haunts..., *Mercury*, Sunday Tas, 6 March 2016. Retrieved 30 Dec 2021.

53 & 54 Postponement Of Flight Led to... (1946, Mar 12). *The Mercury (Hobart, Tas.: 1860 - 1954)*, p. 4. Retrieved 31 Dec 2021 from http://nla.gov.au/nla.news-article26174982

55 Air Victims' Bodies Identified (1946, Mar 12). *The Daily Telegraph (Syd, NSW: 1931 - 1954)*, p. 5. Retrieved 1 Jan 2022 from http://nla.gov.au/nla.news-article248493280

56 Pilot's Condition Was Normal (1946, July 23). *The Mercury (Hobart, Tas.: 1860 - 1954)*, p. 11. Retrieved 31 Dec 2021, from http://nla.gov.au/nla.news-article26188867

Images:

-Headstone of Miss Marjorie Williams kindly photographed and supplied by Linda McKenzie.

-Images of some victims from: Postponement of Flight Led to Former Hobart Man's Death (1946, March 12). *The Mercury (Hobart, Tas.: 1860 - 1954)*, p. 4. Retrieved December 31, 2021, from http://nla.gov.au/nla.news-article26174982

-Miss Correll Grant Allison 1909–1946, from Allison family tree, *Ancestry.* Retrieved 1 Jan 2022 from https://www.ancestry.com.au/family-tree/person/tree/87830580/person/30569049805/story

-Third officer AC Gibson from: 2 Sth. Australians In Hobart Crash (1946, March 11). *News* (Adel, SA: 1923 - 1954), p. 1. Retrieved Dec 8, 2021 from http://nla.gov.au/nla.news-article128349798

-Image of Miss Pauline Trimmer: Fatal Dive of Hobart Plane (1946, March 14). *Chronicle* (Adelaide, SA : 1895 - 1954), p24. Retrieved Jan 4, 2022, from http://nla.gov.au/nla.news-article93157295

-Image of Miss Uta Smith: Converted C47s Not Being Grounded Because Of Air Crash (1946, Mar 13). *The Mercury (Hobart, Tas.: 1860-1954)*, p4. Retrieved Dec 31, 2021 from http://nla.gov.au/nla.news-article26175200

-Image of Mr Cyril Schaedel reproduced with kind permission from Dan Jones, *Find A Grave.* – https://www.findagrave.com/memorial/212999958/cyril-p-schaedel

-ANA Crash at Seven Mile Beach, Tas, 1946. Source: Australian Film and Sound Archive, 9 Oct 2008. Retrieved 30 Dec 2021 from: https://en.wikipedia.org/wiki/File:SevenMileBeach1946_2.png

-Argus newspaper front page: (1946, March 12). *The Argus (Melbourne, Vic.: 1848 - 1957)*, p. 1. Retrieved December 30, 2021, from http://nla.gov.au/nla.news-page1667767

-Scene of crash: 25 Lose Lives When DC-3 Airliner Crashes... (1946, March 11). *Advocate (Burnie, Tas.: 1890 - 1954)*, p. 5. Retrieved Dec 30, 2021 from http://nla.gov.au/nla.news-article68966207

-Image of Captain Thomas Spence: (1946, March 11). *The Telegraph (Brisbane, Qld.: 1872 - 1947)*, p. 1 (City Final). Retrieved Jan 1, 2022 from http://nla.gov.au/nla.news-page19963167

- Passenger list: Report on loss of Douglas C47-DCA 1900 aircraft VH-AET, Seven Mile Beach, near Cambridge, Tas, 10 March 1946. NAA: A8325, 10/3/1946 PART 1, scanned p21. Retrieved from Piggott, Michael, Disasters. Commonwealth Govt Records, Tasmania. National Archives of Aust, 2013.

Above: Eveline rests in an unmarked grave in the Roman Catholic section EE, site number 59, of the Cornelian Bay Cemetery. We have marked the grave with a small rose and cross.

The last man hanged
Frederick Thompson

Interred: **Eveline* Mary Maughan**, 1937 – 8 July 1945 (aged 7).

Location: Roman Catholic, section EE, site number 59 (unmarked grave).

Interred: **Frederick Henry Thompson**, 1914 – 14 February 1946 (aged 32).

Location: Roman Catholic, site number 26, sub location Pauper, (unmarked grave).

Cemetery: Cornelian Bay Cemetery and Crematorium, Queens Walk, New Town, TAS 7008.

*In many references Eveline's name is spelt Evelyn. We have gone with the version her family printed in the death notice of 9 October 1945.

There are some milestones in life where being the first or last might be a badge of honour; being hanged isn't one of them. In Van Diemen's Land, the badge of dishonour for the first man hanged went to Alexander Cullen on 18 August 1857 who, in a drunken stupor, murdered the woman he was living with, Elizabeth Ross, and then attempted to drown himself. Alexander Cullen admitted his crime and was said to be "exceedingly penitent"[1] but that did not stop his appointment with the noose.

The dishonour of being the first woman hanged in Tasmania went to a Scotswoman, Mary McLauchlan, who was hanged early at the start of the week, 8.30am on Monday 19 April 1830. Mary's story was sad but not uncommon. She was convicted of stealing and dispatched to Australia at age 24 with her two young daughters. Upon arrival, Mary was placed with another Scot, Charles Ross Nairne, a settler living in the Coal River Valley, north-east of Hobart Town. In a short time, Mary was pregnant, and Charles Nairne got rid of her as soon as he became aware.[2]

Mary was sent to Hobart's Female Factory, where, in an outhouse she gave birth to a son who did not live. With her work duties and poor diet, the baby may have been stillborn, but Mary was accused of infanticide and sentenced to death. She was hanged at the Hobart Town Gaol and her body dissected. A plaque remains on the footpath reading: "Mary McLauchlan was found guilty of infanticide and sentenced to death. She was the first woman to be executed in Van Diemen's Land." Had the same happened to her in Britain, it is likely the judge would have given her the benefit of the doubt, as history shows was often the case.[3]

It was 89 years after the first man was hanged in Tasmania and 24 years since the last man went to the gallows,[4] when Frederick Thompson was preparing to meet his maker. Thompson met his end at just after 6am, 14 February 1946, inside Hobart Penitentiary.[5] His hanging had been moved forward two hours from 8am as the administrators and wardens tried to avoid protests from members of the public who were anti-capital punishment. To his last breath, Thompson protested his innocence.

A child is missing

Frederick Thompson's crime seven months earlier was unthinkable – the murder of seven-year-old Eveline Mary Maughan, the daughter of Private Bernard and Mrs Nancy Maughan. Young Eveline attended St Joseph's Convent School and was walking to church at St Joseph's on Sunday at 8.30am on 8 July 1945. As she had several younger siblings, it was not uncommon for her to walk to church alone where she would meet her school friends outside the church before mass started.

The walk was not a great distance from Eveline's home at 100 Goulburn Street, West Hobart. To St Joseph's Church on the corner of Harrington and Macquarie Streets was a nine-minute walk of about 750 metres or just short of half a mile. That morning, her brown hair was neat, her complexion fresh, and she wore "a pink woollen dress, brown overcoat, with fawn collar and pockets, cream straw hat, brown shoes, and lemon socks."[6] But Eveline did not arrive nor did she return home. A few hours after she was due home, Eveline's mother contacted the police. No one could recall seeing the young girl at church.[7]

The community's willingness to help saw dozens of reports that took considerable time to work through and provided little assistance locating Eveline. Civilians joined in the search including women, and Mr Biggins, the headmaster of Hobart High School, organised 200 of his male students to participate.[8] Detective Inspector Fleming declared "that the child was either the victim of a pervert or had been kidnapped."[9]

Above: St Joseph's Church on Macquarie Street, looking east.
Source: W.L. Crowther Library, State Library of Tasmania.

Eveline's father, a war veteran, was a patient in a military hospital in Campbelltown and returned home to the family to help with the search. People scoured the bush, the slopes of Mt Wellington and the district, including disused shacks.[10] A week later, the police remained baffled and desperate, but Eveline's mother, Mrs Nancy Maughan, believed her daughter was still alive.[11] The police had four theories – Everlyn had been kidnapped, or murdered, fallen into the river (Derwent) or had become lost in the bush, the latter of which they discounted.[12]

The family suffered the indignity of letters to the police claiming Eveline had been hurt by her family and was buried in the home. Police were quick to assure the public that they had conducted a thorough search of the house and the home life of Eveline Maughan was indeed a happy, normal life.[13]

Days, weeks and even months came and went with no sighting of Eveline. The premier offered a 100-pound reward and it was then, that Frederick Thompson, 31, a wharf labourer, was flagged as a suspect. A member of the public had seen Thompson carrying a body in a bath.[14]

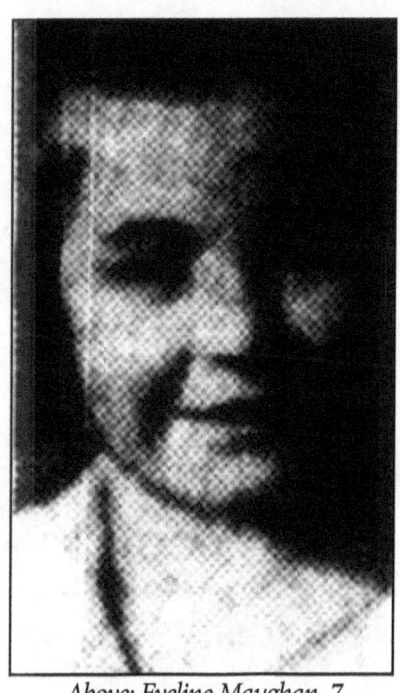

Above: Eveline Maughan, 7.
Source: News, SA, 1945.

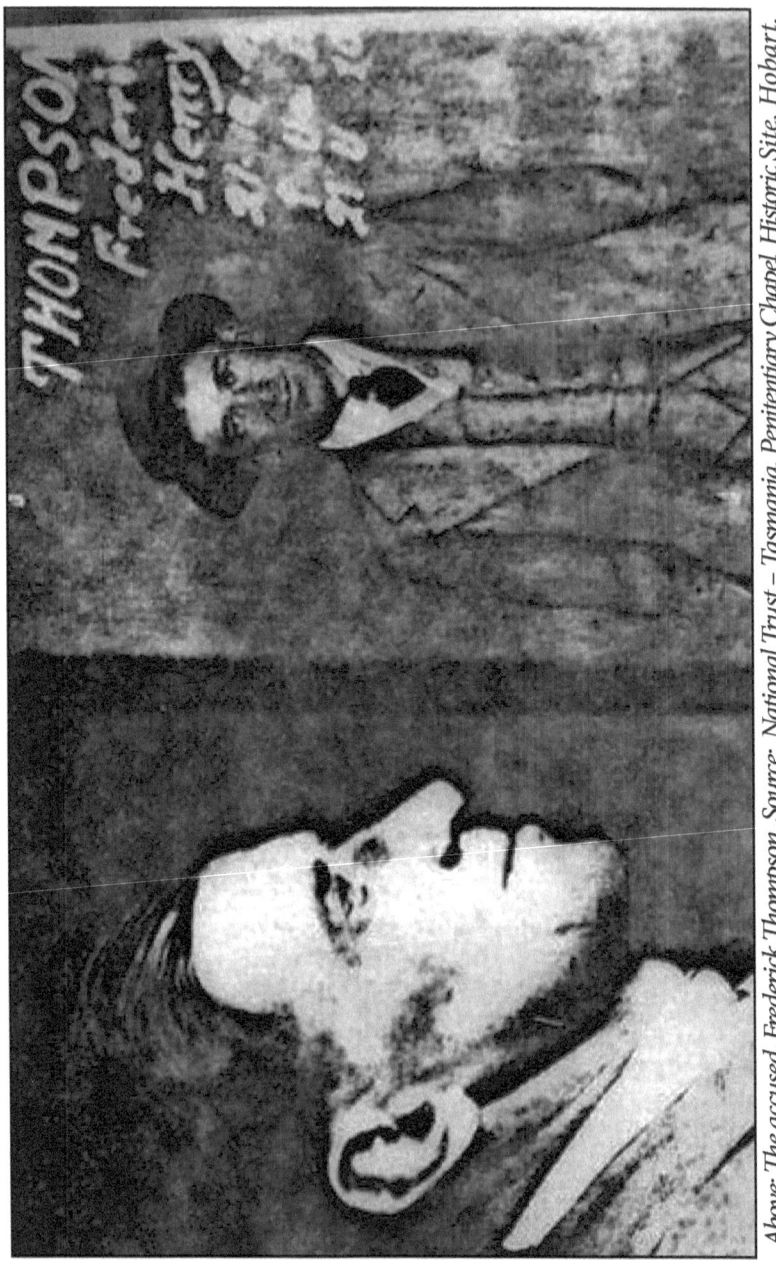

Above: The accused, Frederick Thompson. Source: National Trust – Tasmania, Penitentiary Chapel Historic Site, Hobart.

On hand and nearby

Frederick Thompson was a married man and father to two daughters, aged seven and 12 months. His wife was in hospital and the children were staying with his mother, May Thompson, where he frequented to have tea with his daughters.[15] The Thompson family lived in Harrington Street, a block from St Joseph's church, and it was at their home that police found several stolen items, mind you, none of them pertaining to the disappearance of young Eveline.

But Frederick Thompson was no stranger to the police. Four years earlier, in 1941, he appeared in the Hobart Police Court having been on the premises of a private residence for an unlawful purpose and seen attempting to force a door with a tool. When the police arrived, he was sitting waiting for them. It was noted that Thompson "had been under the control of the Mental Deficiency Board, but was not at the present time."

Newly married, and enlisted, Thompson was remanded for a week for medical observation and the magistrate suggested: "he will have to go to bed early like the rest of us for a week, but that will probably do him good."[16] The lax supervision of Thompson would no doubt come back to haunt that magistrate.

A year later, in 1942, Thompson was back in court and this time for a more serious crime – loitering in a public place with intent to commit indecent assault on a female. He was found guilty and spent the next six months in prison.[17] Jump ahead two years, and in 1944, Thompson, now 28, was charged again, this time for exposing himself in public at Sandy Bay.

Name	Age	Date of Admission	Date of Discharge or Death	Religion	If able to Read or Write	Disease	Where Born	Trade or Calling
THOMAS Robert George	80	1 · 12 · 37	7 · 8 · 46	C. of E.	Yes	Senility	Launceston	Labourer
TAYLOR Joseph	48	16 · 9 · 39	21 · 10 · 40	C. of E.	No	Senility	Seymour	Labourer
TAYLOR Leonard Frank	15	4 · 5 · 41	8 · 5 · 41	C. of E.	Yes	Weak State	Smithton	Messenger
TURNER Malcolm Alexander	69	12 · 5 · 41	31 · 7 · 41	C. of E.	Yes	Destitute	New Norfolk	Labourer
TAGGETT John George	78	31 · 7 · 41	25 · 4 · 44	C. of E.	Yes	Senility	Collingwood	Labourer
THORPE Alfred Benjamin	85	1 · 8 · 41	15 · 8 · 41	C. of E.	Yes	Senility	Franklin	Farmer
TRIFFITT Jack	16	12 · 8 · 41	18 · 8 · 41	R.C.	Yes	Weak State	New Norfolk	Labourer
TUNKS Henry Edward	64	29 · 8 · 41	23 · 10 · 41	C. of E.	Yes	Cardiac	Collingwood	Labourer
TAYLOR Arthur Lewis	14	9 · 10 · 41	22 · 10 · 41	R.C.	Yes	Under Sentence	Melbourne	Butcher
THOMPSON Frederick Henry	26	22 · 10 · 41	22 · 10 · 41	R.C.	Yes	Mental Defect	Hobart	Labourer
THOMAS Henry James	58	10 · 12 · 41	22 · 8 · 42	R.C.	No	Destitute Convalescent	West Tamar	Labourer
TOON Mow	64	24 · 1 · 42	6 · 2 · 42	Chinese	No	Old Age & Disease	China	Gardener
TURNER Thomas Nichol	62	8 · 6 · 42	1 · 10 · 42	C. of E.	Yes	Senility	Longford	Labourer

Above: Frederick's admission record at New Town Charitable Institution, 1941.
Below: The New Town Charitable Institution. Source: Libraries Tasmania.

He pleaded guilty and was remanded for medical examination. A certificate was furnished stating Thompson was feeble-minded and ordered him to be sent to the Government Institution for Mental Defectives at Lachlan Park.[18] While this writer could find no record of him being institutionalised in 1944, Thompson had spent time previously in institutions such as the New Town Charitable Institution in Hobart – six months from July to December in 1938 when he was aged 24, two months from December 1938 to February 1939, and a short stint in 1941.[19]

But each time Frederick Thompson was released back into society, and with his sexual misconduct record, and residence in proximity to the church, Thompson was now a reasonable suspect.

Another potential suspect, Clarence Goldie Gordon Smith, 54, of Sandy Bay – a recipient of the Military Medal in WWI[20] – had been questioned by police about his possible involvement in Eveline's death, but he was charged with indecent exposure and the case adjourned. A week after, Clarence Smith's body was found floating in the Derwent River.[21]

Eveline is found

Three months after her disappearance, dashing all hopes her parents may have held that she might return home safely, Eveline's body was found at the Queenborough Cemetery, a cemetery that was unused. Her body was found by Edmund Mead of Goulburn,[22] New South Wales, who was visiting the cemetery with his wife and 12-year-old son to pay his respects at his father's graveside.[23] Mr Mead

Above: Front page announcing Eveline's body was found, 6 October 1945.
Source: The Mercury (Hobart), p. 1.

found a child's shoe and shortly after, a body wrapped in material lying on a grave – that of a little girl with her hands bound in front of her. It was Eveline's decomposed body that had been there for some time, fully clothed. Only Eveline's hat was missing.[24]

Edmund Mead told the media: 'I was in the cemetery with my wife and son about 12.30pm. Wandering in and out of the lines of tombstones we saw a child's shoe protruding. We looked closer and saw the body of a girl. We did not know of Eveline Maughan's disappearance. We got such a shock we forgot about my father's grave."[25]

Cunningly arranged in a space between two graves, the wooden frame shown in the centre of the picture, camouflaged with weeds, concealed the body of 7-year-old Evelyn Maughan. In the background is Det.-Inspector R. W. Fleming.

Above: the newsclipping and description of finding Eveline's body.
Source: Examiner (Launceston) 6 October 1945.

Police alleged the strips of fabric that Eveline was wrapped in were similar to material found in Frederick Thompson's house.[26] Within a few days, Thompson, 31, was charged with the murder of Eveline Maughan. Due to the decomposition of the body, the pathologist could not conclusively determine Eveline's cause of death or whether she had been sexually assaulted.[27]

Eveline's wrists had been bound together in front with a piece of blanket-like material, the same material that was cut into three pieces, wrapped around her head, and partially knotted at the front and sides. A khaki handkerchief was found loose around her neck, but the pathologist believed it would have been tight when Eveline was alive, and it, along with the fabric around her head most likely resulted in asphyxiation.[28]

The inquest

It is hard to know or understand what might have been going on in Frederick Thompson's mind during the inquest, as he was reported to be calm and watching proceedings as if he were not the chief participant, as if he firmly believed in his innocence and perhaps thought the court would see that, or lack of evidence would see him freed. Or perhaps it was indicative of his mental state. Thompson was tried before Justice Andrew Inglis Clark (Jnr), and in her evidence, Eveline's mother, Nancy, said she knew Frederick Thompson by sight only.[29]

Witnesses came forward at the inquest, including Mr Courtney Trowbridge who claimed to see Frederick Thompson carrying a bath on his back. Mr Trowbridge was tall enough to see into the bath and claimed he saw what appeared to be a child's body covered with material. Mrs Vida Davies agreed she saw the same man in question carrying his load. Mrs Jane Hall bore witness too and spoke with a man she said looked like Frederick Thompson that same day at 1pm when he was pushing a child's stroller up Barrack Street. A bath was on the stroller and she said to him in conversation as he passed: "You have a load on that pusher." Mrs Hall claimed that the man replied, "This is moving on Sunday, but it will be my last move on a Sunday."[30] Mrs Minnie Connacher also saw the man wheeling a child's pusher with a big bundle and entering through the gates of the Queensborough Cemetery but she could not identify him as Thompson.[31]

It was enough evidence for Justice Clark, and Frederick Thompson was committed for trial.

The trial

Above: Edmund Mead.
Source: The Mercury.

No time was wasted. Eveline's body was found on 5 October, an inquest was conducted, and on 12 December 1945, the trial began, with Mr Frederick Carr Mitchell – a solicitor of seven years' experience practising law – representing Thompson, who pleaded not guilty. A string of witnesses recounted seeing Thompson with the bath, entering the cemetery, and Mr Edmund Mead retold of finding

Eveline's body. Eveline's uncle spoke of identifying Eveline, and Mrs Nancy Maughan told again of her daughter leaving for church that morning and never returning.

Aside from the sightings, the only piece of evidence presented was by Detective-Inspector R. W. Fleming who produced three pieces of blanket found soaking in a trough among clothes at Frederick Thompson's residence, along with the same blanket found wrapped around Eveline in the Queenborough cemetery.[32] The Government Analyst, Herbert Eric Hill, spoke of the material found around Eveline's head and in Frederick Thompson's house, saying "the type of weave in the two sets of pieces of blanket, made of wool and cotton, was similar,"[33] but he could not say whether any one piece had been torn from another.

When shown the piece of blanket taken from his home, Frederick Thompson saw the edge was sewn, as it was also on the piece taken from Eveline's body. He claimed that "he did not sew the edge. The blanket did not belong to him."[34]

As to the body seen in the bath he was carrying, Frederick Thompson claimed he was carrying paint he had gotten from the wharves and that he had left the paint at the Sandy Bay Rifle Range. He and a few other men had obtained the U.S. paint while working on the vessel, *James Aswell*, and of the 10 gallons in his possession, he sold five gallons and kept the remaining five. Thompson claimed it was the paint he was moving about on the day in question.[35]

The paint, or evidence that the tins had rested on the soft soil at the rifle range, was not found by police.[36] Oddly, despite the fact it might have saved his life, Thompson refused to give the name of the person to whom he sold the five gallons of paint. He claimed the buyer was a waterside worker, but he would not get thrown into the dock for telling his name. He was, after all, well and truly in the dock.[37]

No evidence was presented by Frederick Thompson's legal representative about Thompson's mental health. On the sixth day of the trial, the jury deliberated and in less than two hours, found him guilty. His sentence – death by hanging.

The last man hanged

One can only imagine the shock to the community when it was declared that Thompson would die by hanging, given the last person to die in the state by the same method did so 24 years prior, in 1922. Frederick Thompson had 14 days to appeal his sentence and he instructed his counsel to do so; it was soon dismissed. Protests sprang up, church leaders believed Thompson to be insane and thus should not be executed,[38] and the government was put under considerable pressure. A letter was then forwarded to the Attorney-General requesting Frederick Thompson's history of mental health be considered, and church groups appealed for a reprieve based on Thompson's mental state. These appeals were considered by an Executive Council but not upheld. The death penalty was to stand.[39] A hangman was brought in from Melbourne to do the deed.

Last-minute attempts at a reprieve and calls to cabinet ministers to intervene failed. On Thursday 14 February 1946, just after 6am, Frederick Thompson was hanged in front of a few officials and wardens. He shook hands with the prison guard but made no statement. Thompson went calmly to the gallows and his death, which according to the gaol medical officer, was instantaneous.[40] Thompson was later buried in the paupers' section of Cornelian Bay Cemetery.

Thirty-two executions took place at the Hobart gallows from when they were relocated to the penitentiary in 1857 and removed from being a public spectacle.[41] Frederick Thompson's was the last but it took another two decades for the Tasmanian government to finally declare the end of capital punishment in Tasmania. It was not for lack of trying from some high in office, including Attorney-General Roy Fagan who commuted 20 death sentences during his time in office and spent over a decade trying to have the law removed.[42] Finally, in 1968, it was abolished and thus, Frederick Thompson remained the last man hanged in Tasmania. Today you can tour the gallows in Hobart and see the site for yourself.

Queensland was the first state to abolish the death penalty as early as 1922. New South Wales abolished the death penalty for murder in 1955 but some offences still carried the death penalty (piracy and treason) until 1985. The Northern Territory and ACT abolished it in 1973, Victoria in 1975, South Australia in 1976, and Western Australia in 1984.[43]

Remembering Eveline and her family

Showing great compassion, Mrs Edith Waterworth, President of the Tasmanian Council for Mother and Child, put the blame for Eveline's death squarely at the feet of those responsible for releasing Frederick Thompson from a mental home. Mrs Waterworth felt strongly enough to sign the petition against the hanging of Thompson, believing that "men with Thompson's record of sexual offences should never be released from mental institutions. Thompson was more sinned against than sinning."[44] Mrs Waterworth actively sought financial provisions for Eveline's family to make a fresh start elsewhere.

Eveline was buried in an unmarked grave in the same cemetery as Frederick Thompson. No public funds appear to have been raised towards her headstone – a community initiative that often took place to assist the family of victims of crime. Today, nothing marks her grave. Mr Edmund Mead, who discovered Eveline's body in the cemetery, was awarded the 100-pound reward.[45]

DEATHS

MAUGHAN.—On or about July 8, 1945, suddenly, at Hobart, Eveline Mary, beloved daughter of William and Nancy Maughan, of 100 Goulburn St., Hobart, grand-daughter of L. S. Mason, of 100 Goulburn St., Hobart, and grand-daughter of Mr and Mrs J. Maughan, of 221 Macquarie St., Hobart, and Mrs G. Mason, of Sydney, aged 7 years. Requiescat in pace.

Above: Eveline's death notice.
Source: Family Notices (1945, October 9). The Mercury.

References:

1 Brand, Ian, Executions at Campbell Street Gaol 1857 – 1946. Retrieved 21 March 2022 from URL: http://www.penitentiarychapel.com/html/executions.htm

2 & 3 Stubbs, Barry, Talking Point: Strong whiff of injustice around the case of Mary McLauchlan, 17 May 2017. *Herald Sun.* Retrieved 21 March 2022 from URL: https://www.themercury.com.au/news/opinion/talking-point-strong-whiff-of-injustice-around-the-case-of-mary-mclauchlan/news-story/8a9b556bf2ad671f92f0d8a8ee6af2f8

4 & 5 Burgess, Georgie, Frederick Thompson was the last man hanged in Tas. but claimed innocence until the end, *ABC Radio Hobart*, Sunday 9 Jun 2019. Retrieved 21 Mar 2022 from: https://www.abc.net.au/news/2019-06-09/frederick-thompson-was-the-last-man-hanged-in-tasmania/11083304

6 £100 Offer for News of Child (1945, July 14). *The Mercury (Hobart, Tas.: 1860 - 1954)*, p. 8. Retrieved March 21, 2022, from http://nla.gov.au/nla.news-article26159825

7 Little Girl Leaves for Church and Not Seen Again (1945, July 9). *The Herald (Melbourne, Vic.: 1861 - 1954)*, p. 3. Retrieved March 21, 2022, from http://nla.gov.au/nla.news-article249159674

8 Unavailing Search for Missing 7-Year-Old Girl (1945, July 12). *The Argus (Melbourne, Vic.: 1848 - 1957)*, p. 3. Retrieved March 21, 2022, from http://nla.gov.au/nla.news-article974777

9 & 10 Women Join Hunt for Missing Child (1945, July 11). *The Daily News (Perth, WA: 1882 - 1955)*, p. 8 (HOM EDITION). Retrieved March 21, 2022, from http://nla.gov.au/nla.news-article78787691

11 Girl Alive Mother Believes (1945, July 13). *The Sun (Sydney, NSW: 1910 - 1954)*, p. 6 (LATE FINAL EXTRA). Retrieved March 21, 2022, from http://nla.gov.au/nla.news-article230455302

12 Four Theories in Girl Mystery. (1945, July 18). *The Herald (Melbourne, Vic.: 1861 - 1954)*, p. 5. Retrieved March 21, 2022, from http://nla.gov.au/nla.news-article249176264

13 Missing Girl's Home Life was Happy (1945, July 19). *Barrier Miner (Broken Hill, NSW: 1888 - 1954)*, p. 5. Retrieved March 21, 2022, from http://nla.gov.au/nla.news-article50004848

14 Burgess, Georgie, *ABC Radio Hobart*, Op.cit.

15 Hobart murder trial. Accused denies that he even knew girl (1945, December 15). *Advocate (Burnie, Tas.: 1890 - 1954)*, p. 7. Retrieved March 22, 2022, from http://nla.gov.au/nla.news-article68954052

16 Police Court News (1941, October 21). *The Mercury (Hobart, Tas.: 1860 - 1954)*, p. 5. Retrieved March 22, 2022, from http://nla.gov.au/nla.news-article25898176

17 Gaol for Six Months. (1942, November 14). *Examiner (Launceston, Tas.: 1900 - 1954)*, p. 6. Retrieved March 22, 2022, from http://nla.gov.au/nla.news-article91524633

18 Police Court News (1944, February 12). *The Mercury (Hobart, Tas.: 1860 - 1954)*, p. 4. Retrieved March 22, 2022, from http://nla.gov.au/nla.news-article26009754

19 Thompson, Frederick Henry, Record Type: Health & Welfare, New Town Charitable Institute. *Libraries Tasmania.* Record ID: NAME_INDEXES:1620837. Retrieved 22 March 2022 from URL: https://stors.tas.gov.au/HSD274-1-3$init=HSD274-1-3_62

20 Accused Man's Body in River (1945, October 2). *News (Adelaide, SA: 1923 - 1954)*, p. 6. Retrieved March 22, 2022, from http://nla.gov.au/nla.news-article128315988

21 Arrest Follows Discovery of Missing Girl's Body (1945, October 7). *The Daily Telegraph (Sydney, NSW: 1931 - 1954)*, p. 5. Retrieved March 22, 2022, from http://nla.gov.au/nla.news-article248027154

22 Brand, Ian, Executions at Campbell Street Gaol 1857 – 1946. Retrieved 21 March 2022 from URL: http://www.penitentiarychapel.com/html/executions.htm

23 Girl's Body Found on Grave (1945, October 6). *The Mercury (Hobart, Tas.: 1860 - 1954)*, p. 1. Retrieved March 21, 2022, from http://nla.gov.au/nla.news-article26154891

24 - 25. Ibid.

26 & 27 Burgess, Georgie, *ABC Radio Hobart*, Op.cit.

28 & 29 Inquest Opened on Death of Hobart Girl (1945, October 20). *Advocate (Burnie, Tas.: 1890 - 1954)*, p. 7 (Edition 2). Retrieved March 22, 2022, from http://nla.gov.au/nla.news-article69095569

30 & 31 Story of Man and "Bundle" (1945, October 26). *The Herald (Melbourne, Vic.: 1861 - 1954)*, p. 3. Retrieved March 22, 2022, from http://nla.gov.au/nla.news-article245669302

32 & 33 Blanket Pieces Produced at Murder Trial (1945, December 14). *The Mercury (Hobart, Tas.: 1860 - 1954)*, p. 8. Retrieved March 22, 2022, from http://nla.gov.au/nla.news-article26157537

34 Thompson Sentenced to Death (1945, December 18). *Advocate (Burnie, Tas.: 1890 - 1954)*, p. 5 (Edition 2). Retrieved March 22, 2022, from http://nla.gov.au/nla.news-article69104185

35 Hobart murder trial. Accused denies that he even knew girl (1945, December 15). *Advocate (Burnie, Tas.: 1890 - 1954)*, p. 7. Retrieved March 22, 2022, from http://nla.gov.au/nla.news-article68954052

36 Blanket Pieces... *The Mercury*, Op.cit.

37 Accused Cross-Examined at Girl Murder Trial (1945, December 17). *The Mercury (Hobart, Tas.: 1860 - 1954)*, p. 9. Retrieved March 22, 2022, from http://nla.gov.au/nla.news-article26147705

38 Burgess, Georgie, *ABC Radio Hobart*, Op.cit.

39 Death Sentence Stands (1946, February 14). *Advocate (Burnie, Tas.: 1890 - 1954)*, p. 5. Retrieved March 22, 2022, from http://nla.gov.au/nla.news-article68962658

40 Thompson Executed (1946, February 15). *Examiner (Launceston, Tas.: 1900 - 1954)*, p. 1. Retrieved March 22, 2022, from http://nla.gov.au/nla.news-article92691395

41 & 42 Burgess, Georgie, *ABC Radio Hobart*, Op.cit.

43 Potas, Ivan and Walker, John, Capital Punishment, February 1987. Trends and Issues in Crime and Criminal Justice, No.3, *Australian Institute of Criminology*. Retrieved 22 March 2022 from URL: https://www.aic.gov.au/sites/default/files/2020-05/tandi003.pdf

44 Should Not Have Been Allowed At Large (1946, February 20). *Advocate (Burnie, Tas.: 1890 - 1954)*, p. 5. Retrieved March 22, 2022, from http://nla.gov.au/nla.news-article68963460

45 Murder of Hobart Child. (1945, October 10). *Cairns Post* (Qld.: 1909 - 1954), p. 6. Retrieved July 25, 2022, from http://nla.gov.au/nla.news-article42462550

Images:

Macquarie Street looking east [picture] Hobart [Tas.] : Anson, ca. 1878, digitised item from: W.L. Crowther Library, *State Library of Tasmania*. Retrieved 1 April 2022 from URL: https://stors.tas.gov.au/ILS/SD_ILS-677335

- Eveline Maughan: Hobart Child was Strangled Police Think (1945, October 6). *News* (Adelaide, SA : 1923 - 1954), p. 1. Retrieved March 30, 2022, from http://nla.gov.au/nla.news-article128316200
- Frederick Henry Thompson. Image kindly supplied by the National Trust – Tasmania, Penitentiary Chapel Historic Site, Hobart - https://www.nationaltrust.org.au/places/penitentiary/
- Institutional record: Thompson, Frederick Henry, Record Type: Health & Welfare, New Town Charitable Institute. *Libraries Tasmania*. Record ID: NAME_INDEXES:1620837. Retrieved 22 March 2022 from URL: https://stors.tas.gov.au/HSD274-1-3$init=HSD274-1-3_62
- (1900). Photograph - New Town - Charitable Institution - later St Johns Park. *Libraries Tasmania*. Retrieved 22 March 2022 from URL: https://stors.tas.gov.au/PH30-1-7641
- Front page: Girl's Body Found on Grave (1945, October 6). *The Mercury* (Hobart, Tas.: 1860 - 1954), p. 1. Retrieved March 22, 2022, from http://nla.gov.au/nla.news-article26154891
- Grave with Detective Fleming: Child's Body Found (1945, October 6). *Examiner (Launceston, Tas.: 1900 - 1954)*, p. 1. Retrieved March 22, 2022, from http://nla.gov.au/nla.news-article91936969
- Edmund Mead: Girl's Body Found on Grave (1945, October 6). *The Mercury* (Hobart, Tas.: 1860 - 1954), p. 1. Retrieved March 22, 2022, from http://nla.gov.au/nla.news-article26154891
- Family Notices (1945, October 9). *The Mercury* (Hobart, Tas. : 1860 - 1954), p. 10. Retrieved March 30, 2022, from http://nla.gov.au/nla.news-article26162859

Above: Eveline's unmarked grave, RC, EE, No 59, Cornelian Bay Cemetery.

Top: *The Lynch family grave courtesy of Cindi Thorn, Find a Grave.*
Below: *Albert Henry Jackson's grave in Cornelian Bay Cemetery.*

The day the river flowed backwards

The Lynch family & Albert Jackson

Interred:
John Patrick Lynch, b. 1913 – 4 April 1929 (aged 16 years).
Ernest Alfred Lynch, b. 1916 – 4 April 1929 (aged 13 years).
Allan Lynch, b. 11 August 1918 – 4 April 1929 (aged 11 years).
Dorithy Gladys Lynch, b. 1920 – 4 April 1929 (aged 9 years).
William Wells, b. 1903 – 4 April 1929 (aged 26 years).
Jane Wells, b. 1921 – 4 April 1929 (aged 8 years).
Mary Louise Lynch, b. 1910 – 4 April 1929 (aged 19 years).
Nellie Margaret Lynch, b. 1912 – 4 April 1929 (aged 17 years).

Location: S-21 R-G, Plot 34.
Cemetery: Ulverstone General Cemetery, 33 Lovett Street,
Ulverstone, TAS 7315.

Interred: **Albert Henry Jackson**, 1894 –12 July 1982 (aged 88).
Location: Roman Catholic, section NC, number 139.
Cemetery: Cornelian Bay Cemetery and Crematorium,
Queens Walk, New Town, TAS 7008.

A massive amount of water containing trees and boulders, including one 10-tonne monster,[1] was hurtling down the river valley towards Derby and the Briseis Mine. This reads like a scene from a disaster movie but it was not on the big screen or fiction, it was happening in a real river valley, heading towards a real town, and its residents' lives would soon be altered forever.

A flood like never before

On 9 April 1929, the *Adelaide Advertiser* reported on a disaster that was sweeping across Tasmania causing widespread damage and mayhem. The paper described it as a calamity, hardly an understatement when the situation was examined in the edition of Tuesday, 9 April: "the deluge which had swept the whole of the north, from Derby on the east to Wynyard on the west, involving already the loss of 23 lives and the destruction of upwards of £1,000,000 worth of property" was far from finished and "Tasmania, with her fifty odd rivers and streams, and her tremendous rainfall, averaging 145 inches (3683mm) a year, with a maximum registered in 1924 of 175 inches, (4445mm) has had floods before, but never one like this."[2]

A situation that will be familiar to many mainland Australians in more recent times developed over northern Tasmania on 4 April 1929, leading to heavy rainfall which, driven by strong north-easterly winds, produced increasing volumes of rain. Tasmania's 'fifty odd' rivers and streams simply couldn't handle the deluge and it overflowed into the surrounding countryside.

Setting for calamity

In the north-east of the state there lies the small and once prosperous town of Derby. It was settled in the 1870s and its financial survival was guaranteed with the discovery of a large lode of tin that led to a mine being established. By the end of the 19th century the Briseis Mine, named after the winner of the 1876 Melbourne Cup, was producing upwards of 120 tonnes of tin a month. Briseis was one of the richest and most profitable tin mines in the world.

The mine relied on water from a dam built above the mine which operated by using high-pressure jets of water to dislodge tin, thus forming a slurry that was pumped through sluice boxes to extract the ore. The Cascade dam, built on the Cascade River, provided high-pressure water for the Briseis Mine. Because the dam was above the mine, it was also above the town of Derby.[3]

Deadly deluge

When on 4 April the catchment above Derby received 125 millimetres (4.9 inches) of rain in ninety minutes, on top of the 450 millimetres (17.7 inches) it had received in the previous two days, it was too much for the dam to take.[4] At 4 o'clock the inevitable occurred. The dam burst, sending seven and a half million gallons, some 34 million litres of water, into the Cascade River. Those who watched what happened reported that in the lead-up to the disaster, water had been violently tumbling over the top of the dam before the breach. Now that massive amount of water containing trees and boulders, including one 10-tonne monster,[5] was hurtling down the river valley towards Derby and the Briseis Mine.

It was a catastrophe in the making for the people of Derby and as far away as Launceston. This 30-metre-high wall of water, debris and mud, out of control in the narrow gorge, had a will of its own and it showed it. So powerful was the torrent that it forced the Ringarooma River to reverse its course and flow uphill for 10 kilometres. It smashed everything in its path including people's homes, the railway station, every bridge over the river, and eventually contributed to damage to the Cataract Gorge Bridge, almost 100 kilometres away in Launceston.[6]

What cost a warning?

And the catastrophe extended to those who were still at work in the Briseis Mine. It seems the first to see the approaching wall of water was the mine's assistant manager, William Beamish, who apparently had a little more notice than others and decided, rather than running for his life, to attempt a warning to his colleagues still in the works and unaware of the impending deluge. One account says that as he attempted to do this, a wave swept him away, dragged him under and he failed to resurface. Another report says he was in the mine office when "Mr. Beamish, who is numbered among the seven men who were reported last night to be missing, was able to warn only those people who were in the mine's office before it was overwhelmed, and he himself, apparently, was carried away."[7] He was a married man and father of two.[8]

Whether or not an individual survived the deluge was a matter of chance… the timely arrival of someone who could help or the inability of those in trouble to extricate themselves. No more so was that demonstrated than in the Briseis Mine disaster where 14 people lost their lives.

Most of the victims were miners, but five were members of the Whiting family whose home was smashed to pieces while they were eating dinner. The water struck the house, washing it and the family away. The bodies of Stephen Whiting, his wife Alice, and children Max, 12, Keith, 10, and Ray, 2 years and five months, were found at various times and recovered at Branxholm, about five kilometres (three miles) from Derby[9] The family members are all buried in Carr Villa cemetery in Launceston.

Top: The Whiting family grave where Stephen, Alice and their three young sons are buried.
Source: courtesy of Julie Henderson and Lacey Milier, Find a Grave.

Rescue for some

Meanwhile, eight workers at the mine were stranded on tailings mounds (leftover material like ground rock) as the water rushed by, threatening to wash them away. Local policeman, Constable William Taylor, hearing of the men's predicament somehow got hold of a very small, not entirely leak-proof vessel, described as little more than a coracle, which he used to rescue all eight of the stranded men, taking them off one at a time. Constable Taylor was promoted to sergeant,[10] awarded the King's Medal for Bravery and the Humane Society's Clarke Medal.[11]

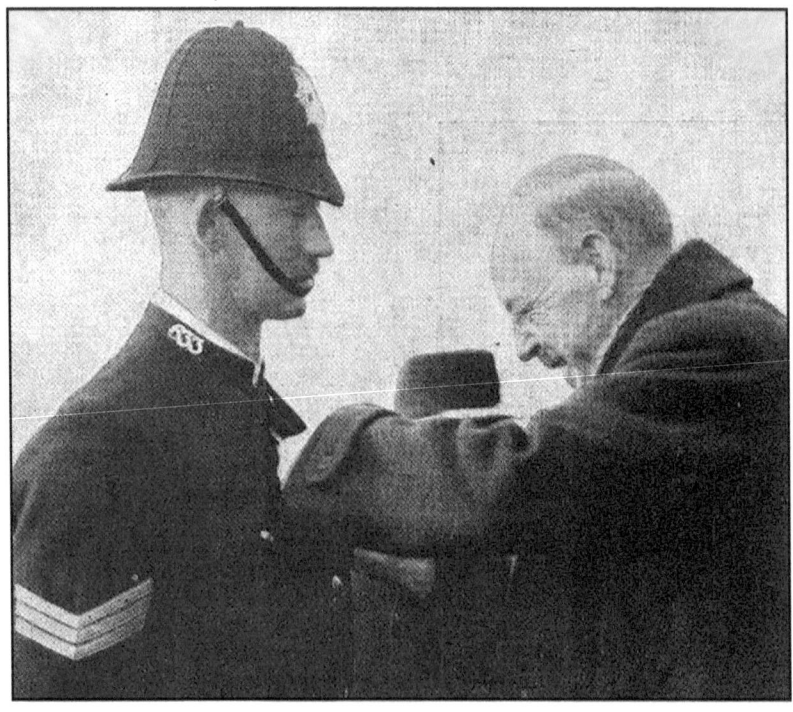

Sergeant Taylor receiving his King's Police Medal in 1930, presented by H. E. The Gov. James O'Grady, 9 July 1930. Source: Tasmania Police Museum.

Above: Residents looking at flooded streets. Below: a woman alights from a row boat with assistance. Source: Libraries Tasmania.

And this terrible time in Tasmania highlighted the brave intervention from members of the 'thin blue line'. Constable Taylor displayed outstanding bravery at the Briseis Mine, while across the state another policeman would be hailed a hero after his actions during the flooding. His name was Senior-Constable Albert Jackson and the events which led to him risking his life several times were also a result of the flooding which all but wiped out much of the north of the state.

The disaster which would engulf the town of Ulverstone, north west of Gawler, and change Senior-Constable Jackson's life forever took place on the flooded Gawler River close to the town. Nine members of the Lynch and Wells families were attempting to return home from a dance, unaware that the bridge they were intending to cross had been washed away and a huge area around where they had hoped to travel was inundated.

Heading towards their fate were John, 16, Ernest, 13, Allan, 11, Dorithy, 9, William, 26, Jane, 8, Mary, 19, Nellie, 17, and George 14. Normally the width of the steam was less than 20 metres, now an area 300 metres by 180 metres was underwater.[12]

Underestimating the torrent

Between 9pm and 10pm, the family's vehicle was overwhelmed as it tried to cross where the bridge should have been. The power of the water washed all but one of those on board downstream, taking their lives one after the other as they struggled against the torrent. The one traumatised survivor was 14-year-old George Lynch, who was washed about 20 metres downstream at which point he was fortunate to be caught in the lower branches of a willow tree, where he remained, trapped, cold and terrified.

Senior-Constable Jackson was one of the first to arrive on the scene. He must have heard the boy's cries as he took off his clothing, tied a rope around his waist and made two unsuccessful attempts to get to George... but the rope was too short to reach the boy. By now it was well and truly dark and car headlights were being used to light up the area where George was stranded.

All the time policeman, Albert Jackson, was in the water he was subject to a battering from debris being washed down the swiftly flowing stream. He suffered lacerations from blackberry thorns, cuts and bruises from the larger logs that came his way and the water was chilly. But he was not going to give up. Someone brought out extra rope which, despite the injuries suffered on his first two attempts, enabled the Senior-Constable to have a third try; he couldn't get any closer than about 10 metres. Some reports list that he did indeed reach the young man in need.

At this time, William Lynch, George's 22-year-old brother arrived on the scene, and was able to reach George from a different angle and was said to have pulled him from the water. George was saved, and Albert Jackson had been in the punishing torrent for an hour. But the policeman did not stop there.

Paying the price

Senior-Constable Albert Jackson spent the next ten days searching for the other missing people. During this time, he was rarely out of the freezing waters as he went above and beyond the call of duty during the searches. In June 1929 the Royal Humane Society of Australasia awarded Senior-Constable Jackson the bronze medal of the society. But the constable would have more to deal with as a result of his rescue efforts.

Following the floods, Senior-Constable Jackson was posted to Bothwell, and one evening, during a routine round at the pub at closing time, he collapsed. What followed was a long stint of two years in the Royal Hobart Hospital, when it was thought he might have polio – a crippling disesase prevalent in that era.[13]

It was a hefty price to pay and towards the end of 1929, Senior-Constable Jackson's physician expressed his opinion that severe mental and nervous strain resulting from his strenuous efforts during the flood rescue work brought about the illness, rendering useless his lower limbs, and seriously affecting his abdominal and lumbar muscles.[14]

DEATHS

WHITING—On the 4th April, at Derby, Stephen Whiting, eldest son of the late S. J. Whiting, of Newstead; also A. M. Whiting, wife of the above and daughter of Mr. and Mrs. Alexander, of Myrtle Bank; Max Whiting, in his 12th year; Keith Whiting, in his 10th year, and Raymond Whiting, 2 years and 5 months, all sons of above.

Below: The tragic funeral notice for the Whiting family that ran 8 April 1929. Source: The Examiner.

The Parliament of Tasmania granted a pension to the invalided man, with legislation bearing his name – the Albert Henry Jackson Pension Act. He received the pension sum of £250 a year.[15]

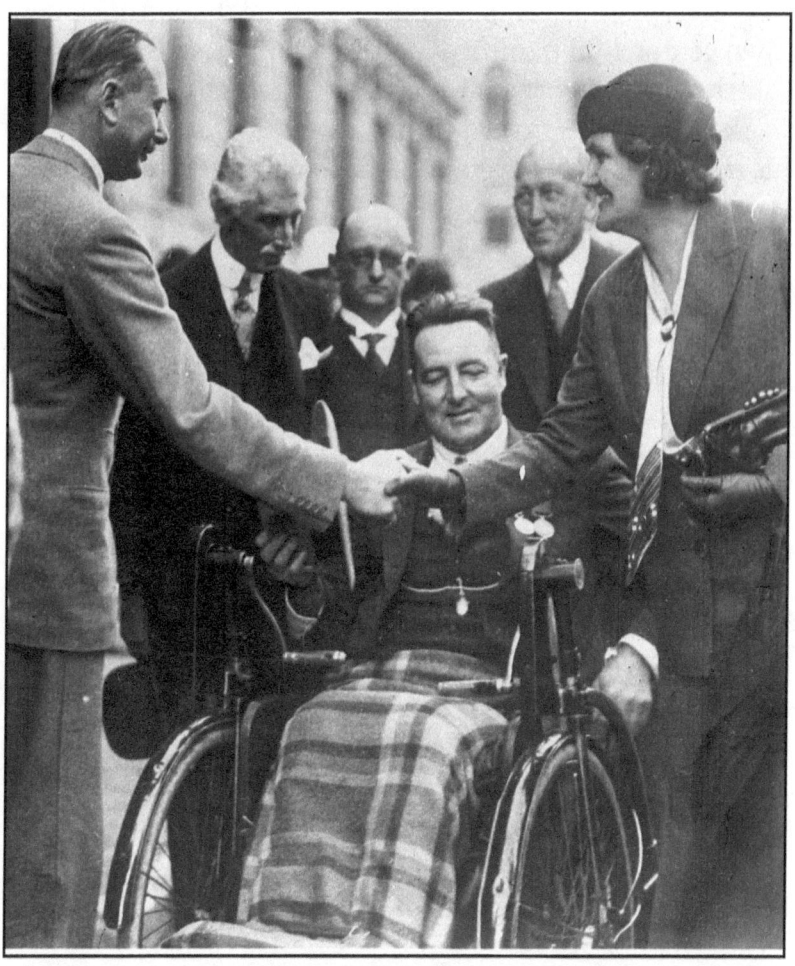

Above: Snr-Constable Albert Jackson who lost the use of his limbs from the rescue trauma, is accompanied by his wife when he meets the Duke of Gloucester, Prince Henry. Source: Tasmanian Police Museum.

In later years, 'Bert' Jackson was to be seen around Hobart in his hand-powered wheelchair. With his cheerful personality and sense of humour, he made light of his disability and took up woodworking as a hobby, selling his souvenir serviette rings turned from Tasmania timbers, and at the end of his day, often getting a lift home in a police car. His grandson, Wayne, said his grandfather "never really talked about his police work."[16] Bert Jackson died on July 12, 1982, aged 88. Although his rewarding career was cut short, his spirit was not.

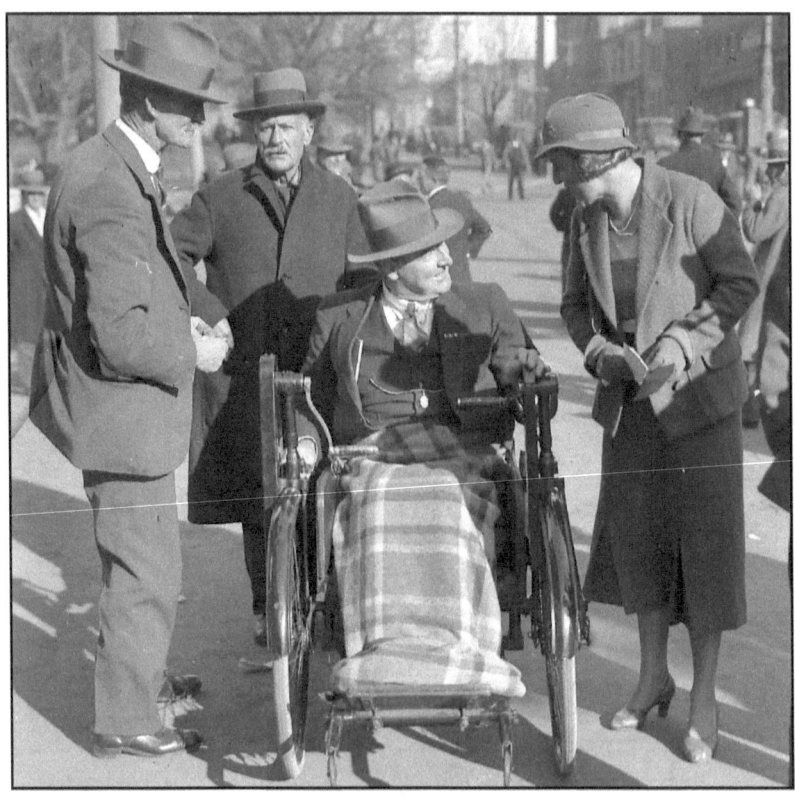

Above: Popular Albert Jackson, a well-recognised face in Hobart. Source: Tasmania Police Museum.

References:

1 *Australasian Mine Safety Journal.* Lessons from the past: Breaking Briseis, 30 May, 2019. Retrieved 28 April 2022 from: https://www.amsj.com.au/lessons-past-breaking-briseis/

2 *The Advertiser (Adelaide, SA: 1889 - 1931)* 9 April 1929: 12. Web. Retrieved 19 April 2022 from URL: http://nla.gov.au/nla.news-article35719551.

3 Wikipedia contributors. (2022, March 1). Hydraulic mining. In *Wikipedia.* Retrieved April 25, 2022, from https://en.wikipedia.org/w/index.php?title=Hydraulic_mining&oldid=1074597560

4 Beswick, John. The Companion to Tasmanian History, Briseis Dam Disaster. 2006. *Centre for Tasmanian Historical Studies.* Retrieved 28 April 2022 from URL:https://www.utas.edu.au/library/companion_to_tasmanian_history/B/Briseis%2520Dam%2520Disaster.htm?msclkid=491af0f6c43811eca58e331fd746bf34

5 - 6 *Australasian Mine Safety Journal.* Op.cit.

7 Terrible Disaster (1929, April 5). *The Mercury (Hobart, Tas.: 1860 - 1954)*, p. 9. Retrieved April 25, 2022, from http://nla.gov.au/nla.news-article24257434

8 Tasmania Swept by The Worst Floods in its History. (1929, April 6). *The Evening News (Rockhampton, Qld. : 1924 - 1941)*, p. 9. Retrieved April 28, 2022, from http://nla.gov.au/nla.news-article201245267

9 Bursting of Dam in Tasmania. (1929, April 9). *The Naracoorte Herald (SA: 1875 - 1954)*, p. 3. Retrieved April 26, 2022, from http://nla.gov.au/nla.news-article147067096

10 The Camera Man's Diary : Doings and People of Interest (1929, August 10). *Examiner (Launceston, Tas. : 1900 - 1954)*, p. 9. Retrieved April 28, 2022, from http://nla.gov.au/nla.news-article51612586

11 Conolly, Pauline. *A Brave and Caring Constable.* Retrieved 28 April 2022 from URL: https://paulineconolly.com/2019/a-constable-with-courage-and-compassion/?msclkid=ec7c6f49c45811ec92268314887b796e

12 Valor Rewarded. (1933, April 28). *Advocate (Burnie, Tas.: 1890 - 1954)*, p. 7. Retrieved April 26, 2022, from http://nla.gov.au/nla.news-article68015702

13 Erwin, Darcy. *ABC News.* 6 July, 2016. Retrieved 28 April 2022 from: https://www.abc.net.au/news/2016-07-06/remembering-albert-henry-jackson-and-the-1929-floods/7573038

14 – 16 Ibid.

Additional notes on Albert Jackson, kindly supplied by the Tasmania Police Museum, May 2022.

Images:

- The Lynch family grave courtesy of Cindi Thorn, *Find a Grave.* Retrieved 3 May 2022 from URL: https://www.findagrave.com/

- Whiting family graves courtesy of Julie Henderson and Lacey Milier, *Find a Grave,* database and images . Retrieved 30 April 2022 from URL: https://www.findagrave.com/

- Sergeant Taylor receiving his King's Police Medal in 1930, presented by His Excellency The Governor, James O'Grady. Extracted from the *Illustrated Tasmanian Mail,* 9 July 1930. Kindly supplied by the Tasmania Police Museum.

- Group of people looking at flooded street, item Number: LPIC84/1/19. *Libraries Tasmania.* Retrieved 28 April 2022 from URL: https://stors.tas.gov.au/AI/LPIC84-1-19

- Woman alighting from row boat, item Number: LPIC84/1/25. *Libraries Tasmania.* Retrieved 28 April 2022 from URL: https://stors.tas.gov.au/AI/LPIC84-1-25

- Funeral notice: Family Notices (1929, April 8). *Examiner (Launceston, Tas. : 1900 - 1954)*, p. 1. Retrieved April 28, 2022, from http://nla.gov.au/nla.news-article51537427

- Snr Constable Albert Jackson meets the Duke; and Albert Jackson. Courtesy of the Tasmania Police Museum.

216

The prisoners' mug shots
Thomas Nevin, photographer

Interred: **Thomas Nevin**, 28 August 1842 – 9 March 1923 (aged 80).

Location: Unmarked grave. Church of England, section DD, no. 277. This is a difficult grave to find as there are no row or plot numbers displayed. Thomas's grave plot lies between the Lewis and Milburn grave plots.

Cemetery: Cornelian Bay Cemetery and Crematorium, Queens Walk, New Town, TAS 7008.

The taking of photographs in the mid-19th century was regarded with much curiosity – it was somewhat time-consuming, expensive and not without superstition. Some feared the camera stole your soul; some cultures believed if three persons were photographed together, the middle person would die first; and of course, there was often no smiling, but this had more to do with the time it took to take the photograph, the necessity to remain still, and manners of the era whereby smiling was seen to be frivolous.

In 1841, the year before Thomas Nevin was born, the first photograph was taken in Australia – a daguerreotype of Bridge Street, Sydney. A daguerreotype was quite the thing – invented by a French man, who discovered that a copper plate coated with silver iodide and exposed to light in the camera, then fumed with mercury vapour and made permanent by a solution of common salt, formed a permanent image. One wonders how he came about that obscure discovery, but as a result, many daguerreotypes, especially portraits, were made in the mid-19th century but largely commissioned by the wealthy, as the process was expensive.

Given an average weekly income in many industries was three pounds a week, it would cost one guinea (1 pound, 1 shilling) to avail yourself of a photographic portrait by George Baron Goodman who established his studio room at The Royal Hotel, Sydney. The art of photography described in his advertisement: "ranked among the greatest scientific achievements of the present age"[1] and he was pleased to advise that the portrait sitting time had been reduced from four minutes as a result of "great improvements that have been made" to "about five seconds on a clear day; but during cloudy dull weather, the operation may require from a minute-and-a-half to two minutes. The portraits taken by this means are really extraordinary as likenesses; they are true to nature, for nature here is her own delineator."[2]

Family and career

Having landed on the shores of Hobart from Ireland with his parents and three younger siblings in July 1852, nine-year-old Thomas Nevin would make Tasmania his home for the rest of his days. From the early 1860s, when he was in his early 20s, Thomas had a passion for photography. Since the first portraits were captured by George and his compatriots twenty years earlier, the techniques had evolved, and Thomas established a studio in New Town and in Elizabeth Street, Hobart, where he produced many stereographs – two identical images side by side, set the same distance apart as Thomas's eyes to create a sense of depth – like a 3D image. He also produced cartes-de-visite – a small photograph often mounted on a calling card, which was very popular at the time.

At the mature age of 28, Thomas took a bride, marrying Elizabeth Rachel Day, 24, on 12 July 1871 – the niece of merchant mariner Captain Edward Goldsmith.[3] One year later, he would become the proud father of a daughter, Mary, and in 1874, a son, Thomas James Nevin Jnr was born. Over the coming decade, the couple had a further four children – three of whom were sons.[4] During these years, Thomas partnered with Robert Smith, another photographic artist – as was the term the two men used in their advertising. But this was dissolved by mutual consent and in 1868, Thomas continued in business alone[5] but successfully.

Above: Thomas Nevin c1866 . Source: ancestry.com.au

He was recognised in the newspaper as a "photographer of this city" at an exhibition attended by His Excellency the Governor in 1869.[6]

In 1875 the Council appointed Thomas as Town Hall keeper, Hobart Town[7] and he received the salary of "30s per week, with free quarters, fuel, and light." Thomas was one of 24 applicants and the newspaper acknowledged "the election was by ballot, and the choice of the Council fell upon Mr. Thomas Nevin, whom many of our readers will know as a photographer, following his profession in Elizabeth Street."[8] Thomas was dismissed from this role five years later for drunkenness, "having received repeated warnings"[9] but it is for his photography work that we remember him.

Above: Some of Thomas Nevin's 1867 studio photographs for those who could afford it. Source: State Library of Victoria.

Mug shots

Thomas Nevin was one of the first photographers to work with the police in Australia, taking photographs of prisoners, and establishing one of the earliest surviving mug shot databases. These were not your conventional mug shots that you see today where the subject holds a numbered card in front of them, faces left, then right, then to the camera and often looks worse for wear or most contrite. These mug shots were in many cases, quite striking portraits.

It is worth noting at this point that there has been some contention that Thomas was the only commercial photographer in Hobart to be contracted by the police to provide prisoner identification photographs for the central registry at Town Hall.[10] There has also been a vigorous debate as to whether the prisoners' photographs were taken by Thomas or another photographer of the time, A.H. Boyd.[11] Contenders claim A.H. Boyd was not a photographer – amateur or professional – and has no claim to the images,[12] whereas Thomas was a professional photographer and his younger brother, John, a constable working at the Hobart Gaol as a messenger, was a handy contact for Thomas. John is said to have assisted Thomas with prisoner admissions in order for him to photograph the subjects from 1875[13] until John contracted typhus and died in 1891, aged 39.

Regardless of which camp you choose to believe, the fact remains that many of these men – prisoners – would never have had their likeness captured due to the expense and their standing in society. Today because of their surviving mug shots, their stories live on, and Thomas and his colleagues photographed some of the most notorious.

Photographing Henry Stock

The paper described the death of Mrs Elizabeth Stock as a domestic tragedy but it is best described as a brutal murder. Elizabeth, aged 21, and her son, Walter, 3, were bludgeoned to death and left in bushland in Tasmania's Victoria Valley by her husband, Henry, stepfather to Walter.[14] Their bodies were conveyed to the town of Ouse.

Henry was not a transported convict, but that didn't stop him from getting on the wrong side of the law. In July 1883 at the age of 19, the local lad faced court for forgery and spent six months behind bars. On his release from prison, Henry Stock was told to take his wife back or pay maintenance. Henry decided he would not do either, and he saw to that. Taking a gun, Henry shot at Elizabeth but missed – the bullets hit her hat and scalp but did not cause damage enough to kill her. Henry went further. Intending to claim they had been murdered, he brutally bashed his wife and stepson to death with a rock.[15] Their remains were not discovered for some time until after an alarm was raised that mother and child had not been seen. The police investigated and questioned Henry, noting a foul smell which he claimed was because "an old cow had died there some time ago."[16]

When they were found, Elizabeth and Walter's remains were unidentifiable[17] and upon his arrest, Henry was said to be so cool about the situation that it was assumed he had not yet fully realised the extent of his position.[18]

Enter photographer Thomas Nevin who took the photo of Henry Stock at his arrest. The oval-mount carte-de-visite showed Henry Stock in his best street clothes.[19] A later report claimed: "the condemned man maintains his

Above: The arrested murderer, Henry Stock in his mug shot by Thomas Nevin. Note his best street clothing. Source: State Library of NSW.

appearance of stoical indifference",[20] yet it was said that when his family visited him, he broke down, unable to control his emotions.[21] Henry Stock "was swiftly served justice. Ten minutes was all it took for the jury to agree he murdered his young wife and stepson."[22] Their duty done; the jury was home in the arms of their own families that evening. Henry Stock was hanged at Hobart Gaol. His portrait remains.

Other mug shots of interest

Amongst the mug shots in Thomas Nevin's collection was that of criminal **Mark Jeffrey**, whose colourful life is the first story featured in this volume.

It is believed that Thomas took this photo of Mark Jeffrey in the first days after Jeffrey was moved to Hobart Gaol from the notorious prison, Port Arthur.[23] Jeffrey looks rather dignified, sitting for his portrait, stern and serious.

Above: Notorious prisoner Mark Jeffrey cutting a fine figure in his mug shot in 1870. Source: Libraries Tasmania.

Above: Mug shot of Richard Copping. Source: State Library of NSW.

Off to the gallows was **Richard Copping** *(above)*, 19, looking very much the sensitive and serious young man in his prison portrait. Copping engendered significant community sympathy and support as he was from a good family, and some claimed his actions were due to an illness of the brain, while others, including the journalist from the *Tasmanian Evening Herald,* blamed his actions on "the frenzy of love in an evil moment."[24]

His crime was the brutal murder of his cousin, Susannah Stacey, 18, whom he killed with an axe. Susannah tried to block the door of the room in which she had hidden, but Copping forced it open and murdered her, striking her down the forehead.[25] He then went and sat on a fence until her distressed father appeared, and accused him of murdering his daughter. Richard Copping replied: "'Yes, I know that I have.' He then jumped off the fence, and said, 'She deceived me, and I'll be hung [sic] for her like a man.'"[26] Copping then shot himself, but not fatally.[27]

In prison, Richard Copping was said to be "completely unmanned, and frequently cried like a child."[28] After his execution, Copping's brain was examined but no evidence of disease was found.[29] To see his portrait taken in May 1878, one might imagine he was gazing into the distance as if envisaging what may have been with Susannah, when five months later they were both deceased. The reason: jealousy.[30]

Teenage murderers James Sutherland and **James Ogden** look confident and full of potential. James Sutherland is even sporting a pipe in his mug shot of 1883. Both young men were no strangers to the police, with previous crime sheets for disorderly conduct and theft. But they left two women widows and were hanged for the separate murders of Alfred Holman and William Wilson.

The attack by Ogden and Sutherland on their second victim, William Wilson, was a terrifying ordeal for a young family. Wilson was a repairer on a railway line, a husband and father of three boys and a girl. Hearing a noise outside his house, he went out to investigate, was shot and stumbled to the door, warning his wife. Ogden and Sutherland then called to Wilson's wife: "Come out here, missis, or I'll put you where he lies."[31] Mrs Wilson said she did not recognise

Above: James Sutherland's interesting mug shot with his pipe!
Source: National Library of Australia.

the voices. She closed the door, terrified, and heard the assailants planning to get sticks and burn the house down.

While Mr Wilson lay dying outside, and inside a woman huddled with her four children, the young men hurled stones through the windows and set fire to the weatherboard house at both ends. When the inhabitants could remain inside no longer, Mrs Wilson ran out with the children, begging for their lives and pushing the children to escape. Odgen and Sutherland spared them but wanted to take the daughter, Lizzie, with them. Mrs Wilson stood between them and they raised the gun to her. The men left with Lizzie, while Mrs Wilson ran to a neighbour for help, hearing her daughter's screams. There she found three men who armed themselves but would not leave the house. Mrs Wilson remained there until daylight and then ran to the neighbour's cottage nearest her own. To her relief she found her three boys and Lizzie were there and unharmed. The police arrived and Mrs Wilson next saw her husband, William, at the hospital. He did not survive.[32]

At their trial, Ogden and Sutherland claimed they did not intend to kill William Wilson, just have a lark with him, but he angrily told them he didn't care who they were and to get off his property. Sutherland said it was then they "let him have it. It was his own fault".[33]

In April 1883, a journalist from *The Herald* wrote that the two young men were "displaying a callousness that is simply inexplicable. They shout and sing ribald songs and when told that hanging was too good for them smiled in the most composed manner."[34] But on the eve and the day of the hanging it was reported: "Neither prisoner slept during the night, saying that they wished to see as much of the world as possible before they left it." Previously James Sutherland

Above: James Ogden's mug shot presents a young man who does not look capable of murder. He went to the noose shaking violently.
Source: State Library of NSW.

had berated James Ogden for showing any weakness but in the end, he softened and requested a Reverend Mace "to ask the wives of the murdered men to forgive them. He complained bitterly of the treatment he had received from the world, which had not been a pleasant place to live in, as he had no parents to look after him, but had been kicked about by those who got all the work they could out of him without caring the least about him… Ogden's features were heavy and swollen. Both walked calmly to the scaffold. Sutherland's step was firm, but Ogden, who carried a bunch of flowers, trembled violently. When standing on the scaffold, they looked more boyish than ever, rendering it difficult to realise that they were the perpetrators of such a dreadful deed as that for which they were executed."[35]

Little did Thomas Nevin know that the men he captured that day with his camera would lead such brief lives. He took a second shot of James Sutherland just before they executed him in June 1883. This time, there was no pipe.

Living on

There were many more criminals – petty and hardened – captured and preserved by Thomas over the years. He hand-tinted some photographs to add realism when they were attached to the criminals' records.

Today, his images, while mug shots to assist the police, are described as "strikingly beautiful with the expressions and poses of the prisoners allowing us a window into the lives of these men."[36] In 1977 when Thomas' photos were first exhibited together at the Queen Victoria Museum, Launceston, the curator, John McPhee, said of them: "These photographs are among the most moving and powerful images of the human condition." Thomas' Tasmanian prisoner mug shots have survived in public collections and are considered among the earliest.

Unlike many of his subjects, Thomas lived a long life, shared with his wife, Elizabeth, until in 1914 Elizabeth, 67, died suddenly at their residence. Nine years later Thomas passed away, aged 80[37], at his residence at 270 Elizabeth Street, leaving behind his print on the city, literally.

Above: Elizabeth and Thomas Nevin c1866 . Source: ancestry.com.au

Images:

- Nevin & Smith (1867). [Studio portrait of two children]. *State Library of Victoria.* Retrieved 21 April 2022 from URL: http://handle.slv.vic.gov.au/10381/49353

- Nevin, Thomas J (1867). [Studio portrait of a woman]. *State Library of Victoria.* Retrieved 21 April 2022 from URL: http://search.slv.vic.gov.au/permalink/f/1cl35st/SLV_ROSETTAIE8414985

- Nevin, Thomas J., [photographer], Henry Stock, Death Warrants V.D.L. Tasmania Supreme Court. Photo courtesy of *Mitchell Library, State Library of New South Wales,* Call nos: C 202 - C 203.

- Nevin, Thomas J., 1842-1923, (photographer.) (1870). Mark Jeffrey. *Libraries Tasmania.* Retrieved 9 July 2021 from URL: https://stors.tas.gov.au/144584489

- Richard Copping, Murder, collection of Miscellaneous Photographic Portraits (1877). *State Library of NSW.* Retrieved 31 Mar 2022 from: https://collection.sl.nsw.gov.au/record/YezVeZW9/NQZKPj2l44ObW

- Boyd, A. H. (1883). James Sutherland, sentenced in Launceston on 29 May 1883, Tasmania. *National Library of Australia.* Retrieved 31 March 2022, from http://nla.gov.au/nla.obj-142918711

- James Ogden. Miscellaneous Photographic Portraits. (1877), *State Library of New South Wales.* Retrieved 31 March 2022 from: https://search.sl.nsw.gov.au/permalink/f/1ocrdrt/ADLIB110312730

- Thomas Nevin and Elizabeth Nevin, *Ancestry* family tree of LHoffman8228. *ancestry.com.au*

References:

1 & 2 Advertising (1842, December 10). *Australasian Chronicle (Sydney, NSW: 1839 - 1843)*, p. 3. Retrieved March 16, 2022, from http://nla.gov.au/nla.news-article31738165

3 Mugshots taken by commercial and police photographer Thomas J. Nevin in Tasmania, 1870s-1880s, *Prisoner Pics Blogspot*. Retrieved 16 Mar 2022 from: https://prisonerpics.blogspot.com/

4 Thomas James Nevin Snr 1842-1923, *Ancestry*. Retrieved 16 March 2022 from URL: https://www.ancestry.com.au/family-tree/person/tree/4101166/person/131498806/story

5 Advertising (1868, February 26). *The Mercury (Hobart, Tas.: 1860 - 1954)*, p. 1. Retrieved April 1, 2022, from http://nla.gov.au/nla.news-article8850754

6 Canary and Cage-Bird Exhibition. (1869, May 20). *The Tasmanian Times (Hobart Town, Tas.: 1867 - 1870)*, p. 3. Retrieved April 1, 2022, from http://nla.gov.au/nla.news-article232868146

7 Municipal. (1876, January 24). *The Mercury (Hobart, Tas.: 1860 - 1954)*, p. 1 (The Mercury Summary for Europe.). Retrieved April 1, 2022, from http://nla.gov.au/nla.news-article8942583

8 The Mercury. (1875, December 29). *The Mercury (Hobart, Tas.: 1860 - 1954)*, p. 2. Retrieved April 1, 2022, from http://nla.gov.au/nla.news-article8942022

9 Colonial News. (1880, December 4). *Launceston Examiner (Tas.: 1842 - 1899)*, p. 2. Retrieved April 1, 2022, from http://nla.gov.au/nla.news-article38265109

10 Mugshots taken by commercial... *Prisoner Pics Blogspot*, Op.cit.

11 Julia Clark. A question of attribution: *Port Arthur's convict portraits in Journal of Australian Colonial History*, Vol 12, 2010, p77-97.

12 Improprieties: A. H. Boyd and the Parasitic Attribution, 2010. *Thomas J. Nevin | Tasmanian Photographer (1842-1923) & KLW NFC Imprint 2003-2022*. Retrieved 17 March 2022 from URL: https://thomasnevin.com/2010/01/17/improprieties-a-h-boyd-and-the-parasitic-attribution/

13 Mugshots taken by commercial... *Prisoner Pics Blogspot*, Op.cit.

14 - 18 Horrible Murder of a Wife and Infant. (1884, April 29). *The Mercury (Hobart, Tas.: 1860 - 1954)*, p. 3. Retrieved March 15, 2022, from http://nla.gov.au/nla.news-article9021391

19 Mugshots taken by commercial... *Prisoner Pics Blogspot*, Op.cit.

20 - 21 The Mercury. (1884, September 29). *The Mercury (Hobart, Tas.: 1860 - 1954)*, p. 2. Retrieved March 31, 2022, from http://nla.gov.au/nla.news-article9093832

22 The case against Henry Stock (var. Stocks), *Thomas J. Nevin | Tasmanian Photographer (1842-1923) & KLW NFC Imprint 2003-2022*. Retrieved 15 Mar 2022 from: https://thomasnevin.com/2021/02/20/the-case-against-henry-stocks-1884-for-the-murder-of-his-wife-and-her-child/

23 Prisoner Mark JEFFREY, a Port Arthur flagellator, Thomas J. Nevin | Tasmanian Photographer, 26 August 2014. Retrieved 31 March 2022 from URL: https://tasmanianphotographer.blogspot.com/2014/08/prisoner-mark-jeffrey-port-arthur.html

24 The Execution of Richard Copping. (1878, October 22). *Tasmanian Evening Herald (Launceston, Tas.: 1878)*, p. 3. Retrieved Mar 31, 2022, from http://nla.gov.au/nla.news-article232957111

25 Shocking Tragedy near Sorell. (1878, May 14). *Tribune (Hobart, Tas.: 1876 - 1879)*, p. 2. Retrieved March 31, 2022, from http://nla.gov.au/nla.news-article201731697

26 The Bream Creek Tragedy. (1878, May 16). *The Mercury (Hobart, Tas.: 1860 - 1954)*, p. 2. Retrieved March 31, 2022, from http://nla.gov.au/nla.news-article8963244

27 Shocking Tragedy near Sorell. (1878, May 14). Op.cit.

28 - 29 Execution of Copping. (1878, October 23). *The Cornwall Chronicle (Launceston, Tas.: 1835 - 1880)*, p. 3. Retrieved 31 Mar 2022, from http://nla.gov.au/nla.news-article66501400

30 Shocking Tragedy near Sorell. (1878, May 14). Op.cit.

31 - 34 The Tasmanian Tragedies. (1883, April 17). *The Herald (Melbourne, Vic.: 1861 - 1954)*, p. 3. Retrieved April 1, 2022, from http://nla.gov.au/nla.news-article241137813

35 Execution of the Tasmanian Murderers. (1883, June 15). *The Burrowa News (NSW: 1874 - 1951)*, p. 2. Retrieved April 1, 2022, from http://nla.gov.au/nla.news-article107932148

36 Scharoun, Lisa (2015) *Ancestors*. [Artefact]. Retrieved 16 March 2022 from URL: https://eprints.qut.edu.au/225498/

37 Thomas James Nevin, Ancestry family tree of LHoffman8228. *ancestry.com.au*

Above: Reverend Knopwood's grave. Source: Find a Grave.

The cannibal and the priests
Alexander Pearce, Rev. Knopwood and Father Conolly

Interred:	Reverend Robert Knopwood, 2 June 1763 – 18 September 1838 (aged 75).
Location:	Saint Matthews Anglican Cemetery.
Cemetery:	King Street, Rokeby, Clarence City, TAS 7019.
Interred:	Father Philip Conolly, 1786 – 3 August 1839 (aged 53).
Location:	Saint Mary's crypt, Saint Mary's Cathedral.
Plaque:	180 Harrington Street, Hobart, TAS 7000.

During his time as a priest and magistrate, Reverend Robert Knopwood had heard some colourful confessions and admissions. But the one uttered from the prisoner, Alexander Pearce's lips, he had not heard before. Pearce – a short Irish man with brown hair and blue eyes[1] – stood resolute, and confessed to having murdered and eaten the flesh of several of his fellow escapees. The year was 1822 when eight men had escaped from a prison on Sarah Island and became lost in the bush. The Reverend refused to believe it, but there was truth in the story.

Before the fatal drop

It was not that he was a naive man by any measure; but Reverend Robert Knopwood had not, to date, struck cannibalism in his confession box or courtroom. He was a man accustomed to the highs and lows of life. Born to wealth in Norfolk, England, his father's considerable gambling debts and his own debts accumulated as a young man moving in his social circle, crippled him. Robert sold the family estate to clear the sums owed, and after studying for the ministry at Cambridge, he eventually joined an expedition to Port Phillip, thus arriving on Australia's shores. In February 1804, the Reverend Robert Knopwood conducted the first service in Tasmania at Hobart Town.[2]

Irish Roman Catholic priest, Father Philip Conolly, served the Lord and his community for five years in the Dublin archdiocese before he became a missionary and arrived at Botany Bay, and next, Hobart Town on 14 April 1821. In a store owned by a potential parishioner, Father Conolly delivered his first mass with nine free settlers in attendance.[3]

Fellow Irishman, Alexander Pearce, a farm labourer, led a very different life. He too knew the struggles of having no money and in an underhanded attempt to gain some, he was sentenced to seven years for stealing shoes. Unlike the Reverend Knopwood and Father Conolly, Alexander Pearce's passage was on a convict ship, when he was sent to Australia to do his time.

The path of these three men would cross when Reverend Knopwood—now a magistrate as well as a minister—charged Alexander Pearce, 34, with murder and sentenced him to be hanged on 19 July 1824. Crimes of this violent nature were not new, especially amongst prisoners, but here was a heinous act that got the attention of the population... an act of cannibalism, as shocking then as it is today.

On the day of the hanging, it was Father Philip Conolly who stood with Pearce a few minutes before the fatal drop. Father Conolly later shared the story of what Pearce had freely admitted to him and wanted to be known "in order to humble himself, as much as possible, in the sight of God and Man"[4] and to give his side of the story. This is Pearce's tale.

An act of survival

Alexander Pearce and his seven fleeing prison companions were prepared for an escape from Sarah Island – an isolated prison on six hectares (15 acres) established before the Port Arthur penal settlement. Many of the prisoners were subject to hard labour, felling trees in the rainforest, and it was a cold, barren and isolated place.[5] The eight men, whose charges ranged from theft to carrying forged banknotes, escaped the prison in two boats with rations amounting to about two ounces of food per day, for a week. But a week's rations were not enough and when the food ran out, there were eight hungry and potentially violent men.

According to Pearce – and he was the only prisoner alive to recount the story, and thus it is his version of events – it was the prisoner Bob Greenhill who had appointed himself leader[6] and suggested the men draw lots as someone must be sacrificed for the good of all.[7] This separated the men, and soon Bill Cornelius, 20, (alias William Kennely[8]), Edward Brown, and Alexander Dalton placed themselves at one fire. Pearce and the rest of the men sat around another.

The three segregated men soon departed, and Pearce could not say on his return what became of them, but Alexander Dalton was believed to have died of exhaustion.[9] As for the other two, a newspaper report of the day – the *Hobart Town Gazette and Van Diemen's Land Advertiser* – wrote on Saturday 16 November 1822 that two prisoners who returned to the settlement made an "ineffectual effort to pass the mountains, so far exhausted from want of food, that they died in the hospital a few days after. These men stated, that previous to their leaving the others, one had been killed to afford sustenance to the rest. Of the farther progress and fate of the five wretched men who survived nothing has been heard, but it may be believed to have terminated in greater horrors."[10] That was indeed to come.

Even with this confession of sorts from one of the escapees that cannibalism took place, Reverend Knopwood either did not hear of it or did not believe it.

Above: A painting of Reverend Knopwood by artists Dunnett, Gregson and Graves (1763-1838). Source: Wikimedia Commons.

Decline and despair

The remaining five starving men, including Alexander Pearce, survived a little longer on wild berries and roasting their kangaroo jackets.[11] They made their way to Gordon's River, and unbeknown to prisoner Thomas Bodenham, he was the next 'nominated' victim to feed the men, all of whom agreed they would partake of his remains to spread culpability. The plan was that Pearce, along with John Mathers, would gather firewood, while Bob Greenhill and Matthew Travers killed Thomas Bodenham. And so, they did.[12]

Pearce then told how a few days later, as they crossed a river – dragging Matthew Travers by a pole as he could not swim – Travers along with Bob Greenhill then suggested John Mathers be killed as their next source of food. Poor Mathers, a baker by trade and all of 24-years-of-age,[13] suffered a much more brutal murder, as Pearce admitted that he and Matthew Travers held Mathers while Bob Greenhill killed him with an axe.

Pearce claimed they could barely taste the flesh of John Mathers, but they ate nevertheless to keep up their strength. Due to weakness, they advanced no more than eight kilometres (five miles) over the next few days. Matthew Travers must have known his time was coming to be the sacrifice for the remaining prisoners, after receiving a snake bite to the foot.[14] The 27-year-old's foot had swollen, rendering him almost lame. Sure enough, Greenhill did the deed which, according to Pearce, took place while Pearce gathered the firewood.[15]

Travers' remains sustained them for some days but then it was just the two of them, and Pearce recounted that both men tried to kill the other when they were distracted or off guard. Succumbing to sleep, Bob Greenhill met his maker at the hands of Pearce, who then ate for the next four days on Greenhill's remains. Now Pearce was alone and had three days without food, scavenging what he could along the banks of the Derwent River.

And so it was that Alexander Pearce, the former farm labourer who was sent to prison for theft, had lost his will to live. He had found himself in this situation, in this land, after stealing six pairs of shoes and being sentenced to seven years transportation.[16] It was over. He claimed to have yelled out, hoping the natives would put an end to him. But it was bushrangers who found him and returned him to the prison. Pearce told of his cannibalistic crimes, but Reverend Knopwood, acting as the magistrate, thought it fanciful and refused to believe him. He assumed the other escapees were alive and had taken up life as bushrangers. Pearce was promptly sent back to prison life on Sarah Island.

Above: (1870) Photograph of Sarah Island. Source: Libraries Tasmania.

The crime to end all crimes

Pearce endured the brutal conditions for another year until Thomas Cox (aged 21 est.) coaxed him into escaping; Pearce and Cox were in the same work gang. Pearce claimed Thomas Cox was always egging him on to escape with him. When Pearce's shirt was stolen and he faced corporal punishment because it was missing, he agreed to go with Cox.

Prepared to brave the elements – it was November, and warmer than the winter months – they made their escape and for two days pushed their way through the forest until reaching the beach by day three. Tired and having not eaten, they became distracted by hunger as they travelled for another two days towards Port Dalrymple, arriving at King's River. The men sought a reprieve for four days, laying low to avoid the troops in pursuit. By now they were starving.

Overcome by famine and no stranger to what had to be done, Pearce decided he would kill Thomas Cox and eat his flesh. Waiting until Cox was asleep, he took an axe and finished him off, and for another night, survived by eating the remains of his former gang mate. The soldiers had gone, but Pearce, with food in his stomach, returned to the settlement and gave himself up.[17]

When he heard in court that parts of Thomas Cox's body were found in Pearce's pockets, the Reverend Knopwood stopped short. Perhaps there was something to the cannibal confession he had heard a year prior. Pearce told the court that "he had killed Cox because when they reached King's

River, he discovered that Cox could not swim."[18] According to Pearce, he struck Thomas Cox three times and young Thomas Cox, seeing that Pearce was walking away, begged him to finish him off, and Pearce obliged him.[19] It provided a solution to his state of starvation.

Pearce pleaded not guilty to Cox's death but told the court "he had cut off a bit of his [Cox's] flesh to show what had become of him."[20] Now the Reverend Knopwood realised some further investigation was warranted into Pearce's previous escape of 20 September 1822 for 113 days, half of it in the wilderness with seven other men. The Reverend asked the question… where were the remaining prisoners – Matthew Travers, Robert 'Bob' Greenhill, Bill Cornelius, Alexander Dalton, John Mathers, Thomas Bodenham and Edward Brown?

But first, to verify what became of Thomas Cox, a small party including Pearce was ordered to find Cox's body and retrieve it. They found a torso with "the hands cut off, the bowels were torn out, and the greater part of the breech and thighs gone, as were the calf of the legs, and the fleshy parts of the arms."[21] The head was soon found nearby, along with the liver, and more damning evidence – a blood-stained axe. Pearce was asked directly if it was the axe he used to kill Thomas Cox and he responded that it was.[22]

The deaths of the other men did not factor in Alexander Pearce's sentencing. He was hanged on Monday 19 July 1824 for murdering Thomas Cox. Father Philip Conolly was by his side. A portrait was drawn of Alexander Pearce after his execution and he did not earn a decent burial.

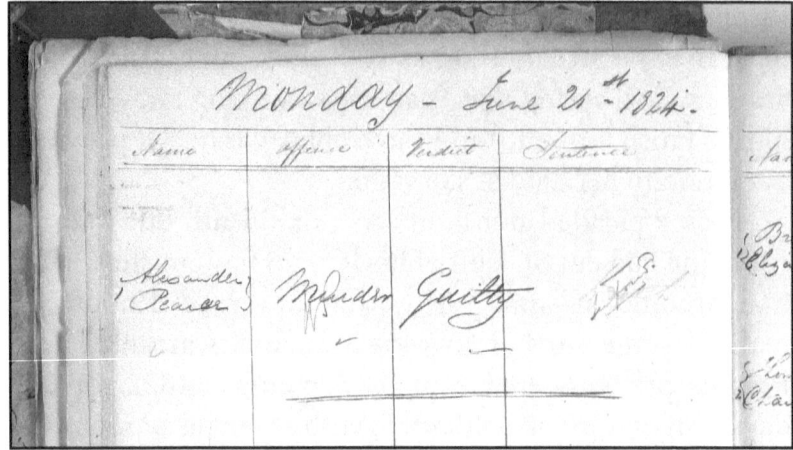

Above: The original court document bearing Alexander Pearce's guilty sentence on 21 June 1824. Source: Libraries Tasmania.

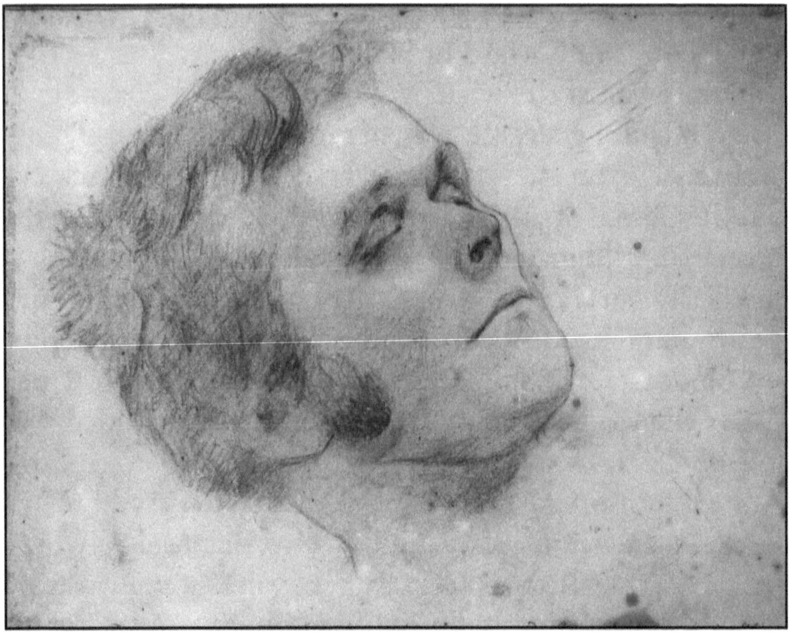

Above: The face of Alexander Pearce sketched, after his execution. Source: Tasmanian Archive and Heritage Office, Libraries Tasmania.

The aftermath

Pearce was not charged with cannibalism.

Father Philip Conolly, who stood on the platform with Alexander Pearce before he was hanged, stated the severity of the sentence was necessary, but he had great empathy for Pearce, believing the punishments Pearce had endured and the lashings received created desperation which made escape an attractive alternative. As Father Conolly stated, sadly: "the unfortunate Pearce was more willing to die than to live."[23]

As for Father Conolly, he passed away 15 years later and was buried in the Roman Catholic burial ground in Harrington Street, Hobart Town. But his remains, along with those of four archbishops, were exhumed in September 2021 from below what was now the floor of the North Transept of the Cathedral and interred in the Cathedral's crypt in December of that year.[24]

After the hanging sentence was completed, Alexander Pearce's body was removed from suspension and taken to the hospital for dissection. His skull was believed to have been sold by the Assistant Colonial Surgeon to an American phrenologist (a person who studies the skull for mental traits) and now remains at the University of Pennsylvania Museum.[25]

During its time as a penal settlement, 112 convicts escaped Sarah Island, of whom sixty-two perished in the attempt and nine were murdered by their fellow escapees. The remaining forty-one were all eventually recaptured. In its years of service, approximately 1200 men and women were sentenced to serve time there.[26]

The Reverend Knopwood, who was shocked by the confession and initially refused to believe it, was a prolific writer and diary-keeper, but if he did make mention of it in his diary it is unlikely to be more than a short notice as most entries were brief, such as: "The day was very hot"; or "Engaged all the morn upon business till 1 pm when I went on board the *Myrtle* to speak to Capt Barber. I returned home to dinner"; "Mr. H. requested that I would marry him as this morn at 8. He was very forward in spirits. I told him that I could not marry him till I had asked the Banns"; and "at half past 10 I went to the Farm with the Governor to inflict punishment upon some men, and returned to dinner."[27]

The Reverend Knopwood died a pauper, with sickness and poverty knocking on his door for the last years of his life. For some time, his grave bore no headstone, until his daughter, adopted as a baby when her mother was abandoned by a sailor, sought to put a headstone on his resting place. She also inherited his remaining property.[28]

Author George Boxall in his 1908 book, *History of the Australian Bushrangers* claimed: "The truth came out after his [Alexander Pearce's] conviction, when he said that man's flesh was delicious, far better than fish or pork" and fellow prisoner and victim, Bob Greenhill said of cannibalism, that he "had seen the like done before, and it eat much like pork."[29] There is, however, no record of this in any of the newspaper reports of the trial, or in Father Conolly's telling of the tale. It was, after all, starvation that drove the men to perform the act of cannibalism and when questioned at his trial in 1824 about how he could do such a deed, Alexander Pearce answered: "No person can tell what he will do when driven by hunger."[30]

References:

1 'Pearce, Alexander (c. 1790–1824)', People Australia, National Centre of Biography, *Australian National University*, https://peopleaustralia.anu.edu.au/biography/pearce-alexander-31474/text38929

2 Monks, Linda, 'Knopwood, Robert (Bobby) (1763–1838)', Australian Dictionary of Biography, National Centre of Biography, *Australian National University*, https://adb.anu.edu.au/biography/knopwood-robert-bobby-2314/text3003, published first in hardcopy 1967, accessed online 19 April 2022.

3 Monks, Linda, 'Conolly, Philip (1786–1839)', Australian Dictionary of Biography, National Centre of Biography, *Australian National University*, https://adb.anu.edu.au/biography/conolly-philip-1915/text2275, published first in hardcopy 1966, accessed online 20 April 2022.

4 Hobart Town Gazette. (1824, August 6). *Hobart Town Gazette and Van Diemen's Land Advertiser (Tas.: 1821 - 1825)*, p. 3. Retrieved April 19, 2022, from http://nla.gov.au/nla.news-article1090286

5 Raynor, Kate, The Last Confession of Alexander Raynor, *ATOM*. Retrieved 20 April 2022 from URL: https://files.clickviewapp.com/v1/files/abc11b8a805f4814b48a29f0b015a1fb

6 'Pearce, Alexander (c. 1790–1824)', People Australia, National Centre of Biography, Op.cit.

7 Hobart Town Gazette. (1824, August 6). *Hobart Town Gazette and Van Diemen's Land Advertiser (Tas.: 1821 - 1825)*, p. 3. Retrieved April 19, 2022, from http://nla.gov.au/nla.news-article1090286

8 No Title (1839, February 8). *The Tasmanian (Hobart Town, Tas.: 1827 - 1839)*, p. 4. Retrieved April 19, 2022, from http://nla.gov.au/nla.news-article232803516

9 'Bodenham, Thomas (?–1822)', People Australia, National Centre of Biography, *Australian National University*, https://peopleaustralia.anu.edu.au/biography/bodenham-thomas-31484/text38939

10 Hobart Town. (1822, November 16). *Hobart Town Gazette and Van Diemen's Land Advertiser (Tas.: 1821 - 1825)*, p. 2. Retrieved April 19, 2022, from http://nla.gov.au/nla.news-article1089800

11, 12 Hobart Town Gazette. (1824, August 6). *Hobart Town Gazette and Van Diemen's Land Advertiser (Tas.: 1821 - 1825)*, p. 3. Retrieved from http://nla.gov.au/nla.news-article1090286

13 'Mather, John (c. 1798–1822)', People Australia, National Centre of Biography, *Australian National University*, https://peopleaustralia.anu.edu.au/biography/mather-john-31483/text38938

14 'Bodenham, Thomas (?–1822)', People Australia, National Centre of Biography. Op.cit.

15 *Hobart Town Gazette*. (1824, August 6). Op. cit.

16 'Pearce, Alexander (c. 1790–1824)', Op.cit.

17 *Hobart Town Gazette*. (1824, August 6). Op.cit.

18 'Pearce, Alexander (c. 1790–1824)', Op.cit.

19 - 22 The Supreme Court of Van Diemen's Land. (1824, June 25). *Hobart Town Gazette and Van Diemen's Land Advertiser (Tas.: 1821 - 1825)*, p 2. http://nla.gov.au/nla.news-article1090236

23 *Hobart Town Gazette*. (1824, August 6). Op. cit.

24 Sheehan, Catherine, Bishops of Hobart laid to rest in St Mary's crypt, *Archdiocese of Hobart*, December 14, 2021. Retrieved 25 July 2022 from URL: https://hobart.catholic.org.au/2021/12/14/bishops-of-hobart-laid-to-rest-in-st-marys-crypt/

25 'Pearce, Alexander (c. 1790–1824)', Op.cit.

26 Raynor, Kate, The Last Confession... Op.cit.

27 Knopwood, Robert 1946, 'The diary of the Rev. Robert Knopwood, 1805-1808. pt.1', Papers... the Royal Society of Tasmania. *University of Tasmania*. Retrieved 20 April 2022 from: https://eprints.utas.edu.au/13550/

28 Monks, Linda, 'Knopwood, Robert (Bobby). Op.cit.

29 The Early Bushrangers. (1899, November 25). *The Australasian (Melb, Vic.: 1864 - 1946)*, p. 49. Retrieved April 19, 2022, from http://nla.gov.au/nla.news-article138611135

30 The Supreme Court of Van Diemen's Land. Op.cit.

Images:

-Reid, D. L. [photographer], Grave of Rev Robert Knopwood, *Find a Grave*, Memorial ID 124198951. Retrieved 20 April 2022 from: https://www.findagrave.com/memorial/124198951/robert-knopwood

-Dunnett, F., T.G. Gregson), JW Graves [artists], Painting of Reverend Robert Knopwood (1763-1838). *Wikimedia Commons*. Retrieved 20 April 2022 from URL: https://commons.wikimedia.org/w/index.php?title=File:Robert_Knopwood_(1763-1838).jpg&oldid=609248604.

-(1870). Photograph - Sarah Island, Macquarie Harbour. *Libraries Tasmania*. Retrieved 20 April 2022 from URL: https://stors.tas.gov.au/AI/NS1013-1-1866

-Court document, Alexander Pearce guilty, 21 June 1824. Prosecutions Project ID: 270962. *Libraries Tasmania*. Retrieved 20 April 2022 from URL: https://stors.tas.gov.au/NI/1522737

-(1860). Photograph - Sketches from the Dixson Library, Sydney, of the face of Pearce, Alexander, after his execution. Tasmanian Archive and Heritage Office, *Libraries Tasmania*. Retrieved 19 April 2022 from URL: https://trove.nla.gov.au/work/235060379

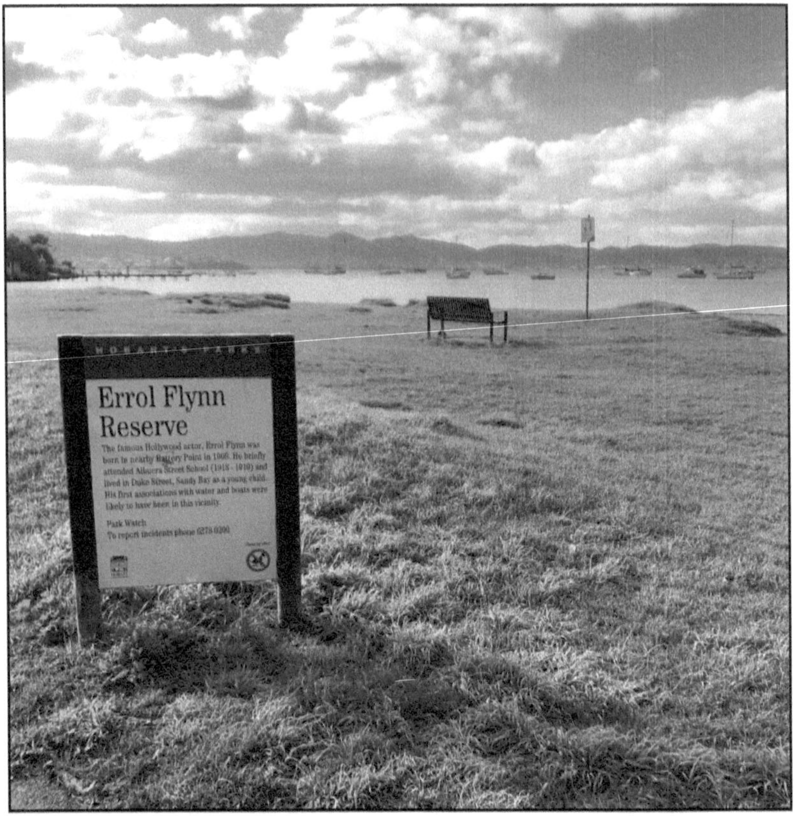
Errol Flynn
Reserve
Park Watch

1909

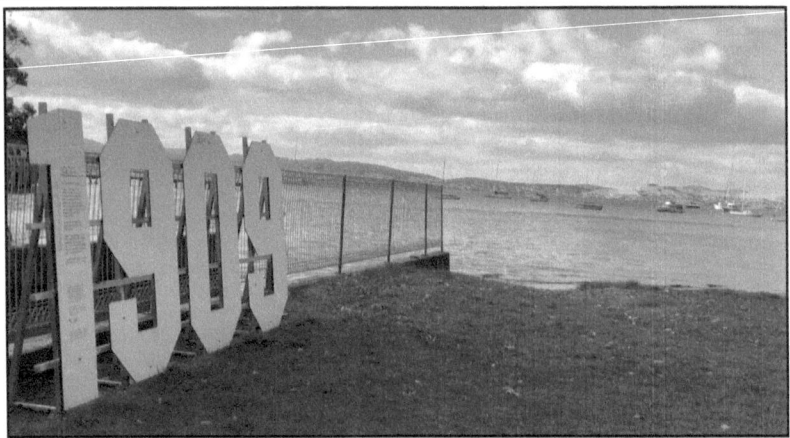

The Flynns of Sandy Bay
Errol and Theodore Flynn

Memorial: **Errol Flynn Reserve**
Named after Errol Leslie Thomson Flynn,
20 June 1909 – 14 October 1959 (aged 50
years).

Location: Marieville Esplanade, Sandy Bay, TAS 7005.

Above: Portrait of Errol Flynn c1940s. Source: National Library of Australia.

"I shall return"[1] were the prophetic last words of debonair, larger-than-life actor, Errol Flynn, who at the age of 50 in 1959, passed away from a massive heart attack. In his 50 years, Flynn had set hearts on fire, travelled the world, and was arguably Australia's most successful acting export of the early to mid-20th century. But it began humbly in 1909 in Tasmania, when a university professor and his wife gave birth to their first son and the first Flynn to be born in Tasmania.

The Flynns in the community

Proud parents, Theodore and Lily welcomed Errol Leslie Thompson Flynn, born in the relatively new Queen Alexandra Hospital, on Hampden Road, Battery Point in the chilly month of June 1909. It had been a whirlwind time for the family. Not only did Errol arrive, but the pair were only in their first year of marriage, their first year in Tasmania, and Theodore was in the first year of his new posting as a lecturer at the University of Tasmania. Had he known then his son would become one of the world's most famous actors, he no doubt could have been knocked down with a feather from one of the native birds he studied (although marsupials were his major line of study).

The Flynn family actively participated in their new Tasmanian community. Not long after he arrived, Theodore joined the Field Naturalists Club which fuelled his interest in marine biology. The year after, he led the club on an excursion to Wineglass Bay. His long ten-year involvement with the group culminated in his election as Chairman in 1918 and 1919. His out of office involvement also included an appointment to the Council of the Royal Society in 1911, and curator and Trustee of the Tasmanian Museum and Botanical Garden in 1911.[2]

It was green pastures for Theodore Flynn who was initially appointed as a lecturer to the University of Tasmania, but a generous bequest to the university two years later, saw the creation of a new discipline – a biology department, with funds to endow a chair (professor), a brand new laboratory and equipment. Thus, Theodore Flynn was appointed the inaugural Professor of Biology in 1911 with a remit to research

Above: The Field Naturalists Club. Theodore is far left and inset above.
Source: Tasmanian Archive and Heritage Office, Libraries Tasmania.

diseases of plants and animals, Tasmania's unique marsupials, and other research projects that the trustees approved.[3]

In 1912, when Errol was three, Theodore joined Mawson's Australian Antarctic Expedition as the biologist in charge (he had met Mawson at school and university). What Theodore lacked in experience, he made up for with enthusiasm and a year later he delivered a presentation to the Royal Society on the findings and results. As a consequence, his involvement was commemorated with the naming of Flynn Lake on the west coast of Macquarie Island.[4]

As he grew, young Errol became actively involved in catching bettongs (rat kangaroos) for his father's research on their reproduction process, and making a few shillings at the same time. He wrote in his autobiography: "When school finished, I raced home to be at his side, to hurry out into the back yard, where we had cages of specimens of rare animals... Through Father's activity I made my first venture into commerce. He bought all the kangaroo rats [bettongs] he could get hold of for Hobart University. I learned to set box traps in the hills of near-by Mount Wellington. He paid a shilling a head."[5]

In return, his father described him as "a happy, sunny little fellow, always getting into boyish scrapes" such as the time Errol went to a children's birthday party at the bishop's house. Errol's mother received a call from the bishop's wife saying "I'm terribly sorry, Mrs Flynn, but I will have to send your little boy home. We left him in the garden for a moment and he has tipped all the little girls into the ornamental fountain."[6] Even then Errol liked to tease the girls but perhaps on this occasion, they did not think as fondly of him. In later years, Theodore would say of his son that it was Errol's charm that got him into trouble.[7]

Flynn's mother, Lily (who later changed her name to Marelle), loved the outdoors but also had a love for the arts. Errol said: "Mother played the piano. She sang. She danced. Apparently she had theatrical ambitions. Once a theatrical group came through Hobart, and mother was paid to do a swimming bit."[8] At the age of nine, Errol took on a minor role as a page boy to Enid Lyons as 'Queen of the Public Service' in Hobart's 1918 Queen Carnival.

Dame Enid's husband, Joseph, would become Prime Minister and in her book, *So We Take Comfort*, she recalled young Errol and described him as: "Dressed in his mauve satin suit with lace ruffles at his wrists and silver buckles on his shoes, he was a dashing figure – a handsome boy of nine with a fearless, somewhat haughty expression, already showing that sang-froid for which he was later to become famous throughout the civilised world."[9]

But the cherubic looking young lad then returned to his outdoor adventures, and he remained a doted-on only child until the age of ten when his sister, Rosemary, was born. Later in life, Errol

Above: Errol with Enid Lyons. Source: Museum of Australian Democracy.

Flynn recalled: "The two main streams of thinking in the family were of the earth; the primordial creatures in the nearly impenetrable Tasmanian wilderness, and the eternal oceans. My primary interest became the sea. I would listen to anyone who would talk of it."[10]

Learning and lessons

Theodore may have been noted for his studious and learned nature but he cut a dashing figure like his son and was also somewhat eccentric. He was remembered as "full of pranks", "a flamboyant teacher", a man who stood "tall among his successors being a stronger character than most of them", "an excellent teacher who took a great interest in his students: at least those who showed an interest in the subject", "very industrious but also gregarious and friendly" and a "very powerful personality full of drive and energy that led him into many adventures, credible or otherwise".[11]

Errol's description of Theodore showed the love between father and son when he said: "The rapport was with my father. He looked Irish. He had red, bushy eyebrows, black hair; he was lean, angular, full of charm, goodwill, and a certain professorial quietness. He spoke with a clipped British accent, tinged with touches of Irish brogue."[12]

But despite the studious and learned nature of his father, Errol – who grew to be a tall, robust boy – was rebellious in the classroom and one wonders if it embarrassed his father.[13] Young Flynn railed against authority which saw him expelled from several Hobart schools including the Hutchins School – an Anglican College in Hobart; the Friends School; and Albuera Street Primary School.[14] His education continued at boarding schools in London and Sydney.

Off to 'sea' the world

As soon as he turned 18, Errol departed to discover the world, beginning in Sydney. The year was 1927, and the world was his oyster. He secured a job with a shipping company and sailed to New Guinea. Not afraid of hard work and trying something new, he worked as a tobacco plantation overseer, did some gold prospecting, and penned several articles for the *Sydney Bulletin* on life in the 'jungle'. Three years later he returned home, excited to learn his father had bought him a yacht, '*The Sirocco*'[15]. Now aged 21, he sailed from Sydney back to New Guinea (some 1660 nautical miles) with friends. The Tasmanian *Mercury* reported on the unknown young man's adventure on 13 March 1930, notably as his father's son:

> "*To set sail from Sydney for New Guinea in a 13-ton yacht is something of an undertaking, and certainly it is not an adventure most people would face with equanimity. Yet the crew of the good ship Sirocco, which has just set out on this venture, will not fail through lack of keenness. The navigator is Errol Flynn, a son of Professor Flynn, of Hobart. Another Tasmanian – an ex-Cambridge man – T. Adams, is one of the four. Flynn has a plantation 200 miles from Rabaul, and he has undertaken the voyage as a means of returning home, while the others are seeking adventure and wealth.*"[16]

Errol told his father that they ran short of food and oil and funds, so went ashore at a small port to earn some money to keep the trip afloat. Theodore recalled his son's story: "Outside a boxing booth at a travelling fair a gorilla of a man called Battling Bilson was offering five pounds to anyone who would stand up to him for three rounds... Errol's companions looked at each other, then at Errol, who at six-foot two stood head and shoulders above them. He ducked under the ropes... stripped to his underpants, started a slogging match. Errol told me later, 'I got the five pounds and we bought food, but I'd taken so many punches on the chin that I wasn't able to eat for a week.'"

Back in Tasmania, Theodore found himself without a chair when in 1931, the funding was cut for research and only enough remained to support a lectureship. Thus after 22 years, Theodore and the family left Tasmania and took up a university chair at the Queen's University, Belfast, where he remained, conducting research until retiring in 1948.[17]

Meanwhile, Errol's financial management skills were found lacking. He said in his autobiography, *My Wicked, Wicked Ways*: "My problem lies in reconciling my gross habits with my net income"[18] and never a truer word was spoken – he had racked up debts of some concern. Errol needed a new venture, and his mother's interest in the arts rubbed off on him. His acting experience amounted to a small part in a documentary, but his looks were certainly a drawcard. The timing was just right on his return as a Sydney-based production of '*In the Wake of the Bounty*' was being cast – the story of the mutiny on the *Bounty*.

Errol claimed an interesting connection with the mutineers – his mother's ancestor was Midshipman Edward Young, who was on the *Bounty* and a participant in the mutiny. Young was dispatched to Pitcairn Island with Fletcher Christian. Supposedly, a sword that hung in their Tasmanian home had been one of the infamous Captain Bligh's and bequeathed to Lily.[19] An interesting connection but one that is disputed. Errol – with his dashing looks – was cast in the role of Fletcher Christian. Despite the best efforts of the director Charles Chauvet and three long months of shooting on location on Pitcairn Island, the film released in 1933 did not set the world on fire, and neither did Errol's performance. Two years later, the film *Mutiny on the Bounty* starring Clarke Gable enjoyed box office success. Nevertheless, Errol was an actor, and it lit a flame within him for more acting roles.

Finding his acting chops

A move to England was on the cards now, and Errol, 24, spent the year of 1933 picking up roles as he could get them before securing a place the following year at the Northampton Repertory Theatre. Here he enjoyed roles and training, of which he'd had little to that point. Parts in British films followed including 'Murder at Monte Carlo', which opened doors for him. Irving Asher, a talent scout from Warner Bros., saw Errol in action and while the role was not award-worthy, he saw Errol's charisma radiating off the screen and signed him.[20] His career had begun in earnest.

Many films followed, in part thanks to Errol's first wife (he was engaged once before but never married). While on a ship from London, Errol met Lili Damita, a fellow actor five years older than himself, and they married in 1935. Lili was an established French-American actress and singer, and Errol was relatively unknown by comparison. Her networks would prove most useful to him. He scored a minor role in *The Case of the Curious Bride* and *Don't Bet on Blondes* in that same year (1935).

Above: Errol and his first wife, Lili Damita, at Union Airport, 1941.
Source: Los Angeles Times, UCLA digital collection.

Then came his break – 'Captain Blood'. Warner Bros. considered several actors for the role, including Leslie Howard and James Cagney, but Errol won the lead opposite 19-year-old Olivia de Havilland with whom a screen passion was obvious. The film was an enormous hit, and so were its two leads; it made the studio a fortune. Olivia would go on to star in Gone with the Wind in 1939 but would partner with

Above: Errol in Captain Blood, 1935. Source: Wikipedia.
Below: Errol and Olivia de Havilland in the hit movie, The Adventures of Robin Hood, 1938. Source: Wikimedia.

Errol for seven more films. Errol was off and running – an international movie star, and more successes followed, with films one after the other including *The Charge of the Light Brigade* (1936) with Olivia de Havilland again. It was Warner Bros.' No. 1 hit movie of 1936.[21] Next came *Green Light* (1937), Errol playing a doctor; *The Prince and the Pauper* (1937); *Another Dawn* (1937); and *The Perfect Specimen* (1937).

During this time, despite the frenetic film schedule, Errol published a book about his adventures sailing around Australia as a youth, titled *Beam Ends*. And at the peak of his bankability as a star, he travelled to Spain in 1937, impassioned by the Spanish Civil War, to work as a war correspondent and inform objectively on the conflict. Unfortunately, his travelling companion was the photographer, Hermann Erben, whose Nazi connections blackened Errol's reputation. No evidence exists that Errol knew of Hermann's loyalties, and as "esteemed Hollywood director Vincent Sherman says, Flynn was not racist or harboured prejudices of any kind … he just didn't care what you were."[22]

The following year Errol was back in the studio with *The Adventures of Robin Hood* (1938), again opposite Olivia de Havilland, which was a global hit made in Technicolor and with the highest budget for a Warner Bros. film to date. It returned its budget investment with a huge profit.[23] Following was the unsuccessful *Four's a Crowd* (1938) again with Oliva, but *The Sisters* (1938) with Bette Davis did reasonably well. Next, *The Dawn Patrol* (1938) with co-stars Basil Rathbone and David Niven which, with an all-male and predominantly British cast, was said to be one of "fraternal good cheer".[24]

Larger than life

Despite his enormous profile, Errol tried to enlist to fight in the Second World War (with the US armed services) but failed because of illness. He threw himself back into his work, with reporters calling him a draft dodger. However, the studio would not allow to be known that their athletic, dashing and handsome box-office star had health problems.[25]

There were many more films to follow including the 1940 western film, *Santa Fe Trail*. Errol was paired with Olivia de Havilland again. It was another hit, ranking among the higher grossing films of the year, and the seventh Flynn–de Havilland film. Next came a step in a different direction – a mystery where Errol played an amateur detective – *Footsteps in the Dark* (1941). His co-star, Ralph Bellamy, said of the then 32-year-old Errol, he was "a darling. Couldn't or wouldn't take himself seriously. And he drank like there was no tomorrow. Had a bum ticker from the malaria he'd picked up in Australia. Also a spot of TB. Tried to enlist but flunked his medical, so he drank some more. Knew he wouldn't live into old age. He really had a ball in *Footsteps in the Dark*."[26]

In that same year, he and his actress wife, Lila, gave birth to Errol's only son, Sean Flynn. The year after, he and Lila divorced, bitterly, after seven years of marriage. Over the years his family remained a constant in his life – his mother, father and little sister visited him on the set of his films and on his yacht, and despite the divorce, his parents remained in touch and friendly with Lili and the wives to come.[27] He continued his prolific film schedule and in 1942 Errol played an Australian in the WWII film *Desperate Journey* (1942); it was a huge hit.

Above: Errol and Olivia de Havilland in Santa Fe Trail. Source: Wikimedia.
Below: Advertising for Errol's motion picture, 'Footsteps in the Dark', 1941.
Source: State Library of Victoria.

But he claimed his favourite role was that of the boxer, Gentleman Jim Corbett in the film *Gentleman Jim* (1942) which Warner Bros. purchased the rights to make from Corbett's widow, specifically for Errol to play.[28] Errol trained extensively and did most of his own boxing scenes. Again, it was an enormous hit for Warner Bros.

Perhaps it was the Australian way of being self-deprecating or because he was not formally trained and felt a lack of confidence in his ability, but Errol Flynn was said to be never confident in his acting skills. The director, Lewis Milestone, said: "Flynn kept underrating himself. If you wanted to embarrass him, all you had to do was to tell him how great he was in a scene he'd just finished playing: He'd blush like a young girl and muttering 'I'm no actor' would go away somewhere and sit down."[29] Yet, he was consistently Warner Bros.' biggest box office star in many varied roles, from mystery to adventure.

Health in decline

On set in 1942, at 33, Errol collapsed, claiming in his autobiography it was a mild heart attack. But it would be another seventeen years until his heart did claim him. The remaining years of Errol's life were in keeping with his nature displayed as a wild young Tasmanian scholar – adventurous, rebellious and often pushing the envelope. Bouts of successes, fighting and public drunkenness (possibly embellished by the studio), charges of rape (of which he was acquitted) were all media fodder. He famously said: "It isn't what they say about you, it's what they whisper"[30] and he did little to discourage the whispers.

Above: Errol as James J. Corbett in "Gentleman Jim", ca. 1942.
Source: National Libary of Australia.

In 1943 Errol remarried, taking Nora Eddington, 19, to be his second wife (*pictured right*) and at 36 fathered Deirdre and at age 38, another daughter, Rory. His marriage to Nora ended in 1949 when he was 40, and he remarried in 1950, aged 41, to another actress, Patrice Wymore, 24, (*pictured left*) with whom he had a daughter, Arnella Roma. In his autobiography, Errol described Patrice as "reserved, she had beauty and dignity. [She] typified everything I long for…everything I am not." [31] Patrice was widowed at 33 and never remarried.

Left: Errol's wife/widow, Patrice Wymore. Source: Pix, National Library Aust.
Right: Second wife, Nora Eddington. Source: Los Angeles Times, UCLA.

Errol died before his wives and children; his parents also survived him. In 1959 while visiting a friend, Dr Grant Gould in Vancouver, intending to sell the doctor his yacht, Errol complained of back pain. He told Dr Gould and their guests that he was going to lie down, but "I shall return".[32]

Two hours later, he suffered a heart attack and could not be revived despite the valiant efforts of his friends and medical staff. His guest, Miss Beverly Aadland, 17, was "deeply shocked"[33] but remained by his side, even travelling with him in the ambulance when his body was removed to the hospital. Errol was still married to Patrice at the time.

Above: Errol's coffin on Los Angeles Union Station train platform, Calif., 19 October 1959. Source: Los Angeles Times, UCLA collection.

His death was not a shock to the family. Theodore told of Errol's doctor warning them their son's heart was weak and to expect the worst; Errol did not tell them.[34] But Errol's daughter, Rory, 12 at the time of his death told *Cinema Retro* magazine "shortly before he died, he told my mother [Nora] that he was only given a year to live, but he only made it three more months."[35] She also told of receiving the letters her father had written to her mother and being delighted: "I realised what a romantic man he was. He definitely romanced my mother through words in his letters, and kept her intrigued with his adventures... I grasp at it."[36]

Errol was buried at Forest Lawn Memorial Park Cemetery in California – a place he was said to have hated. His plaque reads: "In memory of our father from his loving children." His legacy remains – an astonishing portfolio of stage and

Above: Errol's grave and plaque in California. Source: Wikimedia.

screen work including more than 64 films and TV roles, and a life that lived up to his motto: "I intend to live the first half of my life. I don't care about the rest."[37]

A father's pain

After the death of his son, Theodore wrote a series of articles titled, *My Son Errol*, that were printed in various publications including the *Women's Weekly* in Australia in December 1959. In the articles he bemoaned Errol's reputation as a womaniser, blaming the studios for fuelling the lie, including a story of one occasion when Rosemary visited her brother – she was then 15 – and soon stories claimed Errol was in a hotel room with a young girl.

Theodore claimed Errol was "more sinned against than sinning."[38] He recalled another incident when the family and guests were dining out together, including daughter Rosemary, when the conversation got lively. "Errol made some strong remarks. Somebody touched him on the arm and rebuked him mildly. He calmed down at once and changed the subject. The next day I was shocked to read a newspaper headline: '*Errol Flynn drunk and disorderly in Hollywood cafe: famous star in uproar again.*' The story gave a graphic and wholly imaginary description…. Errol's reaction to this calumnious story surprised me. 'Nothing to worry about,' he said. 'Don't blame the newspaper. Someone in the studio has put them up to it. It's all publicity.'"[39]

When Theodore and Marelle first received the telegram from Errol, advising Warner Bros. had signed him, Theodore was not surprised, saying of his son, "he was marvellous to look at. They all said he was the most handsome man they had ever had in Hollywood. And his manners were perfect. Inevitably, I suppose, women were attracted to him… They simply could not leave him alone."[40] Of their relationship, he wrote that the family's love for Errol "ran like a golden thread through his all-too-short life. He telephoned his mother only a few days before his death."[41]

Above: Errol and Theodore Flynn aboard Errol's yacht, c.1946.
Source: National Library of Australia.

What became of…

Marelle (Lily) Flynn, Errol's mother, died eight years after her son, in 1967 (some reports list December 1966 and 1968). Aged 77, she was hit by a car while crossing the street.[42] His father, **Theodore** died on Wednesday 23 October 1968, nine years after his son, Errol. Theodore, 85 at the time of his death, was a resident at a nursing home in Hampshire, England.

Errol's sister, **Rosemary**, who was also born in Hobart, went on to study art at Queen's University Belfast where her father, Theodore, was a professor of zoology. At age 20, she announced her engagement to solicitor James S. Elliott, and was said to be working in the Belfast naval canteen when a telegram of congratulations arrived from Errol.[43] Rosemary did not complete her degree and her marriage did not last.[44] She remarried in 1947 to Airforce Officer Charles A. Warner, and lived a life abroad at numerous military posts. Rosemary loved and actively supported the arts, particularly the opera and orchestra. She died of cancer in Germany, aged 61, survived by her husband.[45]

Sean Flynn: Errol never knew the torment that befell his ex-wife, Lili, with the mysterious disappearance of their son, Sean. Like his father, Sean took to acting, but soon was bored with it, and also like his father, took a keen interest in news and politics. He became a photojournalist and secured a contract with *Time* magazine, covering the Vietnam War. Travelling with the US Army Special Forces units, he often faced danger and in April 1970 on assignment in Cambodia, communist guerrillas captured Sean, 28, and fellow photojournalist Dana Stone. They were never heard from again and declared dead in 1984.[46] **Lili** died of Alzheimer's disease in March 1994, in Florida, aged 89.[47] When Errol's biography was brought to the screen, actress, Barbara Hershey played Lili.

Errol's second wife, **Nora Eddington** died in 2001, aged 77, having fought a long battle with kidney disease. She is buried in Los Angeles. His third wife, **Patrice Wymore**, lived to the age of 87. She contracted a pulmonary disease and passed away in Portland, Jamaica a year later, in 2014. She is survived by her grandson, Luke Flynn.[48] At the time of going to print, two of his three daughters are still alive and living overseas.

Remembering the Flynns of Sandy Bay

Errol Flynn remembered the hearty years of his youth spent on a beach in Tasmania. He recalled: "A beach, Sandy Bay, was not far away and I was often there, swimming from the age of three. The beach was of hard brown sand, the water freezing cold. Mother was a good swimmer, and she took me there very often,"[49] And the residents of the birthplace of one of the world's biggest stars have not forgotten him either. On the foreshore in Sandy Bay you will find '*Errol Flynn Reserve*'. There is also the large lettering 1909, a sculpture celebrating the year of Errol's birth and a 'Hollywoodesque' tribute to where Errol's star shone.

Maffra, a stately Victorian weatherboard house built in 1885 that the Flynn family once lived in, is still a private residence but you can drive by at 12 Aberdeen St, Glebe to see the home where Errol Flynn spent some of his childhood.[50]

After her brother's death, Rosemary gave her father

a note that Errol had written to his parents, knowing he would die soon. Theodore shared the note in his tribute articles. It read:

"I am more sorry than words can tell for any trouble I have caused you or for any shame you have ever felt about my life. I love you as I have always loved you. I close my eyes and relive the days when we were all together in Tasmania, in Belfast, and in England. All the glitter and the girls who have been associated with my name mean nothing compared with these memories."[51]

Above: Portrait of Errol Flynn (1930). Source: National Library of Australia.

References:

1 In Vancouver, Errol Flynn dies of a heart attack, *Desert Sun*, Volume XXXIII, Number 26, 15 Oct 1959.
2 - 5 Flynn and Flynn, Biography of Theodore Thomson Flynn, UTAS, *University of Tasmania*, 29 January, 2013. Retrieved 26 April 2022 from URL: https://www.utas.edu.au/library/exhibitions/flynn_and_flynn/ttFlynn.html
6 - 7 My son, Errol (1959, December 30). *The Australian Women's Weekly (1933 - 1982)*, p. 3. Retrieved April 26, 2022, from http://nla.gov.au/nla.news-article44024191
8 Remarkable Characters, Errol Flynn: The Most Famous Tasmanian. *The Museum of Lost Things*, 29 July 2017. Retrieved 25 April 2022 from: https://www.museumoflost.com/errol-flynns-birthplace/
9 Rhodes, Campell, Oh Errol! —what does Errol Flynn have to do with democracy? *MOAD* (Museum of Australian Democracy), 20 Jun 2013. Retrieve 25 April 2022 from URL: https://www.moadoph.gov.au/blog/oh-errol-what-does-errol-flynn-have-to-do-with-democracy/
10 Remarkable Characters, Errol Flynn. Op.cit.
11 - 12 Flynn and Flynn, Biography, Op.cit.
13 Remarkable Characters, Errol Flynn. Op.cit.
14 Wikipedia contributors. Errol Flynn. In *Wikipedia, The Free Encyclopedia*. Retrieved 25 April 25 2022, from https://en.wikipedia.org/w/index.php?title=Errol_Flynn&oldid=1083829330
15 My son, Errol (1959, December 30). Op.cit.
16 The Mainland Day by Day (1930, March 13). *The Mercury (Hobart, Tas.: 1860 - 1954)*, p. 6. Retrieved April 25, 2022, from http://nla.gov.au/nla.news-article29158164
17 Flynn and Flynn, Biography. Op.cit.
18 Quotes, Errol Flynn, *Goodreads*. Retrieved 25 April 2022 from URL: https://www.goodreads.com/author/quotes/14017.Errol_Flynn
19 - 20 Remarkable Characters, Errol Flynn. Op.cit.
21 Glancy, H (1995). "Warner Bros. Film Grosses, 1924–1951: The William Schaefer Ledger". *Historical Journal of Film, Radio and Television*. In *Wikipedia*. Retrieved 25 April 2022 from URL: https://en.wikipedia.org/w/index.php?title=Errol_Flynn&oldid=1083829330
22 Nasht, Simon, Tasmanian Devil: The Fast and Furious Life of Errol Flynn" (PDF). *Flaming Star Films*. Retrieved 25 April 2022 from: http://www.flamingstarfilms.com.au/presskits/Tasmanian_Devil.pdf
23 Mark Glancy Warner Bros. ledgers from Wikipedia contributors. Errol Flynn. In *Wikipedia*. Retrieved 25 April 2022 from: https://en.wikipedia.org/w/index.php?title=Errol_Flynn&oldid=1083829330
24 Kennedy, Matthew. Edmund Goulding's Dark Victory: Hollywood's Bad Boy Genius, Madison, Wisconsin: University of Wisconsin Press, 2004, p. 177. In Errol Flynn. In *Wikipedia*, retrieved 25 April 2022 from: https://en.wikipedia.org/w/index.php?title=Errol_Flynn&oldid=1083829330
25 Wikipedia contributors. (2022, April 21). Errol Flynn. In Wikipedia. Retrieved 04:57, April 25, 2022, from https://en.wikipedia.org/w/index.php?title=Errol_Flynn&oldid=1083829330
26 Bawden, James; Miller, Ron (4 March 2016). Conversations with Classic Film Stars... University Press of Kentucky. p36. In *Wikipedia*. https://en.wikipedia.org/w/index.php?title=Errol_Flynn&oldid=1083829330
27 My son, Errol (1959, December 30). Op.cit.
28 Tony Thomas, Rudy Behlmer* Clifford McCarty, The Films of Errol Flynn, Citadel Press, 1969 pp116–117 in Errol Flynn, *Wikipedia*, https://en.wikipedia.org/w/index.php?title=Errol_Flynn&oldid=1083829330
29 Higham, Charles; Greenberg, Joel (1971). The celluloid muse; Hollywood directors speak. Regnery. p184, in Errol Flynn, *Wikipedia*. https://en.wikipedia.org/w/index.php?title=Errol_Flynn&oldid=1083829330
30 Quotes, Errol Flynn, *Goodreads*. Op.cit.
31 Patricia Wymore Flynn Dies at 87 in Jamaica, The Errol Flynn blog. Retrieved 27 April 2022 from URL: https://www.theerrolflynnblog.com/2014/03/23/patricia-wymore-flynn-dies-at-87-in-jamaica/
32 - 33 In Vancouver, Errol Flynn dies of a heart attack, *Desert Sun*, Volume XXXIII, Number 26, 15 October 1959.
34 My son, Errol (1959, December 30). Op.cit.
35 - 36 Thomas, Nick, Cinema Retro Exclusive Interview with Rory ... November 2009, *Cinema Retro magazine*.
37 Errol Flynn, *Quote Master*. Retrieved 25 April 2022 from URL: https://www.quotemaster.org/qfdff1b2be5fe9cf61e1927489bf1ab47
38 My son, Errol (1959, December 30). Op.cit.
39 He was not a Lothario (1960, January 6). *The Australian Women's Weekly (1933 - 1982)*, p. 10. Retrieved April 26, 2022, from http://nla.gov.au/nla.news-article48530779
40 - 41 My son, Errol (1959, December 30). Op.cit.

42 Tracing footsteps of a swashbuckler, The Argus, 27th November 2000. Retrieved 27 April 2022 from URL: https://www.theargus.co.uk/news/5156435.tracing-footsteps-of-a-swashbuckler/
43 Film Star's Sister Engaged (1941, May 3). *Saturday Evening Express (Launceston, Tas. : 1924 - 1954)*, p. 3. Retrieved April 27, 2022, from http://nla.gov.au/nla.news-article264983943
44 McGonagle, Suzanne Appeal unearths idol's Irish roots, *The Irish News*, 19 Nov 2013. Retrieved 27 April 2002 from: https://www.irishnews.com/news/2013/11/19/news/appeal-unearths-idol-s-irish-roots-76211/
45 Obituary: *Washington Post*, July 1, 1981. Sourced from Nora Rosemary (Flynn) Warner (abt. 1920 - 1981), *WikiTree*. Retrieved 27 April 2022 from: https://www.wikitree.com/wiki/Flynn-2091
46 Kennedy, Helen, Remains of Errol Flynn's son... , *Daily news*, 29 March 2010. Retrieved 25 April 2022 from URL: https://www.nydailynews.com/news/world/remains-errol-flynn-son-photographer-sean-flynn-found-cambodia-mass-grave-article-1.171326
47 Wikipedia contributors. (2021, November 19). Lili Damita. In *Wikipedia*. Retrieved 25 April 2022, from https://en.wikipedia.org/w/index.php?title=Lili_Damita&oldid=1056034542
48 Woo, Elaine, Patrice Wymore Flynn dies at 87... *Los Angeles Times*, 24 March 2014. Retrieved 25 April 2022 from: https://www.latimes.com/local/obituaries/la-me-patrice-wymore-20140325-story.html
49 Remarkable Characters, Errol Flynn. Op.cit.
50 Bevan, Jarrad, A Tasmanian home... *Mercury*, 21 November 2016. Retrieved 26 April 2022 from URL: https://www.themercury.com.au/realestate/a-tasmanian-home-once-lived-in-by-actor-errol-flynn-has-hit-the-market/news-story/c2ff72fbb37af932e65a1b25b9f2bbb4
51 He was not a Lothario (1960, January 6). Op.cit.

Images:

-([194?]). Portrait of Errol Flynn Retrieved April 26, 2022. *National Library of Australia*. Retrieved 26 April 2022 from URL: http://nla.gov.au/nla.obj-136388967

- Tas Field Naturalists Club. Sir William Crowther Collection, Tasmanian Archive & Heritage Office, *Libraries Tasmania*. Retrieved 26 April 2022 from https://stors.tas.gov.au/PH30-1-8972J2K$init=PH30-1-8972

-A young Errol Flynn (right) in costume. *MOAD* (Museum of Australian Democracy), 20 Jun 2013. Retrieve 25 April 2022 from URL: https://www.moadoph.gov.au/blog/oh-errol-what-does-errol-flynn-have-to-do-with-democracy/

-Errol Flynn and his first wife, Lili Damita, at Union Airport as he returned from Honolulu trip, 20 February 1941, *Los Angeles Times Photographic Collection*. Retrieved 25 April 2022 from URL: https://digital.library.ucla.edu/catalog/ark:/21198/zz0002tv21

-Captain Blood: Wikipedia contributors. (2022, April 21). Errol Flynn. In *Wikipedia*. Retrieved 25 April 2022, from https://en.wikipedia.org/w/index.php?title=Errol_Flynn&oldid=1083829330

-The Adventures of Robin Hood (1938) with Olivia de Havilland, by Warner Bros. - Original trailer, Public Domain. *Wikimedia*, retrieved 25 April 2022 from URL: https://commons.wikimedia.org/w/index.php?curid=34085625Wikipedia contributors.

-On the set of the movie, *Santa Fe Trail*, De Havilland Flynn.jpg. (2020, September 1). *Wikimedia Commons*. Retrieved 26 April 2022 from URL: https://commons.wikimedia.org/w/index.php?title=File:Santa_Fe_Trail_De_Havilland_Flynn.jpg&oldid=446716790

-Stainer. (1941). Advertising for Errol Flynn in the motion picture, 'Footsteps in the Dark'. *State Library of Victoria*. Retrieved 26 April 2022 from URL: http://handle.slv.vic.gov.au/10381/248616

-(1940). [Errol Flynn as James J. Corbett in "Gentleman Jim", ca. 1940]. *National Library of Australia*. Retrieved April 26, 2022, from http://nla.gov.au/nla.obj-136642628

-A star gives a party (23 Sept 1950) Patrice Wymore and Errol Flynn. *Pix* Magazine, National Library of Australia. Public domain. Retrieved April 27, 2022, from http://nla.gov.au/nla.obj-468508830

-Errol Flynn and his second wife Nora Eddington Flynn, Calif., 9 Aug 1946, *Los Angeles Times Photographic Collection*. Retrieved 25 April 2022 from https://digital.library.ucla.edu/catalog/ark:/21198/zz0002rswk

-Errol Flynn's coffin on L.A. Union Station train platform, 19 Oct 1959, *Los Angeles Times Photographic Collection*. Retrieved 25 April 2022 from https://digital.library.ucla.edu/catalog/ark:/21198/zz0002qtgd

-Errol's grave. Meribona [photographer], CC BY-SA 3.0 *Wikimedia Commons*. Retrieved 26 April 2022 from URL: https://creativecommons.org/licenses/by-sa/3.0

-Photograph by Lloyd MacLean of Errol Flynn and his father Theodore aboard Flynn's yacht, Zaca, c.1946. *National Library of Australia*. Retrieved 26 April 2022 from http://nla.gov.au/nla.obj-297272775

(1930). Portrait of Errol Flynn, Maroussia Richardson collection. *National Library of Australia*. Retrieved April 27, 2022, from http://nla.gov.au/nla.obj-224117315

The gentleman bushranger
Martin Cash

Interred: **Martin Cash**, 11 October 1810[1] – 26 August 1877* (aged 67 years).

Location: Roman Catholic, section A, site number 110.

Cemetery: Cornelian Bay Cemetery and Crematorium, Queens Walk, New Town, TAS 7008.

* While Martin's gravestone lists his year of death as 1878, all sources, including newspapers of the day, list it as 1877.

Above: Portrait of Martin Cash as it appears on his book cover.
Source: State Library of New South Wales.

If there was one thing that the fledgling nation of Australia had, it was a fascination with the sometimes cruel, at other times unfortunate, mostly escaped prisoners who took to the scrub and attracted the title of 'bushrangers'.

What's in a name?

They wore appellations like 'Mad Dog' Morgan, 'Captain Thunderbolt' and 'Black Douglas'. Perhaps the most callous of them all were the Clarke Brothers who plied their trade where Canberra now stands. The two brothers who carved out a career of crime which included the murder of a policeman, also shared a final fate, hanged simultaneously on twin gallows at Darlinghurst Gaol on 25 June 1867. Others like Ned Kelly, who had won a degree of popular support, were executed for their crimes and sometimes their gang members died with them. In 1841 bushranger Edward "Teddy the Jewboy" Davis was executed in Sydney along with five other members of his gang.

All this goes to show the man who is the subject of this story, a fellow called Martin Cash, was a rare creature... an Australian bushranger who died of old age. But that doesn't mean getting there wasn't something of a trip for Martin Cash and that the hangman's rope didn't swing very close.

The changing face of bushranging

The bushranging industry, if it can be described that way, went through stages. As almost all the early bushrangers in this country were escaped convicts who were forced to steal what came their way, traveller's bounty from people who walked the roads, raids on farm properties, small gold shipments and the occasional stagecoach became their prey. But as small settlements grew to become towns and cities, many as the result of gold rushes, the criminals were given illegal access to great wealth – gold – which, because shipments were largely inadequately protected, they plundered at will.

Many were caught, and as we have seen, many paid the full price for their crimes, but Martin Cash was a different kettle of fish. While he might have been guilty of having 'sticky fingers' it was what might be described as 'crimes of passion' which got him into strife, and women were to be his downfall.

Early days

Martin grew up in a fairly well-to-do family in Enniscorthy, County Wexford, Ireland and wanted for little. Adequately supplied with pocket money, he spent a great deal of time at the races and drinking with his friends. His serious run-ins with the law started when at the age of 18 he attempted to murder a rival for the affections of his sweetheart, Mary. The young woman in question had borrowed or been given money by the young Cash and when he was informed that she was also seeing another man by the name of Jessop, he was "stung to madness with jealousy"[2] and resolved to have his revenge.

After seeing Mary and Jessop through a window, Martin went to his home and returned, gun in hand, to the place where he had seen the couple. According to Martin, Jessop had his arm around Mary's waist, sufficient proof of her treachery. At this point, Martin took a couple of steps back from the window through which he was observing proceedings between the pair and fired his weapon at his rival, who immediately fell to the floor.

There are several accounts of what happened that resemble Martin's version of events. One of them says that young Jessop, the interloper, was actually shot in the buttocks.[3] Likewise, when the law dealt with Martin Cash by sentencing him to seven years transportation, the official records show it was actually for house-breaking, not attempted murder. Regardless of the actual charge, about six months later, Martin and 169 others found themselves aboard the transport ship the *'Marquis of Huntley'* bound for Botany Bay, where it arrived on 10 February 1828.

Upon arrival in what he described as "the dreaded receptacle of all human depravity,"[4] Martin was assigned to a Mr George Bowman, a leading pastoralist in the Hunter Valley who bred sheep and Shorthorn cattle, owned some fine race-horses and found time to act as a member of the Presbyterian School Board at Singleton. Martin Cash worked for him as a stockman on several of the family properties for many years, even after he attained his ticket-of-leave[5], a permit that "allowed convicts to work for themselves provided they remained in a specified area, reported regularly to local authorities and attended divine worship every Sunday, if possible. They could not leave the colony."[6]

Mixing marks

Now according to Martin, while he was working for Bowman he made the acquaintance of one John Boodle, who asked Martin to assist him and his brother in the branding of some cattle, and not suspecting for a moment that there was anything wrong, Martin had no hesitation in assisting. While the cattle were being branded, two more men joined him for a brief time and then departed. It was at that time that Boodle broke the bad news that the cattle they were branding did not belong to him or his brother and that the two men who dropped in briefly were aware of that fact. Boodle, his brother, and an unwitting Martin Cash had in fact been cattle duffing, even if Martin wasn't aware of it. Boodle suggested, given their circumstances, that the best plan would be to leave the colony immediately.

Martin didn't have to be told twice and fearful of what may happen to him, he and the woman with whom he had struck up a relationship, Bessie Clifford, headed for Van Diemen's Land, sailing aboard the 'Francis Freeling' on 10 February 1837. It was exactly nine years after Cash arrived at Botany Bay. Predictably, it wasn't all that long before he became the subject of police investigations again and two years later, he was sentenced to seven years at Port Arthur, the so-called escape-proof prison. It was a claim that Martin Cash would show to be less than accurate. Over the next 18 months, he escaped three times and at one stage was on the run for almost two years. When he was sent back to Port Arthur this time, he had another four years added to his sentence.

While he was in Port Arthur, Martin Cash became close to a pair of convicted bushrangers, Lawrence Kavenagh and George Jones and with them planned what was believed to be the impossible. The scheme was an elaborate escape plan to be executed by swimming across the shark-infested waters of Eaglehawk Neck, the narrow isthmus where Eaglehawk Bay joins Pirates Bay. The waters on either side of the neck were reportedly shark-infested and half-starved hounds were chained together along the exposed banks of Eaglehawk Bay to repel any would-be escapees.

On Boxing Day, 1842, the trio bundled their clothes together and tied them onto their heads and took to the deadly waters. They all got to the other side in one piece, but all of them lost their clothes. Now naked, the trio robbed a road gang's hut for clothing, and so began a twenty-month spree of bushranging – robbing mail coaches, homesteads

Left: Portrait of Martin Cash by Thomas Bock c1823–43. Source: State Library of NSW. Right: Bushranger portrait believed to be Lawrence Kavenagh, c1843. Source: Tasmanian Archive and Heritage Office.

and inns, which threw much of Tasmania into fear and consternation.[7] They were involved in several dramatic shoot-outs which only enhanced their notorious reputation.

Shoot out in Hobart Town

Their status grew amongst the lesser classes whom they left alone, and their deeds were seen much as a Robin Hood adventure, where they took from the rich but didn't distribute to the poor. They earned the nicknames 'Cash, Kavenagh and Jones' or 'Cash & Co.'[8]

The three pursued a bushranging career on foot, robbing inns and the houses of well-to-do settlers with seeming impunity, and without the use of unnecessary violence, thus earning them the reputation of 'gentlemen bushrangers'.

But while their reputations grew, Martin got word that his girlfriend, Bessie, had left him for another man, and enraged by this news he vowed to kill them both. They were in Hobart and that was where Cash headed from his hideout, with murderous intent. Matters came to a head on the evening of 29 August when Martin Cash was spotted with fellow bushranger, Kavenagh, in Brisbane Street, Hobart, and a gunfight broke out. A police constable, Peter Winstanley was shot by Cash and subsequently died two days later from the injury he suffered.

Kavenagh was injured and caught early in the piece and soon Cash was being chased by as many as 100 people, all keen to collect the bounty on his head. The events that followed were re-printed in 1946 from the original *Launceston Express* newspaper reports of 1837: "(Cash) Forcing his way through the crowd into Brisbane St., he arrived outside the old Commodore Inn, where he ran into the arms of a tall, powerful constable named Winstanley. Cash flung him off, and as he came in to attack again shot him. The mob was upon him now, and he slipped on the roadway and fell. Two others, Cunliffe and Oldfield, he wounded, but the crowd bore him down and he was beaten senseless with pistol butts. After a trial lasting two days, in which public interest was intense, he was sentenced to death for the murder of Constable Winstanley."[9]

So how was it that Martin Cash, gentleman bushranger, escaped the hangman's rope?

Power of the press

Certainly, he had the support of many locals at the time of the Hobart shooting who argued for his reprieve, notably R.L. Murray, the editor of the *Review* who was said to be largely responsible for Cash's eventual reprieve. And when Martin Cash's sentence was challenged and postponed, the governor wrote to the authorities in London seeking guidance.

A reprieve was eventually granted but not before Cash had spent 15 months in the scaffold's shadow and he was sentenced to the place where all three of the Cash and Co. gang ended up, Norfolk Island. For two of the three members, it would be more permanent than for Martin Cash, who would be granted a ticket-of-leave allowing him to return to Tasmania.

Once Cash and Kavenagh were captured after the Hobart fiasco, George Jones remained on the run for several months, committing robberies with other escaped convicts. He was executed on Norfolk Island in April 1844 for armed robbery.

Lawrence Kavenagh was tried for serious crimes, including murder, on five separate occasions. He was executed in 1846 at Norfolk Island.

More front than Myers

Few Australian bushrangers survived to tell tall tales and to die at home in their beds as did Martin Cash – and in association with Lawrence Kavenagh and George Jones he was one of a few Australian bushrangers who had the temerity... the effrontery if you prefer...to challenge the authorities of the day and to win the admiration of many of their fellow Tasmanians.

Such was the impudence that while they were on the run, Cash and Co. actually issued a memorandum to the Governor of the colony, John Franklin. It read:

"Messrs Cash & Co. beg to notify to His Excellency, Sir John Franklin and his satellites, that a very respectable person named Mrs Cash is now falsely imprisoned in Hobart Town, and if the said Mrs Cash is not released forthwith and properly remunerated, we will, in the first instance, visit Government House, and, beginning with Sir John, administer a wholesome lesson, in the shape of a sound flogging, after which we will pay the same currency to his followers. Given under our hands, at the residence of Mr Charles Kerr, at Dunrobin, Cash, Kavenagh, Jones"[10]

The gentleman bushranger retires

When transportation stopped in 1853 and Norfolk Island was shut down, Martin Cash and Mary Bennett, the local woman he had married, moved back to Hobart and Martin took up the role of gardener at the Government Domain. In 1855 Martin and Mary had a son, who they also named Martin. In June 1856 Martin senior was granted a conditional pardon which was promoted to a full pardon in July 1863. Martin Cash was 52 years old and a free man.

After Martin spent the next four years in New Zealand, he returned to Tasmania and with Mary bought a small farm at Glenorchy which he farmed until his death on 26August 1877. He was survived by his wife; their only child, Martin, had died in his teens.

Martin Cash is buried in Cornelian Bay Cemetery; Catholic, section: A, site number 110. He is still talked about today in Tasmania, no doubt because of his reputation and Robin Hood-like popular scoundrel approach to life.

References:

1 *"Martin Cash" His personal narrative as a Bushranger in Van Diemen's land.* Published by J Walch and sons Pty Ltd, Hobart, Tasmania. 1870.

2 *"Martin Cash" His personal narrative...* Ibid.

3 L. L. Robson and Russel Ward, 'Cash, Martin (1808–1877)', Australian Dictionary of Biography, National Centre of Biography, *Australian National University*, https://adb.anu.edu.au/biography/cash-martin-1885/text2217, published first in hardcopy 1966, accessed online 1 April 2022.

4 *"Martin Cash" His personal narrative...* Op.cit.

5 Nancy Gray, 'Bowman, George Pearce (1821–1870)', Australian Dictionary of Biography, National Centre of Biography, *Australian National University*, https://adb.anu.edu.au/biography/bowman-george-pearce-3034/text4455. Retrieved online 4 April 2022.

6 *National Library of Australia.* Ticket of leave. https://www.nla.gov.au/research-guides/convicts/tickets-of-leave

7 "Hobart Crown Police Report." *Colonial Times (Hobart, Tas.: 1828 - 1857)* 4 April 1843: 4. Web. 10 Apr 2022 http://nla.gov.au/nla.news-article8753464

8 Death of Martin Cash. (1877, August 29). *Tribune (Hobart, Tas.: 1876 - 1879)*, p. 2. Retrieved April 10, 2022, from http://nla.gov.au/nla.news-article201732686

9 End of Martin Cash (1946, January 26). *Saturday Evening Express (Launceston, Tas.: 1924 - 1954)*, p. 3. Retrieved April 7, 2022, from http://nla.gov.au/nla.news-article265059047

10 Death of Martin Cash. (1877, August 29). *Tribune.* Op.cit.

Images:

- Martin Cash book cover - J. Walch & Sons: Walch Bros. & Birchall - Now Ready. Price One Shilling. Martin Cash, The Bushranger of Van Diemen's Land in 1843. *State Library of NSW*, Call No. 356/7, Item 11. Retrieved 29 April 2022 from https://archival.sl.nsw.gov.au/Details/archive/110329979

- Bock, Thomas [artist]m Sketches of Tasmanian Bushrangers, ca. 1823 – 1843. *State Library of NSW*, Call No. DL PX 5. Retrieved 29 April 2022 from https://archival.sl.nsw.gov.au/Details/archive/110327187

- Bushranger believed to be Lawrence Kavenagh, c1843. Charles Henry Theodore Costantini -- Allport Library and Museum of Fine Arts, Tasmanian Archive and Heritage Office. Retrieved from *Wikipedia*, on 29 April 2022 from URL: https://en.wikipedia.org/wiki/Lawrence_Kavenagh#/media/File:Bushranger_Lawrence_Kavenagh.jpg

Acknowledgements:

We are grateful to everyone who shared their time, wisdom, photographs and enthusiasm to help us with this volume:

- Joanne James for professionally proofreading our first take and always picking up more than we ever will.
- Nicholas J. Bunning who discovered us, and then could not escape us! Thank you NickJ for ensuring our work is the best it can be and for your amazing attention to detail. You amaze us.
- Lindsay Smith for voluntarily reading and proofing with no arm twisting required! We're grateful.
- Linda McKenzie for venturing to Campania Cemetery for us on her holidays to snap the photographs of Mrs Marjorie Williams' grave.
- Edie McArthur, Rob McArthur and the McArthur family descendants for generously sharing knowledge and photos to help us tell young Sylvia's story.
- Patrick Bakes, Balfour historian for sharing his wisdom, sourced via the Circular Head Heritage Centre.
- Libraries Tasmania – we so appreciate that you had all the early newspapers such as *The Weekly Courier* scanned and available online – wonderful.
- Elayne Blake, Circular Head Heritage Centre.
- Tony Grincais, President, Tasmania Police Historical Group, The Tasmania Police Museum, for his generous and kind assistance.
- The Tasmania Police Museum.
- David Berry, State Library of NSW – thank you for your persistence.

- Russell Perkins, Imaging Services, State Library of NSW.
- Arthur Garland, photographer King Island memorials for the *Neva*, via Find A Grave.
- Kent Watson, Monuments Australia (a wonderful website worthy of support).
- Heather Excell, Special & Rare Collections & Digital Library Services & Infrastructure, University of Tasmania.
- Janine Tan, Libraries Tasmania.
- Scott Carlin, Managing Director, National Trust of Australia (Tasmania).
- Tony Sweeney for generously providing us with his extensive research on John Sweeney.
- While we endeavour to visit the graves and photograph them ourselves, Covid has made that difficult. Our sincere thanks to *Find A Grave* and *BillionGraves* contributors who readily share their images with us including:
  - Dan Jones, Elizabeth Rosenberg, Julie Henderson, Lacey Milier and Tanya V.

We would love to connect with you:

Website: www.gravetales.com.au

Podcast: https://www.gravetales.com.au/tune-into-the-podcast/

Facebook: www.facebook.com/gravetalesAUS/

YouTube: https://www.youtube.com/gravetales

Instagram: https://www.instagram.com/gravetales/

Email: enquiries@gravetales.com.au

About the Grave Tales team:

Helen Goltz, Author: Helen is a journalist and producer with a 30-year history of working for newspapers, magazines, in marketing, and producing television and radio programs for clients including News Ltd, the Seven Network and Macquarie Media. She is the author of 20 books, and eight non-fiction titles co-written with Chris Adams. Helen is published by Next Chapter, Wild Hearts, and Atlas Productions. She is postgraduate degree qualified with majors in Literature and Communications.

Chris Adams, Author: Two-time Logie Award winner, Chris started his journalism career in radio before spending over thirty years in broadcast current affairs including working as a journalist and producer for Channel Nine's *Today Tonight* and Executive Producer of Channel Seven's *State Affair*. In 1991 he was a War Correspondent for the Persian Gulf War and in 1993 for the Civil War of Somalia. He is credited with over forty television documentaries before returning to radio as News and Program Director of 4BC. He is now engaged full-time in writing projects, and speaking engagements and golf!

Hastings Goltz-Adams: sadly, our beloved Boxer-boy passed away during the writing of this volume. Always in our hearts.

Joanne James, Editor: Joanne's editing experience extends from proof-reading university handbooks and course guides to editing annual reports and publicity brochures for local government. With a background in primary school teaching, noticing spelling errors is second nature to her – she has been known to correct take-away menus and return them!

Nicholas J. Bunning, Editor: Heralding from Melbourne, Nick has enjoyed a lengthy career in the advertising industry and worked independently as a book and magazine editor. In his spare time, Nick enjoys reading historical true crime and biographies, as well as indulging his passion for 70s and 80s dance music! He lends his expertise to the *Grave Tales'* team with their grateful appreciation.

Also in the *Grave Tales book* series:

Brisbane Vol.1   Melbourne Vol. 1   Sydney Vol. 1

True Crime Vol.1   Great Ocean Road   Bruce Highway

Qld's Great South West   Scenic Rim & Surrounds, Qld.

Coming next – *Grave Tales: Adelaide.*

291

Grave Tales on YouTube

Check out our *Grave Tales* 10-minute video episodes and news clippings on our *Grave Tales* YouTube channel.

Episodes include:
- The *Grave Tales* trailer
- The Jack the Ripper suspect
- The Mystery of Mollie
- The Pearl Ferry Disaster.

Visit at – https://www.youtube.com/gravetales

Grave Tales The Series Podcast

Enjoy more than 40 episodes in our *Grave Tales* podcast series. Listen wherever you enjoy your podcasts by searching for *Grave Tales Australia,* including:

Apple –
https://podcasts.apple.com/au/podcast/grave-tales-australia-the-series/id1434500488

Podbean –
https://gravetales.podbean.com/